Religion and Social
Justice for Immigrants

Religion and Social Justice for Immigrants

EDITED BY
PIERRETTE HONDAGNEU-SOTELO

RUTGERS UNIVERSITY PRESS

NEW BRUNSWICK, NEW JERSEY AND LONDON

LIBRARY OF CONGRESS CATALOGING-IN-PUBLICATION DATA

Religion and social justice for immigrants / edited by Pierrette Hondagneu-Sotelo.
    p.   cm.
    Includes bibliographical references and index.
    ISBN-13: 978-0-8135-3908-9 (hardcover : alk. paper)
    ISBN-13: 978-0-8135-3909-6 (pbk. : alk. paper)
    1. Church work with immigrants—United States. 2. Immigrants—Religious
life—United States. 3. Social justice—Religious aspects—Christianity. 4. Social
justice—Religious aspects. 5. Christianity and justice. 6. Religion and justice.
7. United States—Emigration and immigration—Religious aspects. I. Hondagneu-
Sotelo, Pierrette.
    BV639.I4R45 2006 2007
    200.86'9120973—dc22

                                           2006005582
                                                  CIP

A British Cataloging-in-Publication record for this book is available
from the British Library.

Manufactured in the United States of America

In memory of Brother Ed Dunn (1949–2006),
Franciscan friar and dedicated advocate
for immigrant social justice

CONTENTS

ACKNOWLEDGMENTS

This book comes out of a collective endeavor, one that has been generously supported by the Center for Religion and Civic Culture at the University of Southern California, which is funded by the Pew Charitable Trusts. Around 2001, Professor Don Miller, a scholar of religion and the director of the center, invited me to convene a campus-wide faculty working group on the topic of religion and immigration. With funding he had secured from the Pew foundation, our group of about a dozen faculty met regularly for three years. Only two of the initial working group members were scholars of religion; most of us had expertise in immigration, so we initially began as a reading group, seeking to deepen our knowledge of the ways religion and immigration intersect. Generous funding from the Pew Charitable Trusts allowed us to invite national scholars of religion and immigration to share their work with us at the University of Southern California, and it also funded our research. Many of us brought to the table an interest in race and politics, and our individual research projects evolved in a common direction, analyzing the ways in which religion is involved in immigrant social justice. In February 2005, we hosted a conference featuring our individual work, as well as that of various invited scholars, and the result is this volume, which features the original work presented at that conference. The book began through dialogic meetings among a group that included anthropologists, political scientists, religion and race scholars, and sociologists, and it is our hope that it goes full circle to spur more discussion across disciplinary boundaries, and that it may be of interest to practitioners as well as academics.

There are many people to thank along the way. First, thank you to Don Miller, Jon Miller, and Grace Dyrness, at the University of Southern California Center for Religion and Civic Culture, and the Pew foundation for making our project possible. Pew funding allowed our working group to benefit from the seemingly tireless efforts of Kara Lemma, a graduate research assistant. For three years, she coordinated our working group meetings and meals, copied and distributed readings, researched and wrote an annotated bibliography, made all arrangements for the visiting speakers, and organized the conference with tremendous professionalism. Thank you, Kara! Near the tail end of this project,

Genelle Gaudinez worked as the graduate student research assistant in charge of manuscript preparation, and I am grateful for the celerity and thoroughness of her work. My deepest thanks are to those who participated in the working group. Besides the USC faculty who wrote chapters for this volume, the working group included the valuable participation of Professors Maria Aranda from the School of Social Work, Nora Hamilton from the Political Science Department, Roberto Lint-Sagarena of the School of Religion and the Program in American Studies and Ethnicities, Ed Ransford of the Sociology Department, and Apichai Shipper of Political Science and International Relations. This book reflects their contributions to the working group discussions and their input on the research presented in this book. On a more personal note, many thanks for the patience shown by the guys who manage to live with me and my projects: Mike Messner and our sons, Miles Hondagneu-Messner and Sasha Hondagneu-Messner.

PART I

Diverse Approaches to Faith and Social Justice for Immigrants

1

Religion and a Standpoint Theory of Immigrant Social Justice

PIERRETTE HONDAGNEU-SOTELO

Religion has jumped into the public sphere of global and domestic politics in ways that no social theorist could have imagined fifty or a hundred years ago. Religion, after all, was supposed to die as modernity flourished. Instead, it now stares at us almost daily from the newspaper, but it is usually the extremist fundamentalisms of the Christian right or conservative political Islam that grabs the headlines. Meanwhile, religious activists of other political persuasions remain active outside of the pews and prayer halls, working quietly in numerous social justice campaigns in the United States and elsewhere around the world. This book examines a segment of this group, namely those working for immigrant social justice in the United States.

The late twentieth and early twenty-first centuries are proving to be an age of global migration. The world is on the move, with nearly 200 million people worldwide now living in countries other than those where they were born; about 34 million of them are in the United States. And as anyone who has not been living under a rock knows, immigrants and refugees have met with a deeply ambivalent and often mean-spirited public reception in the United States. We see this in institutions across society, in the media, in workplaces, in the legislature, and in the campaign platforms of politicians at election time. It is an era marked by xenophobia, racialized nativism, the perception that immigrants are draining social welfare coffers, and by a new nationalism that conflates immigrants with terrorists and national security threats. To be sure, the United States is still celebrated as a nation of immigrants, and it is widely perceived as the land of opportunity for new immigrants. There is much to recommend this view, particularly with regards to economic mobility. Yet one suspects that when historians of the future reflect on it, the current period will not be seen as a felicitous one for immigrant communities.

Immigrant newcomers in the United States hail predominantly from Asia, Latin America, and the Middle East, and religion is salient in their lives both prior to and after migration. Indeed, research reveals that many immigrants become more religious in their new destinations. Coupled with the fact that religion remains more palpably present in American daily life than in any other postindustrial society, this means that religion is deeply implicated in immigration and its outcomes—including the reactions and responses to hostile contexts of reception that often greet immigrants. This book brings together studies of different immigrant groups and faith-based activists to examine how religion enables the pursuit of social justice for immigrants in American society today. In this regard, the chapters here analyze religion as a domain currently providing immigrants and their supporters with, alternatively, a sanctuary for coping; an arena for mobilization, civic participation, and solidarity; an ethical and moral basis for action; and possible resources for resistance and collective well-being.

Religion in the United States Today

If the first big surprise for the secularly inclined social observer is the staying power of religion, then the second surprise is the transformation of religion and its many contemporary variations. Religion is a rapidly changing moving target in the United States, so it is challenging, perhaps even foolhardy, to attempt a summary of the changes and continuities in a few paragraphs—but these need to be acknowledged. Even without taking into account the contributions to religious diversity added by the post-1965 immigrants, who include Buddhists, Hindus, Muslims, and other non-Judeo Christians among them, religion in the United States has diversified beyond simple belief and belonging. In recent years we have witnessed the decline of the old "hell, fire and brimstone" view of sin and salvation and the emergence of less-judgmental, more therapeutic, flexible religion among mainline Catholic, Protestant, and Jewish followers, as well as among evangelical Christians. This is accompanied by a loosening of both congregational belonging and strict, formalistic liturgical worship (Wolfe 2003). Spiritual seekers and religious converts are replacing "cradle to grave" religious adherents (Roof 2000; Wuthnow 1998). Christian churches of different sizes have sprung up, running the gamut from megasize, postdenominational "new paradigm" churches that meet in converted warehouses (Miller 1997) to small, inner-city, storefront churches run by Pentecostals and other Christian fundamentalists. And, of course, the geometric growth in evangelicalism is perhaps the most obvious public mark of contemporary change in American religion.

Meanwhile, religion has become more publicly prominent in the United States and around the world. An important body of scholarship today examines the political and civic influence of American religion (Ammerman 2005; Wuthnow and Evans 2002; Lichterman 2005). This scholarship starts with the observation that it is in church that many Americans learn civic skills, the key knowledge and practices that facilitate political participation (Ammerman 2005). This research also underscores that religion is an important domain for contesting market and state institutions (Casanova 1994), and that religion often motivates public and civic action. Many American political mobilizations, from abolition, to the civil rights movement of the 1950s and 1960s, to the Christian right, started in or gained momentum in American churches.

The impact of the Christian right extends far beyond their religious adherents, as they have become primary supporters, lobbyists, and a policy influence in the regime of George W. Bush. While the faith-based initiatives for privatizing social welfare provisions have garnered much attention, the primary social and political efforts of the Christian right in the national political scene have concentrated on issues having to do with the regulation of bodies and sexuality. This includes efforts to restrict abortion, homosexuality, and gay marriage and to police the place of men and women in families. These efforts can be read, as commentators have suggested, as fallout from the social change of the 1960s and 1970s, particularly those practices and values promoted by the women's liberation and gay rights movements. And this warrants another observation and an important point of departure for this book: The Christian right has not collectively thrust itself into the immigration restrictionist movement to restrict and control immigrants, refugees, and the national border. It is important to acknowledge that the fastest-growing, ostensibly most conservative, powerful political force in the American religious front is *not* a key voice in the debates around immigration regulation. Similarly, it is important to look at the religious groups and faith-based immigrant groups that *are* taking a stand on immigrant issues—and that is the task of this book.

It is well known that representatives of the major faith traditions in the United States have been stalwarts of civic action, volunteerism, and social justice work. They have proven to be highly active and sometimes influential in a number of public issues (e.g., homelessness, environmental campaigns, and peace and justice issues). These efforts are well-documented among Catholics, Protestant mainline churches, and Jewish organizations (Weigert and Kelley 2005; Wuthnow and Evans 2002). Not everyone applauds these efforts, but until now the critique of religious involvement for immigrant and refugee social justice has been muted.

Conservative cultural critics and those in favor of immigration restriction are only now beginning to expand the backlash against immigrants to include a backlash against religious-based advocates for immigrant social justice. In one publication, a critic bemoans not only the pro-immigration lobbying and activism of churches but also the ways in which churches have broadened Christianity to encourage tolerance for racial and ethnic difference and acceptance of immigrants: "The Christian churches have not only become steadfast advocates of immigration expansionism, but are propagating their liberal social justice brand of Christianity throughout their school systems. ... most Christian colleges appear to be ... advancing an agenda of diversity, multiculturalism, and social justice, which usually includes a sympathetic view of immigration, both legal and illegal" (Russell 2004, 89). And in the immigration restrictionist legislation pending in Congress at the beginning of 2006, one bill proposes to make it a federal crime to offer assistance or services to undocumented immigrants. The *New York Times* reported that Bishop Gerald R. Barnes, speaking for the U.S. Conference of Catholic Bishops, warned that "This legislation would place parish, diocesan and social service program staff at risk of criminal prosecution simply for performing their jobs," jobs that regularly entail providing humanitarian aid and social services (Swarns 2005). In Los Angeles, California, Cardinal Roger M. Mahoney, the religious leader of the nation's largest Archdiocese, urged Catholics to fast and pray for social justice in immigration reform, and he publicly stated that if the proposed anti-immigrant legislation went into effect, he would tell his priests to resist orders to ask immigrants for legal documentation before providing services. Mahoney supported his viewpoint by citing both Hebrew and Christian scriptures, and he dismissed the proposed legislation as "un-American." "If you take this to its logical, ludicrous extreme," he said, "every single person who comes up to receive Holy Communion, you have to ask them to show papers" (Watanabe 2006:A1). On top of calling for a Lenten fast for parishioners to reflect on the contributions of immigrants, he sent informational packets on immigration to all parishes. That same spring of 2006, in response to the proposed legislation, organizers from both secular and faith-based groups mobilized the largest immigrant rights marches ever seen in this country, with half a million people taking to the streets in Dallas, and in Los Angeles, and hundreds of thousands in other cities around the nation. These largely Latino mobilizations peaked on April 10, 2006, "The National Day of Action for Immigrant Social Justice," with marches and rallies in over sixty cites, but organizing by students, labor unions, Spanish language media, community based organizations, and church groups continued afterward. It is noteworthy that in many cities these marches convened or ended at churches. Joining the Roman Catholic Church in favor of legalization programs for the estimated 11 million undocumented immigrants and against the criminalization of immigrants and those who serve them, were clergy from Episcopal, Lutheran, and even Pentecostal denominations. Clergy and laity have been involved in immigrant rights and social justice work for decades, but clearly, this was a period characterized by new momentum. It remains to be seen whether priests and ministers will be jailed for offering English classes or Holy Communion wafers to immigrants, and whether there will be a populist backlash from the pews against the mainline church hierarchy's active pro-immigration lobbying. These reports do suggest that the role of religion in advocating for immigrants is becoming increasingly visible and contentious.

The goal of this book is to analyze how particular sectors of these mainline religions, as well as those working from Caodaist, Muslim, Christian evangelical, and Buddhist religious traditions, are working for social justice for and with immigrants. The essays here promote an inclusive view of religion, one that not only spans beyond Judeo-Christian confines but also includes the various *forms* that religion takes in the United States. It is necessary to look beyond churches and temples to comprehend the multiple ways that religion is involved in seeking social justice for immigrants. Besides congregations there are religious supranational organizations such as the Catholic church and the national organization of U.S. Catholic Conference of Bishops actively pursuing legislation and policies on behalf of immigrants and refugees (Mooney, this volume). An array of nonprofit, nongovernmental organizations (NGOs) rely on religious affiliations and funding to offer services and advocacy for immigrants and refugees—including organizations such as Lutheran Social Services for Refugee Rights, the U.S. Baha'I Refugee Office, and the Interfaith Refugee and Immigration Ministries. As Nawyn notes in this volume, a majority of the staff at these organizations consists of immigrants and refugees. There are non–Judeo Christian religious groups, such as the Vietnamese Caodai, who are striving for the rights of recognition for their religion and addressing community problems such as racism, economic issues, and the politics of diaspora (Hoskins, this volume).

Religion is implicated in diverse projects for immigrant social justice. There are also ostensibly nonreligious community groups, such as the Saul Alinsky–inspired Pacific Institute for Community Organizing (PICO), which strategically moved toward a faith-based organizing model. As Palacios notes in this volume, this strategy has met with success in immigrant congregations. And then there are interfaith groups, such as the California statewide Interfaith Coalition for Immigrant Rights (Hondagneu-Sotelo, Gaudinez, and Lara, this volume), and the interdenominational Humane Borders (Menjivar, this volume) that organize religious people into immigrant civil rights activism at the U.S.-Mexico border. Prayer, blessings, and devotions to the saints are also important religious practices as well (Hagan, this volume). This list is not exhaustive, but the point is that religion is present at various organizational levels in the pursuit of social justice for immigrants.

Religion is fundamentally about human connection with the divine and the search for transcendence. Yet because religion is a human practice, it takes profoundly social forms, and these social constructions are involved in many pursuits and outcomes. While there are powerfully transcendent, spiritual, and intangible facets of religion, this book takes an overtly instrumentalist view of religion—not to deny the spiritual, but rather to enable an examination of how religious beliefs, scriptures, practices, institutions, and organizations enable groups, both immigrants and their supporters, to work for immigrant social justice.

Religion and Immigrant Lives

Immigrants have constructed and defined the diversity of American religion. Founded by Puritans in search of religious freedom, the United States has no legacy of a mandatory nation-state church, unlike, say, European or Latin American nations. Instead, the United States was based on the concept that people are free to practice their religion of choice, and religion has flourished and diversified with each subsequent wave of immigrants. As historian Will Herberg noted in his classic book *Protestant, Catholic, and Jew* (1961), it was the Russian Jewish and Italian Catholic immigrants of the early twentieth century who helped to eventually transform the United States from a Protestant nation to a Judeo-Christian one. Prior to the age of multiculturalism, religion was seen as an acceptable marker of ethnic identity. This, after all, was an era when immigrants were expected to lose their language and culture. Ethnic churches, such as the Italian Catholic church or the Polish parish, gave way to denominational churches, forming what Herberg referred to as the dominant triad of Protestant, Catholic, Jew. Today, with the post-1965 Muslim immigrants from South Asia and the Middle East, one hears similar expectations that the United States may come to be identified not simply as a Judeo-Christian nation, but as a more inclusive nation of Abrahamic faiths, although this outcome has yet to reach fruition. It is also a narrative that is contested by Hindus, Buddhists, and others excluded from the so-called religions of the book. Complex dynamics are at work, and history is still waiting to be written.

It is clear, however, that today, as in the past, churches, temples, and mosques remain a major institutional point of entry for immigrants. A new wave of scholarship on contemporary immigrants and religion shows the importance of these face-to-face gatherings in congregations, revealing how religious practices and institutions are often strengthened and transformed through immigration (Warner and Wittner 1998). Congregational forms—such as the practice of membership at one temple or church, lay leadership, social services provisions, instructional classes, and clergy acting as counselors—may be adopted by diverse immigrant religious groups, and there is often a simultaneous return to theological foundations as well as efforts to reach out beyond the traditional immigrant ethnic boundaries (Ebaugh and Chafetz 2000; Yang and Ebaugh 2001). In the current era, facilitated with new transportation and communications technology, immigrant congregations often act transnationally, spanning international borders and encompassing people in the societies of origin and destination (Levitt 2001; Ebaugh and Chafetz 2002). Through devotional practices or in congregations, religion remains key in solidifying immigrant ethnic identities (Tweed 1997; Matovina and Riebe-Estrella 2002).

A significant arena of religion and immigrant life involves struggles for immigrant social justice. In the nineteenth and twentieth centuries there were plenty of social advocates guided by their faith traditions to work on behalf of immigrants. Anglo Christian missionaries who had gone to China to proselytize and seek converts returned to the United States to become advocates of Chinese migrant workers during the late nineteenth century. In the midst of severe public racism led by the triumvirate of the American labor movement, WASP Brahmin elites, and eugenicists in universities, these missionaries raised their voices against the dominant view that the Chinese were inferior to whites and should be racially excluded from admission to the United States. Much of the early twentieth century Progressive reform movements, including Jane Addams's settlement house movement for immigrant slum dwellers and factory workers, was influenced by Social Gospel, with its emphasis on improving conditions in society according to Christian principles (Goldstein 2005). And the Italian Bishop Scalabrini championed the cause of Italian immigrants in the United States and in Latin America during the 1890s, founding a Catholic Order dedicated to immigrant pastoral care and social action (Tomasi 2000). Religion has served as an organizational hook not only for immigrant advocates but also for immigrants themselves in their efforts to mobilize around diverse social causes.

Immigrant history is not a finished project, as the United States is still being shaped by immigration. The post-1965 immigrants—the term applied to the current wave of immigrants who ended the mid-twentieth-century hiatus on immigration—hail predominantly from Asia, Latin America, and the Middle East. Unlike the southern and eastern European immigrants who predominated during the last turn of the century, they are extraordinarily diverse with respect to national origins, religion, race and ethnicity, language, social class, and education. Take social class, for instance. These newcomers include both well-to-do professionals who enter the United States with sterling educational credentials and low-wage laborers who may have only finished fourth grade in their countries of origin. Some are captains of corporations and owners of small businesses, but others are illegal immigrant workers who are often highly in debt from the journey. Among the latter, many begin their sojourn in the United States by experiencing intense forms of labor oppression, and in jobs that may involve toxic chemicals or pesticides or dangerous equipment. While a small, privileged group of newcomers inhabits the social worlds of suburban private schools and country clubs, others squeeze into overcrowded inner-city apartments and have their kids exposed to violent neighborhoods.

The 34 million foreign-born people, and their offspring, in the United States account for about 20 percent of the population. In some cities—Miami, Los Angeles, and New York City—they constitute a majority of the population. Although the national origins diversity is impressive, with immigrants coming to the United States from just about every country in the world, Mexico remains by far the largest single source of U.S. immigrants. In fact, Mexicans account for 30 percent of the foreign-born population in the United States, with 9.8 million

Mexicans counted in 2002 (Passel 2004). Moreover, they make up the majority of undocumented immigrants in the United States, and about 80 percent of current Mexican migration to the United States is undocumented. The second and third largest immigrant groups in the United States are the Chinese and the Filipinos, but their numbers trail by comparison—there are only 1.5 million Chinese and 1.4 million Filipino immigrants in the United States today. These groups are followed by slightly fewer numbers of Indians, Vietnamese, Cubans, Koreans, Canadians, and Salvadorans (Passel 2005).

The immigrant population in the United States has grown rapidly, and in addition to the mundane challenges and hardships in the realms of health, jobs, or civil rights, the newcomers encounter a society where the public discourse proclaims deep ambivalence about their presence. Immigrants and their advocates have not been silent in responding. Religion is one important dimension in the response to these lived social injustices.

A Standpoint Definition of Social Justice

Think of the iconic figures of twentieth-century social justice and chances are that Martin Luther King, Cesar Chavez, and Mahatma Gandhi come to mind. These leaders all identified with and drew inspiration from strong religious convictions, albeit from different religious traditions. Martin Luther King's civil rights movement work was guided by his position as a Protestant minister, one imbued with the traditions of African American Christian religious themes of liberation and community solidarity. Cesar Chavez's organizing with the United Farm Workers drew inspiration from religious themes and incorporated Catholic Mexican rituals, such as processions, fasting, enactment of suffering, and the Virgin de Guadalupe, while Gandhi's leadership of the movement against British colonialism was guided by Hindu tenets of nonviolence. Clearly, no one religion enjoys a monopoly over social justice work.

Each of these leaders of social change responded to different kinds of social injustices. Each led groups that faced particular sites of oppressions and injustices—African Americans' struggle against racial oppression and poverty in the segregated South, Mexican migrant farm workers' mobilization against exploitation in western agribusiness, and Hindus's struggle for independence and sovereignty in colonial India. The diversity of religious traditions that inspire social justice work, and the diversity of contexts that situate social injustices, are important points of departure for understanding the chapters in this book. Here I reject the idea that there is one definition of social justice; important but diverse defining statements on what constitutes social justice have been offered by both secular and religious thinkers. Similarly, I believe that no one religious tradition and no one particular immigrant group has a monopoly in defining social justice.

Feminist standpoint theory teaches that women and men, and different racial and class groupings of men and women, are differently situated in the division of labor, and hence these groups experience and see the social world from different standpoints (Collins 1986). So it is with religion and social justice for immigrants. While all immigrant groups share some of the same struggles, they inhabit different social locations, and they face particular social issues and injustices. Hence they have differently situated experience and knowledge about what constitutes social justice. Social class is a major differentiating factor, but there is no guarantee that a relatively well-to-do immigrant group will not face social injustices. Muslim immigrants, for example, include among them many affluent professionals and entrepreneurs from Pakistan, Iran, and Jordan, but in the post-9/11 political and social climate, they have had to work collectively to safeguard their civil rights. While social class may preclude well-to-do immigrants from deprivation in health access and housing, it exacerbates these issues for poor, low-wage immigrant groups such as Mexicans, Cambodians, and Laotians. And while Mexicans are not the only ones surreptitiously crossing the southern border into the United States, they have been the primary targets of the newly militarized U.S.-Mexico border, with one to two Mexicans dying daily in the migration transit. Immigrants are not monolithic. Immigrant groups have particular social locations and hence encounter a different constellation of opportunities and hardships in the United States.

Religion is a multivalent force. It works at the level of belief and theology, sometimes providing the fuel that motivates people to pursue social justice activism, but it also operates as an organizational tool, social network, and resource. In some instances, faith prompts nonimmigrant citizens to rally for immigrant rights and services, while in other cases religion enables immigrant civic and political participation. While religion works in different ways, all of the chapters in this book examine cases where there is an important dialectic between religious faith and social action. They also reveal that a critique of immigrant injustice in society is often based on religion and, importantly, that living as a person of faith requires action. New understandings of social justice emerge in this process when abstract reflections, thought, and beliefs are merged with concrete social actions.

An Introduction to the Chapters

In the following chapter sociologist Rhys Williams shows how the concept of immigrant rights is problematic, bound up as it is with the relatively modern invention of rights discourse, tied to the nation-state and embedded in notions of a liberal state handing out individual rights. Rights, he argues, need to be conceptualized more as a social property. While human rights and social justice may offer competing alternatives, he suggests these too have weaknesses, and he assesses the ability of immigrants to use religion in forwarding these claims.

Both pundits and academics now regularly celebrate religion as an enabler of immigrant civic engagement, civic skills, and democratic participation, but on this point part 2 of this volume draws less sanguine conclusions. Political scientist Janelle Wong and religious studies scholar Jane Iwamura analyze survey data and discover that Asian American immigrants who attend religious services are more likely to hold conservative political views. Many of them attend Christian churches, and they express low tolerance for gay rights and a politics of choice over abortion. Wong and Iwamura concur that religious institutions, Protestant, Catholic, and evangelical ones, may indeed bring immigrants into the political system, but they caution that these newly cultivated political views may in fact be antithetical to those that one might normatively identify with social justice.

Ideas about what constitutes social justice are often rooted in the immediate challenges and social problems facing particular immigrant communities. Members of the same religion, even a minority non–Judeo Christian religion in the United States, are not necessarily united by shared experience and beliefs. This is shown in the chapter by anthropologist Karen Leonard, who underscores the profoundly different experiences of African American Muslims and immigrant Muslims in the United States. Social relations of class and race, as well as the differential impact of the post-9/11 backlash climate, have intensified divisions among American Muslims. While African American Muslim legal scholars are seeking more radical interpretations of Islamic law—which they see as congruent with the race, class, and gender injustices facing their communities—middle-class and upper-middle-class immigrant Muslims are turning to the American legal system to safeguard their civil rights and freedom of speech and assembly.

Religion may also motivate nonimmigrants to collectively organize immigrant groups around social justice issues. This is the case described in the chapter by Russell Jeung, who shows how a multiracial group of Christian community organizers drew on evangelical Protestant faith to sustain themselves as they fomented social action among Mexican and Cambodian tenants living in an Oakland slum apartment. Using Robert Putnam's concept of "bridging social capital," Jeung argues that faith-based organizers brought together diverse immigrant groups, connecting them to outside resources for social change. Giving the lie to the assumption that Christian evangelicals are only interested in evangelizing for conversions and do not work for worldly social justice, this strategy united Latino and Cambodian low-income immigrant tenants in a successful campaign against a slumlord.

Can religion be used by non–faith based organizers in immigrant churches? Based on research conducted in an Oakland, California, Catholic parish with a large Mexican immigrant congregation, sociologist Joseph Palacios suggests that the answer to this question is yes. Mexican immigrants enter the United States, he says, as precitizens, without the prerequisite citizenship rights to participate in politics and voting and also bereft of civic skills. Catholic churches where PICO, a community organizing group that uses religion, is present provide an important venue for civic skill acquisition, thereby allowing Mexican immigrants to conceive of themselves as public persons and as actors in American religious, social, and political institutions. Palacios suggests that faith-based community organizing represents a social justice cultural system that enables immigrant political and civic engagement.

National borders have always loomed large in immigration matters. Since the 1980s, and accelerating since the mid-1990s, the United States has tightened border control enforcement at the southern border. Military helicopters outfitted with radar, electronic intrusion-detention ground sensors, and thousands of Border Patrol agents with night-vision scopes have impeded crossings at the traditional points, leading migrants to attempt the crossing in deserts and mountains, where many of them die of hypothermia and dehydration. Faith-based activists and Mexican communities residing along the border have responded to this situation, and part 3 examines different aspects of this faith-based response.

Jacqueline Marie Hagan draws on research she conducted along the U.S.-Mexico border, the Mexico-Guatemalan border, and in Mexico and Central America. Hagan argues convincingly that church and state are at odds when it comes to regulating migration from south to north. A panoply of mostly Catholic, but also Protestant-affiliated organizations, congregations, and NGOs, clergy, and budding faith-based movements are now in place, actively addressing the spiritual and practical needs of undocumented migrants in transit. Their offerings include shelters, shrines, know-your-rights booklets, water stations, and blessings. While state regulations create an increasingly dangerous landscape, religion steps in to minimize risk, danger, and social injustice.

With the intensification of U.S. Border Patrol enforcement at the California and Texas borders, the Arizona-Nogales area emerged as the new hotspot in the early 2000s. Basing her research in this area, sociologist Cecilia Menjívar examines the social justice teachings and scriptures that motivate and enable a group of largely white, Christian U.S. citizens to mobilize against border violence in Arizona. Themes of Incarnation and the interpretation of migrants as the most authentic contemporary embodiment of Jesus are regularly deployed. Sociologist Pierrette Hondagneu-Sotelo and graduate students Genelle Gaudinez and Hector Lara examine a similar situation in the San Diego-Tijuana area. Here religious activists organize an annual Posada Sin Fronteras, a hybrid political and religious event that condemns violence at the border and commemorates those who died in the border crossing. The authors argue that the emergence of these new hybrid forms of political protest and religious reenactment is the living legacy of biographies rooted in religiously based Latin American–inspired social movements, such as the United Farm Workers, the Sanctuary movement, and those associated with liberation theology. Anchored in long and complex histories of migration, these include processes completely counter to those anticipated by theories of secularization and assimilation.

In the late twentieth century, NGOs, many of them based on religious ideals, emerged as formidable forces in society and politics. Today, most refugees who are admitted to the United States are resettled and assisted by faith-based organizations, and in part 4 sociologist Stephanie Nawyn examines the discourse used by these agencies and their staff. The NGOs rely on explicit statements of Judeo-Christian values, such as showing hospitality to strangers or assisting the needy, and they regularly invoke religious images such as Jewish suffering or Jesus' status as a refugee to encourage Jewish and Christian support for refugee resettlement, creating an interfaith ethic of refuge. Nawyn considers how the power of religious rhetoric and values may alternately work against, influence, or support popular opinion and nation-state policies.

The Catholic church is perhaps the first transnational organization to develop in the world. Sociologist Margarita Mooney examines the Catholic church as a mediating institution between immigrants and the state, enabling new immigrant adaptation and participation in civil society. The Catholic church is also a multitiered institution, and to examine how it operates, Mooney argues that it is important to disaggregate it into three levels: the binational/supranational, the federal, and the local. At the upper echelons, the Catholic church serves as "both a partner of government and a lobbyist," as exemplified by the U.S. Conference of Catholic Bishops and their binational pronouncements on immigration issued in tandem with the Mexican bishops. At the local level, as exemplified by Mooney's case study of Haitians in Miami, the Catholic church is a service provider, advocate, and pastoral provider, allowing Haitians to learn important skills critical for participation in civil society. At the federal or national level, the Catholic church provides resources for local satellite activities, ultimately encouraging immigrant actors in civil society.

The final section considers the relation between theology, redemption, and social justice. Gioacchino Campese, writing from the perspective of a Catholic theologian and as a member of the Scalabrini Order, the only Catholic Order devoted exclusively to the mission of helping immigrants, sketches out the fundamentals of a theology of migration. According to Campese, who has organized two international conferences on migration and theology, such a theology must be fundamentally concerned with transforming and liberating migrant lives. Anthropologist Janet Hoskins introduces Caodaism, a relatively new religion born in Vietnam during the French colonial period. For Caodaists who lived through French colonialism and the postwar Vietnamese diaspora the struggle for social justice includes religious freedom and the right to have their religion recognized; activism that "addresses the wounds of colonialism" as well as racism and hardships encountered in the United States; and political activism directed toward human rights and rebuilding the religion in the homeland. In all of these efforts, Caodaists blend the traditions of Asian spiritualism with worldly activities and commitments.

This volume emphasizes the specificity of immigrant groups and underscores the ways in which different social locations offer them different standpoints from which to define social justice. As we have seen, religion, in its various forms, facilitates these pursuits. Taken together, these chapters begin to reveal that what is at work today in the United States is a large coterie of faith-based organizations, values, and coalitions that constitute a landscape of religion working for immigrant social justice. Some groups work in consortiums and coalitions, while others are dispersed and relatively untethered to similar efforts. But together they constitute an important part of the social and political context of contemporary immigration. Whether working with or against state and market forces, religion is a force to be reckoned with in the arena of immigrant social justice.

Of course, religion does not always serve social justice. As evident from history and the contemporary era, religion can serve nefarious purposes. The intent of this book is not to put religion on a pedestal as the ultimate guarantor of immigrant social justice. Rather, the intent is to recognize—and yes, salute—the efforts of faith-based activists and organizations working for immigrant social justice and to analyze some of the complex processes involved in these efforts.

2

Liberalism, Religion, and the Dilemma of Immigrant Rights in American Political Culture

RHYS H. WILLIAMS

The story of millions of people coming from various old worlds to the promise and potential of a new world is built deeply into American national mythology. Sometimes the narrative emphasizes the Anglo-Saxon origins of the pilgrims, the founding of the city on the hill, and the spread of the newly formed American culture out of New England. Other times the focus is on the waves of new immigrants that traveled through Ellis Island and other points of entry to new lives and middle-class prosperity in an industrializing nation. The recent counternarrative involves the millions of ethnic and racial minorities who came here, often in desperate poverty or enslaved, and struggled for a measure of dignity and opportunity for themselves and their families. But in each case the U.S. national story is one of immigration.

An attendant part of these narratives is the necessary negotiation and adaptation that goes on when living in a new culture. One tradition in immigration scholarship focused on this as a process of assimilation, in which immigrants eventually fit into the social structures and adopt the cultural forms and values of the host society. Other scholars have viewed the same processes as Anglo-conformity and have focused on the ways in which the power of American culture and institutions has pressured immigrants into abandoning their own cultural practices. In this telling, mobility may be available to immigrants, but only to those who have the capacity and the willingness to make themselves into copies of the dominant classes. Recent discussions of globalization and American imperialism testify to the shaping power of American culture, even among people who have not yet emigrated—implying that some significant adaptation to U.S. society has begun even before an immigrant's arrival.

The Shaping Power of American Culture as Liberalism

No matter what the evaluative assessment of the adaptation process—assimilation or pressured conformity—and no matter whether one credits the thrust of that adaptation to American values or to the coercive power of economic and other institutional arrangements, an important dimension of this shaping power is what I will call in this essay "liberalism." I hasten to note that in this essay, as in much academic writing, the term "liberalism" has only some meanings in common with its everyday use in the vernacular.[1] I use it to refer to a particular set of institutional arrangements that developed in the capitalist nations of western Europe beginning in the seventeenth century, and in many ways reaching its apex in twentieth-century Anglo-American society. More specifically for my concerns here, liberalism also refers to the sets of ideological beliefs and assumptions that have undergirded and justified the social, political, economic, and cultural arrangements in the United States.

Noted American political scholar Louis Hartz (1955) once claimed that liberalism was the only ideology legitimately available in U.S. politics. In other terms, and often with different political critiques attached to their analyses, other scholars have basically shared Hartz's view. Seymour Martin Lipset (1979, 1996) noted that the United States was without a significant socialist movement because it was also without a medieval and feudal past—meaning that liberal capitalism was our only real social and cultural tradition. Robert Bellah and his colleagues modified that view slightly but kept its main insight, by calling Lockean individualism—which is one of the philosophical bedrocks of American liberalism—the "first language of American culture" (Bellah 1985, 20, 334). Samuel Huntington (1981) also identified a type of liberal individualism—rooted in American religious culture—as the ideological home territory of reform movement of both the American left and right. One also finds in left-oriented and radical critiques of American society, such as C. Wright Mills's classic *The Power Elite* (1959), a view of a unified power structure, buttressed by a dominant ideology. Jurgen Habermas (1973) constructed a general theoretical account of late capitalist society, largely built on an analysis of liberalism as its hegemonic ideology.

There are differences in the normative assessment of liberalism's dominance. Hartz, Lipset, and Huntington have been generally celebratory about this cultural hegemony, seeing it as a source of political and social stability. Bellah and his colleagues were critical, lamenting the extent to which the instrumental individualism that made for a dynamic economy at the same time corroded dimensions of community in American culture. Mills and Habermas offered radical critiques of liberalism, portraying it as a covering ideology for an avaricious capitalist class.

Nonetheless, all of their claims for a hegemonic liberalism, particularly in American political culture, are fairly similar. And my argument here is a less expansive affirmation of that cultural analysis. In this chapter, I unpack the liberal tradition in politics, economics, and religion, then examine how this dominant culture has produced a bias toward a type of rights talk in social movements. I conclude by considering how the ways in which attempts to press for immigrants' inclusion into American society through the idea of immigrant rights has both positive and negative implications—especially for non-Christian immigrants.

Liberalism as a Philosophical Tradition in Economics and Politics

As a philosophical tradition, liberalism emerged in the writings of English and French thinkers such as John Locke and Thomas Hobbes in the seventeenth century and Adam Smith, Jean-Jacques Rousseau, and the Enlightenment in the eighteenth century. It was a time when the societal order that had supported feudalism was beginning to recede in the face of changes in the economy, politics, religion, science, and culture. The economic, political, and social leadership of the aristocracy, which was built upon title, blood, inheritance, and land, was being challenged by those who made their livings through commerce and manufacturing and justified themselves through their accumulated wealth rather than through aristocratic prestige. Monarchies were slowly giving way to legislative bodies that based their claims to authority on the will of the people rather than an inherited appointment by God. In religion the established Roman Catholic Church—which had been the primary translocal institution in western Europe since the end of the Roman Empire—gave way in many areas to Protestant Reformations.

The grounding assumption of liberalism was what is often called "social contract theory," especially prominent in the work of Hobbes, Locke, and Rousseau.[2] Social contract theory began with the premise that before the development of society humans lived in a state of nature. Life was unregulated by anything but force and, in Hobbes's words, was "nasty, brutish, and short." At some point, people came to realize that they could make their lives better by entering into agreements with one another to refrain from impinging upon others, if others did the same for them. Humans realized that by giving up a little of their freedom (the freedom to plunder others weaker than themselves) they could achieve security and a better life; a social contract developed and society was born. To ensure this security, a form of government was created. Importantly, the optimum form of this government is a minimal one—one that can ensure tranquility but goes no further in abridging the natural rights of the individual.

Note several things about this narrative, which is in effect the creation story of liberalism as an ideology. First, it assumes that humans can and did live at one point outside of society and that the people who came together to form the first society were individuals with wants, needs, preferences, and interests unformed and uninfluenced by growing up or living in community. Second, these presocial individuals are basically rational actors. That is, they calculate that the security and prosperity they can attain by agreeing to the social contract is worth the individual freedoms of action they must sacrifice. Society becomes, for them, a good deal, and they enter into a contract.[3] Finally, the social world, communities and societies alike, are but aggregations of individuals grouped together. The basic unit of society is the individual (rather than, for example, the clan, or tribe, or some other form of community), and all collectivities are merely aggregated extensions of them.[4]

The classical liberal writers were primarily concerned with how a society should organize its political and economic life. In politics, the implications of social contract theory and the minimalist theory of the state led to a theory of individual rights. The assumption is that individuals have natural and inalienable rights, appended to them based on their status as individuals. Rights are not granted by the government—or any other collective entity in society (such as the family or church)—but rather are the individual's entitlements that are to be protected from coercion by collectivities. Importantly, one of the most significant of these rights was the right to own and profit from property.

In economics, the basic organizing institution for human life became the market. In the economic tradition of liberalism, markets are defined by the free exchange of commodities (including personal labor, thought of as a commodity to be bought and sold) between property holders. They are exchanges between equals, each of whom is working to obtain a favorable deal in cost-benefit terms. Since the market equalizes and individualizes, economic relationships are thought to work best with minimal regulation or interference from the government (which would potentially skew the equality of the deal and alter the most efficient exchange conditions). Along with minimal external regulation, markets are thought to work because individuals are able to calculate their own best interests and make deals based on those interests. Thus, individual, autonomous choice is central to economic efficiency and effectiveness, in the same way that political free choice (for example, in elections), is the best way to run democratic governments.

The defense of free market economics, anticollective individual autonomy in politics, and minimal government regulatory power will sound like conservative ideas to many Americans. But when liberalism arose as an ideology in the seventeenth and eighteenth centuries, the conservative position was a defense of traditional institutions—such as the patriarchal family, the Roman Catholic Church, and the aristocratic social order. The idea that one could own property, and do with it what one wanted for personal gain and without having to consider the larger public good, was new and liberal. The notion that one was accorded rights as an individual, rather than duties and responsibilities as a member of a particular social class or ethnic group, and that these rights could not be abridged by political power, was new and liberal. Edmund Burke, the classic voice of precapitalist conservatism, wondered how it would be possible for a society so focused on the rights and privileges of the individual to stay together as a whole. What would provide the necessary glue that would hold communities together, if everyone pursued his or her own self-interest?

Adam Smith provided the most famous answer to that question in his treatise on capitalist economics, *The Wealth of Nations.* Smith argued that the pursuit of *private* interests did in fact produce a *public* good, in that the invisible hand of the market operated to integrate disparate desires into a coherent whole. Smith himself was not particularly in favor of the acquisition of wealth for its own sake. Too much of a Scottish Protestant, he harbored suspicions of the drive for personal gain. But he saw in that drive the tools and processes for the creation of a general prosperity. Similarly, contemporary economics believes that a free market can be self-regulating and promote a general public good. When the supply of any given commodity exceeds demand, the cost of the commodity drops until it becomes a good deal and demand rises to absorb the supply. Conversely, when demand exceeds supply, costs rise, putting a damper on demand (meaning, some portion of the population cannot afford it) until supply and demand balance again. Markets, when left alone to operate freely, tend toward equilibrium—the balance of supply and demand. And thus do private wants and the pursuits of private interests produce public goods, conceptualized as optimally priced commodities where demand is met by adequate supplies.

Key to all this theory—whether in economics, politics, or, by the late twentieth century, culture—is the assumption that individual, autonomous actors are the basic unit of society, and their abilities to make rational choices and maximize their individual interests is in society's best interests. Thus, liberalism as an ideology awards primacy to the autonomous individual and conceives of the public as but an aggregation of those individuals. Institutional arrangements in liberal capitalist societies protect individuals to varying degrees and organize them into markets in economics and interest groups in politics. In liberal societies the difference between private and public has been primarily along the lines of what can legitimately be regulated by the state.

A Culture of Individualism, Autonomy, and Choice

The liberal individualism of American economics and politics has been well documented. Bellah and his colleagues (1985) termed this ideology "utilitarian individualism" in order to emphasize the extent to which the focus on individual choice in economics and politics was geared toward material interests and gain. Such hallowed American mythologies as "rugged individualism" or the "entrepreneurial spirit" suppose that economic individualism explains how a new nation was forged from the wilderness, often by immigrants coming here with little but their determination to create a new and better life. That new and better life was defined as one of comfortable material prosperity and the freedom to be autonomous from the coercive power of institutions (e.g., the ability to practice one's religion without undue pressure from the government).

However, social and cultural changes in post–World War II America expanded these notions of individualism and applied the logic of liberalism to more arenas of social life. The economy grew, suburbs boomed, more people began to attend college, young couples moved away from their families and home neighborhoods, and geographic and social mobility began to loosen the ties that bound prewar society. And groups of people, particularly racial, ethnic, and religious minorities, began to demand release from their positions as second-class citizens.

The paradigmatic case of this type of change is associated with the civil rights movement of the late 1950s through the late 1960s. What is important to note is that what became the dominant interpretations of the cultural meanings, and the substantive accomplishments, of the civil rights movement and the groups that followed it made it coherent with the culturally dominant individualism described above.

In the early years of the civil rights movement, its leaders and allies generally pursued goals that focused on lowering the barriers to inclusion that existed in economic and political institutions. Equality, in the common understandings of the movement's message, meant getting the same *chance* as any other individual to succeed in the competition for economic, political, and social accomplishment within American life. For many white Americans, the problem with the Jim Crow South was that a class of people was being discriminated against based on their membership in a social group. They were not being treated as individuals with inalienable rights. Further, racism in America was largely the problem of the individual prejudices held by unenlightened people. Change individual hearts and minds and we could live in a colorblind society where each person would be treated individually and equally.

As a result of this cultural construction of both the problem and the solution to African American disenfranchisement, equal rights began to be thought of as social arrangements that maximized individual autonomy and institutional rules that treated all people as individuals, regardless of their status in any particular social group (see Williams and Williams [1995] on the master frame of equal rights). By the late 1960s and 1970s the desires for social change expanded beyond disenfranchised minorities and beyond economic and political institutions to a more widespread cultural critique. Many middle-class Americans, particularly college-educated baby boomers, began to chafe under the social mores that governed their parents' lives. Much of this developing critique used the language of liberal individualism to argue against the existing social and cultural restrictions on personal choice in the realms of sexuality, gender, religion, and the like. As a result, older prohibitions against personal vices, such as drug use or drinking, were portrayed as unnecessarily restrictive and were often called victimless crimes. Sexual intimacy was decoupled from marriage and often from romantic love. The decision to have a baby or to terminate a pregnancy became articulated as matter of choice.

During this time, institutional religion—particularly the Protestant and Catholic mainstream—lost a great deal of its cultural authority and for many denominations a fair number of members. Religiously observant people also became more openly selective about which church teachings were acceptable within their own spiritual journey (American Catholics' response to the Vatican's prohibition against artificial contraception is a case in point; see Burns [1996] and Dillon [1999]). Interreligious or cross-racial marriage became increasingly thought of as a matter of individual right to self-expression, while opposition to it became increasingly articulated as personal prejudice.

Bellah and his colleagues (1985, 142) refer to these shifts as the development of an expressive individualism (they find its origins earlier than the 1960s). The preeminent goal of expressive individualism is one of self-fulfillment, often articulated in emotional or psychic terms. Any societal restrictions on that fulfillment, or at least on its quest, is seen as oppressive and coercive—much as societal restrictions on acquisition and profit are seen as interfering in the free market. Individuals are urged to search for and realize their real selves, defined in distinction to social obligations. One motto often attributed to this cultural impulse in the 1960s was "Do your own thing." Like any popular expression, this had many interpretations, but one common idea was that self-realized individuals would be able to deal with and accommodate each other within society without needing restrictive norms and customs. There was for many people a deep idealism in this notion, the assumption that human nature was fundamentally good and could be trusted and that affairs of the heart could be simultaneously free and harmonious. That harmony would be all the more authentic because it would be essentially voluntary. Proponents of these ideas often revealed a faith in a type of invisible hand guiding the personal marketplace—where each individual can pursue his or her own thing and the result will be social and even cosmic harmony, not anarchy or a Hobbesian state of nature.

Cultural individualism has become a favorite target of neoconservative social critics who believe American individualism has gone too far. Glendon (1991, 1998), for example, is critical of rights talk in the contemporary United States because it has become an absolutist claim for individual autonomy and too often legitimates a complete disregard for the common good. Multiculturalism—ideological heir to the tolerance and push for diversity that many associate with the 1960s—is often criticized for emphasizing differences and individual privilege, rather than sacrifice for a coherent national social identity (see the arguments in

Barry [2002] and Kelly [2002]). An intellectual movement known as communitarianism has emerged, primarily composed of political philosophers and social scientists, and has developed critiques of the excesses of both economic laissez-faire individualism and cultural, expressive individualism (e.g., Etzioni 1995). Some opponents of liberal individualism see selfishness and dangerous antisocial tendencies in its basic orientation and philosophy. Others value some aspects of liberal individualism but believe it has become excessive in the United States. Many religious groups in contemporary American society—including some socially conservative immigrant groups—share this concern.

The American Religious Market

Religion in the United States has developed remarkably differently than it has in Europe (western or eastern) or Latin America. Almost all measures of church attendance, religious belief, and economic development show the United States as an outlier compared to these other regions. While there are debates about why this has been true, four basic processes help highlight this development and typify the current American religious landscape: disestablishment, diversity, voluntarism, and consumerism.

The United States, as a nation, never had an established church. Several colonies did, and some state establishments continued beyond the founding of the federal government (Connecticut disestablished in 1819; Massachusetts in 1833). But a national establishment was prohibited by the Constitution—and by the de facto diversity that was already evident in the young nation's religious landscape. By the time of the nation's founding the Congregationalist heirs of the Puritans continued to dominate New England, but Anglicans ruled the South, and the Middle Atlantic states were a mixture of Presbyterians, Quakers, and a few Catholics. This Protestant-based diversity grew dramatically in the first quarter of the nineteenth century as new Anglo-Saxon immigrants brought Methodist and Baptist traditions to an expanding frontier (Hatch 1989; Fisher 1991). Indeed, the ready access to a frontier kept an effective establishment from ever really gaining hold in the United States, and religious diversity flourished wherever the "west" happened to be at the time (e.g., northern New York's famed "burned over district" or the Cumberland frontier of Appalachia; see Finke and Stark [1992]).

The United States was without an official national church, making the religious landscape more open to institutional diversity. And, unlike most of Europe and Latin America, the dominant religious tradition was Protestant rather than Roman or Orthodox Catholic. Thus, the dominant Protestant faiths all had ideological and cultural traditions that legitimated protest, schism, and the founding of new denominations and churches. The Protestant emphasis on belief over ritual, and its focus on purity of community, made ideological conflict a consistent source of religious proliferation.

Because of disestablishment, American churches could not rely upon the government to support them, build their buildings, pay their clergy, or compel members to participate. These tasks could be accomplished only by the willing and voluntary labor of people committed to the faith (recognizing, of course, the powerful role that social pressure and community norms can put on people separate from any governmental coercion).[5] This structural requirement for volunteer member labor aligned nicely with the voluntarism central to many Protestant theologies. Particularly for Baptist, Methodist, Pentecostal, and Holiness traditions—groups that represent what would now be called Protestant evangelicalism—the only authentic religious expression was a voluntary declaration of Christ acceptance and salvation. While Catholics and cradle Episcopalians did infant baptism, these other groups accepted only adult baptisms—seeing only voluntary and free-will commitment as an acceptable path toward salvation.

Thus, much of American religion developed an ethos of voluntarism, equating individual choice, autonomy, and decision with authenticity. Over the past two centuries, this emphasis on voluntary commitment has intersected with the other cultural developments described above that expanded the scope of individualism. By the last quarter of the twentieth century, American religion was even beginning to be described with terms usually used in the economy—the religious consumer who shopped for churches emerged. While encountering criticism—many charge that such consumer-oriented behavior is superficial and geared only to self-fulfillment—many scholars and church leaders recognize its importance in American religious life.

As a result of these developments, it is increasingly common for scholars of American religion to describe it as a market. Indeed, a common approach within the social scientific study of religion is now referred to as the religious economies perspective (e.g., Stark and Finke 2000). Some of the scholars pursuing this approach use the language of economics as a metaphor for the dynamics of American religion behavior, while others take the description quite literally. In any case, much of the language that analyzes American economic behavior, by both organizations and individuals, can be applied to much American religious behavior.

For example, many commentators on American religion have noted that the United States has low barriers to entry to the religious market (Warner 1993). It does not require much to establish a new church, in that one need not have professional certifications, nor pass qualifying exams, nor receive governmental permission. Many churches begin in private homes or rented storefronts, where self-anointed preachers gather small flocks around them and try to expand their congregations through entrepreneurial activities (such as advertising). The religious market can be quite competitive, and many groups work to distinguish themselves from their competitors by emphasizing particular doctrinal and theological beliefs (see McRoberts 2003).

Proponents of a religious economies perspective credit the organization of the American religious market with facilitating religious diversity. Little state regulation and low entry barriers to participants—combined with a culture of voluntarism and an individualist consumerism—has produced a plethora of religious options. Moreover, some hold that these market conditions have produced religious vitality as well as diversity. The competition in the religion field leads suppliers of religious services to work harder to satisfy their customers, which in turn heightens the commitment and loyalty of members (e.g., Finke 1997).[6]

Thus, the language of liberalism, which began in the economy and politics, has spread to culture and religion. This is true of both the concepts used by scholars in understanding American life and the language used by many ordinary Americans in describing their preferences, values, and understandings of how society works.

Liberalism and American Protestantism

The writings of liberalism's founders were often opposed by the reigning religious authorities of their day. This should not be surprising. Liberalism arose in a societal milieu marked by established, officially sanctioned, aristocratic institutions accustomed to inherited privileges accorded by social rank. Liberalism called for a society of individuals with equal opportunity and based the legitimacy of all social arrangements on competition, supply and demand, and profit (however measured). Yet liberalism was not originally, nor is it now, inimically hostile to religion. Liberalism grew up with Protestantism in Anglo-American society and can still accommodate it (indeed, Nelson [2001] claims that economics as a discipline still has many of these moral commitments and that in some key ways economics *is* religion).

However, liberalism is more receptive to some forms of religious expression than it is to others. In the United States, nonestablishment made religion a matter for civil society and mandated a de facto pluralism. Freedom of religion over time became articulated largely as a private matter—noncoercive liberty to worship as one chooses with the attendant freedom from impositions on religious identity by organized institutional actors. This freedom was facilitated historically in the United States because of the cultural hegemony of Protestantism, and then with the growth of Catholicism, a Protestant-influenced Christianity. The dominance of society by one faith tradition made it possible for most of the nation's history to have an officially secular state, but a religiously infused civic and cultural life—because most individual choosers would choose more or less the same thing. The United States developed a desectarianized Protestant worldview and a public religious discourse that supported a generalized universalism, but one built on the assumptions that nonestablishment and individual religious freedom were compatible. They were compatible for most Americans because of a default religious model of individualized, privatized, and culture-adapting Christianity.

So, the institutional arrangements of a liberal, market-organized state protected diversity and religious choice, but these were constrained by cultural patterns and organizational privileges (and, Beaman [2003] demonstrates, by some consistent patterns in case law). In fact, significant religious diversity in American history arrived largely with new immigrants, first evangelical Anglo-Saxons, then Lutheran Germans and Scandinavians, then strings of ethnic Catholic populations, from Irish and German to Italian, Greek, Pole, and Mexican. German and eastern European Jews formed significant populations in nineteenth-century immigration. And, since the 1965 changes in U.S. immigration law, large numbers of Asians and Latin Americans have appeared, bringing with them non-Christian religions such as Islam, Hinduism, and Buddhism, as well as new forms of Christianity such as Filipino Catholicism, Korean Protestantism, and the mix of Pentecostal and Catholic practices that marks much of Central America today.

Non-Christian Immigrants and American Freedom of Religion

Diversity through immigration has encountered various levels of suppression and violence from American civil and institutional authorities. Some of the suppression has been state sanctioned (Mormons, Native Americans, certain cults; see Williams [1995b]), but other episodes of suppression have been nongovernmental and within civil society. Worries about religious diversity have often accompanied anti-immigrant sentiment and have often been racialized. Actual religious pluralism—meaning the normative valuing of the social fact of diversity—has only been established by generational adaptation over time (by both immigrants and native-born Americans), cultural changes in what is regarded as mainstream, and a series of legal judgments that have extended state protections to ever larger numbers of religious practices and identities.

One way in which the United States managed the tension among liberal individualism, religious diversity, and Protestant hegemony was to develop the concept of society as having a public/private distinction. Religious practices and observances were understood as private commitments for home and family and as irrelevant for participation in the economy or polity. Religion could be an important source of personal meaning, raising a family, even maintaining a subcultural identity, but it was fundamentally private. In this context, rights language was designed to protect the private observances of citizens while the public sphere maintained a generic, moralized, desectarian Christianity.

In sum, the incorporation of religious minorities in American culture has not been uncontentious, but it has nonetheless happened. The United States' religious diversity and its pluralism has for the most part been created voluntarily and is understood by many to be the product of our societal commitment to liberalism.

Minority religions have struggled, and continue to struggle (Beaman 2003; Sarna 1998), in a culture and society dominated by Protestantism; but one can argue both that there is less persecution of minority faiths in the United States than many other places and times in history (Beyer 2003; Warner 1993) and, more important to this essay, that liberalism has provided tools for challenging some aspects of this disadvantaged status, although at times with unanticipated consequences.

Rights Discourse and American Political Culture

The primary tool in American history used to create space for disenfranchised or disadvantaged minorities has been rights talk. Particularly since the social movements and cultural changes of the 1960s, rights talk has become a common currency for expressing political claims and social movements' demands. As such, rights language has been a useful wedge for many groups seeking to open the public sphere for full inclusion and citizenship. The cultural repertoire (Williams 1995a) of interpretation in American politics has a significant space for rights language, and claims for individual rights against discriminatory institutions resonate with Americans. This resonance legitimates claims for individual rights. At the same time, many groups find that rights talk channels them into positions or demands that incompletely express their situation or needs. This paradox bears some explication.

Over the course of American political history, the concept of rights has developed some important nuances (Shapiro [1986] and Rodgers [1987] analyze these changes). In many ways, the term "rights" is equated with the idea of liberties. The basis for this equivalency is the idea that rights are things that may not be abridged or taken away—they are inalienable. This is a common reading of the U.S. Constitution's Bill of Rights; it is a list of things government cannot do, particularly to the individual (e.g., prohibit the free expression of religion or imprison a person without due process). In this view, rights are civil liberties in that they are protection from the arbitrary power of government. Many social movement groups have argued that certain social arrangements do infringe on individual rights and they urge changes in law to remedy that inequity.

This use of the term "rights" has noble historical pedigree, with two of the most famous progressive American social movements engaged in just this type of action. The women's suffrage movement and the civil rights movement both wanted legal change—the former to establish for women the right to vote and the latter to establish that laws could not discriminate against people based on the ascriptive category of race. In both cases, legal codes enforced by the state kept a category of people from exercising full citizenship. Part of the reasoning for challenging these laws was that they violated individuals' rights—the government was unfairly abridging women's and African Americans' ability to pursue life, liberty, and happiness.

Many will point out that the suffrage and civil rights movements had broader agendas than just individual rights. But the point is that popular *interpretations* of these movements, and the changes they effected, is that individuals should not be penalized for possessing ascriptive group characteristics over which they have no control. Martin Luther King Jr.'s famous hope that people should be judged for the content of their character rather than the color of their skin is thought by many to call for a type of meritocracy, where individuals rise or fall based on their individual attributes, not for accidents of birth—a clearly liberal perspective on individuals in society. Rights, in this vernacular, are appended to individuals as individuals, helping to guarantee that they may participate in society unfettered by illegitimate external constraints.

However, another interpretation of rights equates them with what might be termed "entitlements." This construction of the term's meaning became more common after the mid-1960s as the target of rights-based social movements moved from changing the legal strictures of the state to enjoining the state to ensure nondiscrimination and full participation in culture and society. As the civil rights movement moved out of the Jim Crow South in the mid to late 1960s, and the civil rights and voting right acts dismantled the legal structure of apartheid, M. L. King was quoted as saying something to the effect of it does us little good to be able to sit at a lunch counter if we don't have the money to pay for a hamburger. This was recognition that liberty from legal restrictions was only the first step toward equality—such formal equality was a necessary, but not a sufficient, step to make African Americans full citizens and participants in American society.

Thus did the focus of the civil rights movement—and other movements that followed—shift from ending differential legal statuses toward getting government to enforce equal treatment and provide for equal opportunities. In Chicago, for example, King pushed for fair housing—by which he meant getting the government to keep real estate agents, banks, mortgage companies, and landlords from discriminating against African Americans. The farm workers movement, for another example, worked to get the government to pressure agricultural businesses to negotiate, sign, and then enforce a union contract. They were urging the state to act on behalf of a minority population.

Understanding rights as entitlements assumes that full citizenship requires more than just being left alone by the state. Full citizenship requires the opportunity for employment at a livable wage and the opportunities for economic and social mobility similar to those enjoyed by members of dominant social groups. This may require government's assistance in overcoming historical patterns of disadvantage, by first outlawing discrimination and then enforcing those laws within society. Policies such as those generally labeled affirmative action have that as a rationale—first the state needs to end its legal discrimination, then the government needs to provide a legal framework that ensures members of formally disenfranchised groups have places in civil society and the economy in order to achieve full lives. Formal legal equality must be supplemented by substantive conditions that allow equality to happen in fact.

The shift in the connotations of rights has produced, perhaps not surprisingly, declining support for rights movements among nonminorities. Partly, this is a straightforward matter of material interests; for example, it was easier for northern white Americans to support King when he was protesting Alabama's laws than when he was pushing for fair housing in the North (Platt and Williams 2002; Williams 2002). But another significant component of the increased opposition is that to many people, thinking of rights as entitlements seems nonindividualist and thus violates liberal assumptions (Williams and Kubal 1999; Williams and Williams 1995). Kymlicka (1989, 140) claims that "there seems to be no room within the moral ontology of liberalism for the idea of collective rights." To many critics, anything other than formal legal equality through the protection of civil liberties threatens to privilege ascriptive statuses and groups. American culture's interpretive push to define rights as individual properties has meant that some social movements have had their own rhetoric used against them and have found that their current needs, as a group, are not well served by rights claims.[7]

Social Justice and Immigrants Rights

There are clear implications here for recent immigrant groups, especially those who are not Christian. Recent organizing for immigrants has often used the term "immigrants' rights." This is not too surprising, given the history and success of many rights-based movements. But there are perils as well. Fujiwara (2005) studied the social movement claims surrounding a recent mobilization in California to restore benefits to Asian immigrants following 1996's national welfare reform. The campaign adopted the slogan "immigrant rights are human rights" and had some notable successes. Rights talk can be an effective political language in the United States.

But that framing had some accompanying limitations. It was not able to capture all the people who had lost benefits, nor all the benefits that had been lost. There was a "narrowing construction of immigrants," and the campaign could not "transcend to broader categories of people in poverty" (2005, 82). The category of deserving people were portrayed as suffering due to unfair ascriptive conditions, taking advantage of the universalism of rights talk. But that category (i.e., the deserving immigrant) did not reframe the basic categories or dimensions of community, commitment, or entitlement. Fujiwara shows that the rights talk was in part a tactical decision made by organizers in the face of disastrous impending changes in the welfare rules; but any later mobilization was also going to be bound by these initial framings and categories. And rhetorically the beneficiaries were severed from their immigrant community's collective needs.

Speaking of immigrants rights has some obvious advantages. It can be quickly understood in public politics and it resonates with many Americans. But it is better at achieving some goals than others. And, just as important, a rights-based discourse may not suit well the cultural assumptions and precepts of the immigrant groups who are being represented.

As noted above, liberalism as a cultural formation is better suited to some religious traditions than to others. Many Catholics who came to this country, and many of the *shtetl* Jews who came from eastern Europe, found that part of the process of adapting to the United States meant negotiating with American liberal individualism (Sarna 1998). Kraut (1998) outlined four strategies that Jews used to survive in Protestant America and makes a point of noting that these are not inherently Jewish strategies. They were strategic responses to an alien cultural setting, and they have great relevance for today's non-Christian immigrants. Many Asian religions are much more communally rather than individualist-oriented. Protestantism's emphasis is often on individual salvation and the personal transformations that accompany conversion and the commitment to Christ. Other religious traditions, such as Islam, focus on the relationship between the community and the divine. Individual liberties are not the issue, particularly in a Protestant Christian country where private religious freedoms are often well protected; the issue is the social and political space to live as a faithful *community* according to their own traditions and beliefs.

Warner (1999) notes that in broad strokes American religion has changed since the 1950s in two important ways. Most crucially for this essay, religion, according to Warner, is no longer a public force able to express universal and consensual sentiments in society. Now it functions primarily as a vehicle for subcultural reproduction for groups within society—importantly, ethnoracial or religious minorities. At the same time, religion is no longer considered part of an ascriptive social and personal identity; it is now an achieved status governed by the expectations of voluntarism and choice.

The implications for non-Christian immigrant communities are clear. More than most native-born Americans, religion is likely to be an ascriptive category for them, an identity they are born into. And it is more likely to be central to the reproduction of their subculture. As a result, many of the needs experienced by non-Christian immigrant communities are not for individualized assertions of rights, but for public social space in which they can live comfortably and worship fully (it is worth noting that many non-Christian groups have patterns of dress and language that make them distinct—a type of religious expression that spans the boundary lines between public and private and that needs more than just a civil liberties style of being left alone). American religious pluralism is giving more nonmainstream religious communities the opportunity to establish themselves in the United States, and enjoy some protections of their beliefs and practices. And yet, the principles of voluntarism, and the assumption that persons may need individualized rights that give them autonomy from their *home* communities, may make the actual reproduction of a subculture more difficult. It is a dilemma not easily contained in the rights language that most Americans are prepared to hear.

Conclusion

Language matters in trying to produce social change. Social movements need a language that can effectively persuade sympathetic people to participate actively in the movement, and that can persuade bystander publics of the movement's legitimacy and claims. The capacity to be persuaded, however, depends upon having the cultural meaning apparatus that can make sense of and incorporate a movement's language. But reigning cultural repertoires make some political languages available and legitimate, while they make other rhetorical claims less likely or less plausible. So, social movements find from the very beginning that their arguments may be limited to what is available in political culture (Williams 1995a), as dominant meanings limit how the public perceives the movement. Further, a social movement group can become boxed in by the rhetoric it uses, once it becomes publicly identified with a particular set of claims or arguments. Shifting position too much may appear insincere or opportunistic. Thus, in a political culture dominated by a particular ideological tradition—such as American liberalism—there is a tendency for all reasonable arguments to get pushed into preexisting molds.

Movements that want to promote the interests of recent and non-Christian immigrants find a clear tension between (1) the shaping power of an individualist consumer culture, with a political culture capable of hearing claims only in terms of individual rights and choice, and (2) the religious ethos and community needs of faith traditions that are best expressed in other religious and political discourses. The language of immigrant rights can open doors to political change due to our cultural resonance with rights language. But it may at the same time misrepresent some of the basic precepts of non–American born, nonliberal communities, and in turn push them into situations that are not comfortable for them.

What advocates for immigrant communities need is a language that is perhaps complementary to rights talk but that works at a communal level. Immigrant groups need a set of arguments that does more than just protect them from unfair practices by governments. They need a language with which to make a case for their entitlement to share a piece of public life. If American religious pluralism now provides a place for what Warner calls "subcultural reproduction"—which in practical terms is religious freedom—within civil society, there needs to be a language that preserves that idea when immigrant groups enter the political arena and want to influence the polity. Immigrant rights may well be effective at providing some civil liberties for individual Hindus, Buddhist, Muslims, or Sikhs, but a social justice language that respects religious communities will be needed to provide these groups the lives that this nation, in its brightest moments, promises.

NOTES

Rhys H. Williams is professor of sociology at the University of Cincinnati, Rhys.Williams @uc.edu. The author thanks Pierrette Hondagneu-Sotelo, Kelly Moore, R. Stephen Warner, and Richard L. Wood for discussions about these ideas or comments on earlier drafts of this chapter.

1. In contemporary American political speech, liberalism is a combination of a commitment to civil liberties in the political sphere, to cultural individualism and multiculturalism in civil society, and to a type of social democracy on economic issues. This constellation of issues and positions is a result of the political coalitions that emerged in the United States after Franklin Roosevelt's New Deal in the 1930s and the realignments in the body politic during and after the 1960s. Both the current Democratic party's liberalism and the current Republican party's conservatism are some distance from the ideological traditions that used those names in the eighteenth century (Platt and Williams 1997).

2. There are a number of excellent accounts of the rise, development, and implications of liberalism as ideology. Several from which I have greatly profited are Hall (1987), Kymlicka (1989), Rosenblum (1989), and Shapiro (1986).

3. For this reason, many have described liberalism's basic conception of humans and human nature as *homo economicus.*

4. Several prominent sociological theorists have taken as their primary theoretical antagonists this type of individualist, economistic theory. For example, Karl Marx had David Ricardo, Emile Durkheim had Herbert Spencer, and Talcott Parsons had Alfred Marshall.

5. Importantly, disestablishment also served to unhook religious dissent from political dissent. Without a legally established church, a religious dissenter did not become a criminal or a political protester. In my view, this decoupling of religion and political establishments kept American politics from developing a serious anticlericalism (as one can see in Europe).

6. While many credit nonestablishment and voluntarism with creating the market in which many different theological ideas and beliefs flourish, there has been less variety in American religion's *organizational* forms. This is true in the contemporary United States largely as a result of state regulation—tax-exempt status requires certain types of organizational arrangements, leading to an institutional isomorphism that has generally coexisted with theological and doctrinal variety (Williams and Massad, forthcoming).

7. That liberalism should have some difficulty accommodating certain dimensions of collective life and communal culture is evident just by measuring the considerable scholarly literature devoted to examining just that subject—only a fraction of which is cited in this essay.

PART II

Religion, Civic Engagement, and Immigrant Politics

3

The Moral Minority

Race, Religion, and Conservative Politics in Asian America

JANELLE S. WONG WITH JANE NAOMI IWAMURA

In Flushing, Queens, John Park often appears as a one-man voter registration campaign, and quite an effective one at that. As the president of the Korean American Community Empowerment Council, Park has registered nearly 4,500 people since he began the organization in 1998. His strategy: setting up a table at one of the community's many Christian churches. Park has visited over seventy-five churches and views these religious institutions as the best recruiting grounds (Nealon 2002). Such grassroots efforts have contributed to united voting blocs that have had significant effects in recent elections. With a population that is overwhelmingly Asian American (53 percent), the citizens of Flushing are responsible for voting the first Asian American into New York City office (Councilman John Liu in 2001) and the first Asian American to the New York state legislator (Jimmy K. Meng in 2004) (Hicks 2004; Kilgannon 2004).

Voter registration has become a significant organizing tool and rallying cause for immigrants and immigrant rights activists. As Park contends: "This is the only way we can get attention from the (wider) community—especially politicians. . . . All immigrants need a path. My role is to make that path" (Nealon 2004).

While forging such a path can be viewed as an exercise in American democracy, one may perhaps ask where it eventually leads. On the other side of the country, Rev. Peter Kim gathered the signatures of his parishioners at the Oriental Mission Church in Los Angeles in support of the California Defense of Sexual Responsibility Act of 2000 (CDSRA), which sought to bar public entities from endorsing, recognizing, or promoting homosexuality as acceptable moral behavior. In alliance with the California Christian Coalition, Kim and other Korean American pastors led a fervent effort to get the anti–gay rights initiative on the November ballot. While the "first statewide political campaign by Korean

Americans" (Ma 2000) ultimately failed, it did highlight the conservative side of Asian American faith-based political organizing.

These examples underscore two important trends within the Asian American community. First, attendance at religious services is associated with greater rates of participation in politics. Second, Asian Americans represent an increasingly active and visible part of the larger evangelical movement. How do we best understand the implications of these two trends and the role that evangelical Asian Americans may play in the American political sphere as their numbers continue to grow?

Religion and religious institutions have long been considered an important resource for political organizing for minority groups, such as African Americans (Harris 1994) and Latinos (Jones-Correa and Leal 2001). For immigrant dominant groups such as Asian Americans, religion may constitute an especially critical resource for political participation. Churches, temples, mosques, and gurdwaras can act as mediators between the immigrant community and American society (Miller et al. 2001), as they did in the case of registering voters in Flushing. Furthermore, these institutions help endow members with important civic skills that can be transferred into the political sphere (Verba, Schlozman, and Brady 1995; Palacios, this volume). The mobilization of Korean American churches in California in support of the CDSRA represents such a practice. However, the latter example also raises a difficult yet important question with which few studies have fully dealt: What are the *substantive political orientations* that are associated with religious attendance and affiliation for the immigrant-dominant Asian American community, particularly the growing numbers of traditional evangelical Christians?

For Asian American Studies scholars and community organizers who work with Asian immigrant groups and interpret their experience from a social justice frame, the potential relationship between religion and ideological conservatism among Asian Americans is troubling. And it is often assumed by these scholars and activists that religious belief and practice only contribute to this conservative outlook that interprets social problems as individually rooted rather than systemically caused. But is this view warranted? Or simply biased concern? Or both? In this chapter we begin to tackle these difficult questions and explore the impact that evangelical Christianity may have on social justice work within the Asian American community. Because approximately six out of every ten Asian Americans in the United States are immigrants, we consider immigration-related factors throughout much of the analysis that follows.

The Political Orientations of Evangelical Asian Americans

We lodge our query within the larger context of Asian American religious and political practice. Although exact numbers are difficult to attain, an increasing number of Asian Americans participate in the evangelical movement today (Busto 1996; Carnes and Yang 2004; Jeung 2004). When referring to such a movement, we speak in conventional terms in which Christian evangelicalism is defined by the following features: an emphasis on sharing one's faith; a reliance on the Bible as the ultimate authority; the importance of Christ's redeeming work through his sacrifice on the cross and the need to accept Christ in order to achieve salvation, an act of faith commonly referred to as being "born again" (Emerson and Smith 2000; Noll 2001; Yang 2004). Scholars estimate that about 25 percent of Asian Americans are evangelical Protestants and Catholics (Carnes and Yang 2004). One widely reported statistic from an evangelical polling firm is that the number of Asian Americans who identified as born-again Christians grew from 5 percent in 1991 to 27 percent in February 2000 (Lattin 2004b). Also that same year, Koreans made up fully one-third of the student population at Fuller Theological Seminary, one of the country's largest and most prominent evangelical training centers (Lattin 2004b). It appears that Asian Americans are not only filling the pews but also taking on leadership roles in evangelical institutions (Lee 2000).

If Asian American evangelicals follow the larger trend, then their religious commitments will play a role in shaping their political orientations as well (Lee 2000). Several studies have found that self-identified evangelicals are more Republican and conservative in their political attitudes than the general population (Noll 2001; Pew Forum on Religion and Public Life 2005); this is especially true of those who identify as traditional evangelicals—those who hold on strongly to the belief that the Bible is the unerring word of God and who go to church weekly (as opposed to centrist evangelicals, who are less fervent in both their beliefs and their attendance). Michael Emerson and Christian Smith (2001) explain why conservative religion lends support to conservative political ideologies. They argue that evangelical tenets that focus on individual effort and the redemptive power of Christ lead many to ignore structural, institutionalized, and systematic sources of racial inequality.

Russell Jeung (2004) and Fenggang Yang (1999) draw attention to the explosion of Asian American Christian churches in the United States. Far from exhibiting a singular profile, these churches demonstrate a range of political commitments and concerns. Jeung (2004) argues persuasively that political orientations among members of these churches depend upon whether the institution is a mainline Protestant church or an evangelical church. Both kinds of churches promote political activism (Jeung 2004). However, mainline churches are more likely to adopt a liberal egalitarian social justice frame that orients parishioners toward civil rights, direct action, and confronting racial discrimination, while evangelical churches are more likely to "seek social change though individual moral conversion" and to promote individualism and social conservatism (Jeung 2004). In a more recent study that includes interview data with

Asian American evangelical pastors, Jeung (2005) hones his initial findings and contends that while these evangelicals may be morally and politically conservative like their white counterparts, they are "socially liberal on racial issues" and "tend to be more color conscious in their approach."

Consistent with the larger American evangelical community, the leadership of many Asian American evangelical churches and organizations often adhere to conservative religious values, emphasizing "the authority of the Bible [and] a negative view of non-evangelical Protestantism" (Alumkal 2003). Scholars assert that Asian American evangelicals also "tend to support conservative Christian political causes such as opposing both abortion and gay/lesbian rights" (Alumkal 2003). Thus, similar to the larger evangelical community, religious, political, and social conservatism characterizes the majority of Asian American evangelical churches and parachurch organizations (Alumkal 2003; Carnes and Yang 2004; Kim and Kim 2001; Noll 2001). Moreover, like many traditional American evangelical churches, traditional Asian American evangelical churches tend to sit comfortably with certain forms of gender hierarchy and inequality (Alumkal 2003; Lee 2000; Yang 2004). In his examination of Asian American evangelical churches, Antony Alumkal (2003) describes congregants as generally supportive of the principle of male headship in the church. Such attitudes can extend to congregants' beliefs about patriarchy within the family as well.[1] Based on his case study of a Chinese Christian Church, Fenggang Yang (2004) also notes gender conservatism among U.S.-born second-generation Chinese Christians—a legacy of their parents—but further argues that such conservatism is even more widespread due to the influence of American Christian fundamentalism.

Ideological commitments, a fundamental aspect of religious life, may mean that a given religious organization is hostile to certain segments of American society, such as gays and lesbians. Don Lattin, a writer for the San Francisco Chronicle, described a protest at San Francisco City Hall following Mayor Gavin Newsom's issuing of marriage licenses to gay and lesbian couples in the spring of 2004. At the protest, "more than 100 evangelicals stood on City Hall steps and unfurled a banner that proclaimed, 'We All Agree—Marriage = 1 Man and 1 Woman." According to Lattin, many of the protesters were Asian American Christians. One spokesperson at the protest, Rev. Thomas Wang, of the Bay Area Chinese Ministerial Prayer Fellowship, claimed that radical gay rights activists had hijacked the civil rights movement (Lattin 2004a). The sentiments and actions of Reverend Wang are consistent with the role that many traditional evangelicals have taken across the country. For example, David Coolidge describes the growing conservative position within the evangelical community as perceiving a "fundamental contradiction between the 'gay agenda' and the traditional view of sexuality and marriage . . . 'compromises' with the gay agenda are bad for evangelicals and bad for American society in general" (Lattin 2004a, 94). The widespread support of the CDSRA by Korean American Christians in California further emphasizes how this is an especially salient view for the Asian American faithful (Lee 2000).

Observers also emphasize the large numbers of Asian American students who are disproportionately involved in evangelical parachurch organizations on college campuses (Busto 1996; Kim 2004). A writer for the *Boston Globe* describes Asians, especially those from China and Korea, as "the roaring engine of growth for campus evangelical groups" (Swidey 2003). As early as 1996, Rudy Busto documented that Asian Americans accounted for nearly two-fifths of the 17,000 attendees at a 1993 national conference for InterVarsity, an evangelical campus parachurch organization (Busto 1996). And published reports claim that the number of Asian InterVarsity members has grown 300 percent from 1986 to 2003 (Swidey 2003). According to Rebecca Kim (2004), Asian Americans predominate in the major campus evangelical organizations of top-ranked American colleges and universities. She writes: "About 80 percent of the members of more than fifty evangelical Christian groups at UC Berkeley and UCLA are now Asian Americans. At Yale, one of the largest campus Christian organizations, Campus Crusade for Christ, was 100 percent white in the 1980s, but now the members are 90 percent Asian. At Stanford, InterVarsity Christian Fellowship, another large campus organization, has become almost entirely Asian" (Kim 2004, 144).

Will younger Asian American evangelicals follow the conservative political path of the larger campus evangelical movement? In their discussion of religion among college students, Carnes and Yang (2004) emphasize findings from a 1997 study that show 39 percent of born-again college freshman did not think homosexual relations should be made illegal, and the same percent agreed that abortion should be legal. However, when compared to the general freshman sample in that same survey (66 percent did not think homosexual relations should be made illegal and 53 percent agree that abortion should be legal), it is clear that evangelical college students are much more conservative than their peers (Higher Education Research Institute 1998).[2]

Anecdotal evidence suggests that younger generation Asian American evangelicals may deviate from the hard-line conservative stances on social and political issues adopted by their evangelical parents. Some younger Asian American evangelicals have devoted themselves to social justice issues, such as obtaining high-quality, affordable housing for low-income racial and ethnic minority groups (Jeung, this volume). In their attempt to forge a middle ground between the public statements against homosexuality advanced by their parents' generation and the views of their more liberal peers, Asian American evangelical students often remain silent on issues like gay marriage while privately condemning homosexuality (Swidey 2003).

Data from a multicity survey of Asian Americans, the Pilot National Asian American Political Survey (PNAAPS), provides some limited support for the idea that religion can be a conservative force in the lives of Asian American Protestants and Christians.[3] Although we were not able to examine ideology and partisan-ship among evangelical Asian Americans specifically, we can assume from previ-ous discussion that many of those who identify as Christian or Protestant *and* attend church services frequently are also evangelicals. The analysis below, though not conclusive, supports the contention that even when controlling for other factors such as socioeconomic status, age, and length of residence in the United States, evangelical Asian Americans may be more conservative and Republican than the general Asian American population.

Asian Americans on the whole tend to exhibit a moderate political ideology and lean toward the Democrats in their party affiliation. Overall, survey respon-dents claim that they are very or somewhat liberal, 32 percent indicate that they are middle of the road in terms of political ideology, and 22 percent identify as politically conservative. About 35 percent of Asian Americans in the survey answered that they did not think in traditional party terms or were uncertain about their party affiliation, while 36 percent identified as Democrat, 16 percent identified as Republican, and 13 percent identified as Independent (Lien, Conway, and Wong 2004).

Although Asian Americans tend to be ideologically moderate and lean Democrat in general, there is variation within the community in terms of polit-ical attitudes and the way in which these attitudes are connected to religion. The data from the survey shows that the relationship between religion and political orientations among Asian Americans is complex. Asian American Christians/Protestants and Catholics tend to be more ideologically conservative than other Asian Americans. Similarly, Asian Americans who affiliate as Christ-ian/Protestant and Catholic also tend to identify as Republican more often than their fellow Asian Americans. Perhaps what is most striking, however, is that across every religious category, more Asian Americans tend to identify as Democrat than Republican and more tend to identify as liberal rather than con-servative. This is in stark contrast to the general American population. Accord-ing to a report from Pew Forum on Religion and Public Life (2005), more Christians (evangelicals, mainline Protestants, and other Christians) identify as Republicans than Democrats. Among American Catholics, 41 percent identify as Republican, while 44 percent identify as Democrats. This suggests that there may be important differences across racial groups in terms of the role that reli-gion plays in determining political orientations. Unlike the general population, the survey results suggest that more Asian Americans who affiliate as Christ-ian/Protestant and Catholic are Liberal versus Conservative and Democrat ver-sus Republican. However, Christian/Protestant and Catholic identifiers are more conservative and Republican compared to Asian Americans as a whole.

Why are Asian American Christians/Protestants more conservative and Republican than their fellow Asian Americans? One possibility might have to do with attendance at religious services. Past research suggests that the direction of Asian Americans' political attitudes depends in part upon the frequency of attendance at religious institutions. Lien (2004b) shows that for all Asian Americans in the survey, those who attend services most frequently are also more likely to be ideologically conservative. This is also the case for Asian American immigrants. When asked "how would you describe your views on most matters having to do with politics? Do you generally think of yourself as very liberal, or somewhat liberal, or middle of the road, or somewhat conservative, or very conservative?" 29 percent of Asian American immigrants who attend services frequently claim that they are politically conservative (as opposed to middle of-the road or somewhat or very liberal), compared to 16 percent of those who attend services infrequently or not at all. Further, those who frequently attend religious services are more than twice as likely as those who do not identify as Republican. The survey data show that along with Asian American Muslims, Asian American Christians/Protestants and Catholics exhibit especially high rates of attendance at religious services.

Multivariate analysis clarifies the relationships between religious affiliation, attendance at religious services, and political orientations and also illustrates the complexity of those relationships. In terms of political ideology, the data in table 3.1 (Model I) suggest that attendance at religious services in and of itself is not associated with self-identified conservative outlook. The analysis also reveals that once other potential influences are taken into account, Christian/Protestants who never attend religious services are *less likely* to be conservative compared to other groups. Rather, the effects of attending religious services *depend upon* religious affiliation and vice versa. The interaction between Christian/Protestant identity and the frequency of attendance at religious institutions is both positive and statistically significant. Based on this result, one can conclude that once other variables such as party identification, strength of partisanship, education, income, age and migration-related factors are accounted for, those Christians/Protestants who *also* attend religious services at least once or twice a month are more likely than others to be conservative. Those who attend services almost every week or more are significantly more likely than others to be conservative.

In terms of Republican Party identification, the analysis shows that, controlling for attendance at religious services and other possible influences on party identification, Christians/Protestants who do not attend religious services are less likely to be Republican than those who do. Controlling for other factors, there is a positive, statistically significant association between the interaction term for Christian/Protestant and attendance at religious services, suggesting that those Christians/Protestants who *also* attend church almost every week or every week are more likely to be Republican than others. (Surprisingly, those who claim no religious preference but attend religious services at least once or twice a month are also more likely to identify as Republican than most other

TABLE 3.1
Religious Affiliation, Attendance at Religious Services, and Political Orientations

Independent Variables	Model I Conservative (Dependent Variable) b	Standard Error	Model II Republican (Dependent Variable) b	Standard Error
Religious attendance[†]	0.01	0.12	0.04	0.14
Christian/Protestant[††]	−0.73	0.61	−1.81*	0.84
Catholic	−0.17	0.66	−0.12	0.82
No religious preference	−0.11	0.54	−1.64*	0.80
Interaction between Christian/Protestant and religious attendance	0.32*	0.17	0.53*	0.21
Interaction between Catholic and religious attendance	0.19	0.18	0.08	0.21
Interaction between no religious preference and religious attendance	0.20	0.26	0.61*	0.32
Strong partisan	0.37*	0.07	0.96*	0.11

Democrat	−1.44*	0.22		0.08
Education	−0.10	0.06	0.06	0.07
Family income	−0.11*	0.06	0.06	0.01
Age	0.00	0.01	0.00	0.01
English language use	0.27	0.18	−0.16*	0.23
Percent of life in U.S.	0.35	0.30	0.18	0.37
Constant	−1.76*	0.58	−4.86	0.83
	N = 954		N = 956	
	Nagelkerke R-Square = .14		Nagelkerke R-Square = .31	

Source: Lien 2004.

[†] Religious attendance is a categorical variable constructed from the question "How often do you attend religious services?" Response categories include "Never," "A few times a year," "Once or twice a month," "almost every week," and "every week."

[††] The comparison religious affiliation category is non-Western religious affiliation, including those who affiliate as Buddhist, Muslim, and Hindu.

Note: Missing values are imputed for the family income measure.

* p ≤ .10

groups and such an interaction does not hold true for Asian immigrant Catholics, who otherwise fit the criteria of the conservative faithful.)

Although the reasons for such a relationship between religious affiliation, church attendance, and political attitudes among Asian Americans might intuitively seem obvious, they are in fact complex. Asian Americans, in relation to each of these factors, appear to hold a high regard for institutional authority—whether that authority be linked with the church or the U.S. political system. One plausible explanation for the connection between the two—church authority and political conservatism—might be traced back to Asian ethnic cultural influences. As Fenggang Yang (1999) and others have argued, Confucian values that permeate Chinese and Korean immigrant cultures can be quite in tune with those values embraced by evangelical Christians in the United States—for example, family, respect for elders, and the importance of education. In fact, Asian Americans may actually choose to attend an evangelical Christian church because they believe that the institution not only upholds the ethnic values they feel are significant but also that it is the best way to transmit these values to their children (Chen 2002). A Confucian outlook also helps reinforce hierarchical structures in which authority figures such as a pastor or church elder may carry unusually high influence, whether they are preaching the gospel or promoting certain political agendas.

As Kwang Chung Kim and Shin Kim (2001) point out in their overview of the Korean immigrant church in the United States, the elders and deacons of these churches tend toward a theological conservatism (e.g., the material existence of heaven and hell, the immaculate conception of Jesus, the return of Christ to the world) that is greatly informed if not identical with their evangelicalism. They note: "Three items dealing with personal relations with God—'studying the Bible regularly,' 'spending time in prayer,' and 'attending church regularly'—received more than 60 percent 'essential' rating. At the same time, 'actively seeking social and economic justice' received the lowest 'essential' rating with 19 percent. Even 'taking care of those who are sick or needy' earned only slightly more than 25 percent 'essential' rating" (86). Following Fenggang Yang's lead (1998), the authors go on to say that the evangelical focus on "absolute moral belief and strict moral standards" provides a stable foundation for immigrants in particular in an otherwise unstable world. The Asian immigrant's life is portrayed as a "life of double jeopardy," in which she experiences trials as both a newly arrived racial-ethnic minority in the United States and as a Korean living abroad. Korean and Chinese immigrants therefore "find the certainty in evangelical belief attractive and try to maintain a firm hold on it" (92).

A parallel argument could be made in relation to these Asian Americans' political conservatism and Republican affiliation. The attitudes associated with evangelical Christian culture in the United States, as well as Republican right-wing conservatism draw from similar claims of stable foundations (church, family) and unerring truths (Bible). Theological and political conservatism become inextricably wed and infuse the Asian immigrant's life not only with meaning but also with a sense of security.

For Asian Americans, religious affiliation maps fairly closely onto national origin. For example, most Koreans in the survey affiliate as "Christian/Protestant" and most Filipino respondents affiliate as "Catholic."[4] As such, it is difficult to disentangle the effects of national origin from the effects of religious affiliation. This suggests that just as national origin may partially account for the relationship between religion and political orientations, ethnic differences among Asian Americans may also be partially driven by religion. Our analysis suggests that scholars who focus on ethnic diversity among Asian Americans must also carefully consider the role of religion in explaining group differences.

It is important to keep in mind that this analysis highlights only general trends. Like the larger American evangelical community (Noll 2001; Smith 2000), Asian American evangelicalism encompasses a significant amount of diversity in terms of beliefs, political orientations, and demographic characteristics.[5] Jeung's work (this volume) reminds us that there may be variation in the political attitudes of Asian American evangelical community and that some evangelical churches and organizations adopt more liberal approaches to politics. Further, the data do not allow us to examine attitudes toward specific political issues such as same-sex marriage, abortion, or racial equality. They do show, at least in terms of self-reported ideology and party identifications, that Christians/Protestants who attend religious services frequently exhibit distinct political attitudes from the general Asian American population, and these attitudes tend to be more conservative and Republican in nature.

Religion, Immigration, and Social Justice:
What Asian Americans Have to Tell Us

Qualitative and quantitative studies posit a strong connection between religiosity and civic engagement for Americans generally (c.f. Verba, Schlozman, and Brady 1995) and groups made up of a large proportion of immigrants in particular (Jones-Correa and Leal 2001; Lien 2004b). In their study of Latino political participation based upon the 1989–90 Latino National Political Survey and the 1990 American National Election Study dataset, Michael Jones-Correa and David Leal (2001) find a strong relationship between church attendance and voter turnout. Some scholars argue that civic skills, such as the ability to communicate and organize effectively, are fostered in religious institution and that these skills aid people in the political realm as well (Palacios, this volume; Verba, Schlozman, and Brady 1995). Others contend that religious institutions function as civic associations, bringing people together to share information about opportunities for civic engagement (Jones-Correa and Leal 2001).

According to Lien (2004b), Asian Americans who attend religious services frequently are more likely to participate in politics by becoming citizens and voting. Consistent with Lien's research, additional analysis of the survey data shows that for both Asian American immigrants and U.S.-born Asian Americans, frequent attendance at religious services is indeed associated with more participation. Those who attend religious services frequently are more likely to *register to vote, vote,* and *take part in a nonvoting activity* (such as attend a public meeting, write a letter to an editor, take part in a demonstration, or protest) than those who do not attend services frequently.[6]

Political scientists and general observers tend to assume that more political participation is better because it contributes to democracy and representation. Political theorists since Alexis de Tocqueville have claimed that involvement in civic life provides the foundation for a strong democracy. Carole Pateman (1970), among others, asserts that civic engagement fosters the skills and attitudes necessary for the democratic process and facilitates the acceptance of collective decisions. Further, participation in politics, in particular, is the mechanism by which citizens influence their government (Verba, Schlozman, and Brady 1995). Through participation, citizens further their political representation by communicating their needs, interests, and preferences to the government. Thus, because more religious involvement is associated with more participation, there are compelling reasons to assume that religion plays an important positive role in political participation.

In fact, religion does seem to encourage more political participation for Asian Americans, a group that has historically exhibited low rates of registration and voting (Lien, Conway, and Wong 2004). Immigrants, especially those from Asia and Latin America, often find themselves on the periphery of the American political system, especially in terms of their political participation. For Asian Americans, frequent attendance at religious services is associated with greater rates of political participation, particularly in terms of registering to vote and nonvoting political activities. Hence, religion can contribute to political equality and the health of American democracy by helping to increase participation among those who have been marginalized in the political system. Or for political entrepreneurs, such as John Park and the Korean American Community Empowerment Council, religious institutions can become crucial sites for political recruitment and engagement.

For many engaged in social justice work, greater political involvement among the historically disenfranchised is a worthy goal. And there is no doubt that Asian American evangelical organizations are critical for promoting the involvement of Asian Americans in the American political system. It is not uncommon for the pastor at one Asian American evangelical church in Los Angeles to encourage congregants to vote during the presidential campaign seasons (Wong 2006). However, the substantive nature of that participation should also be taken into account. Some traditional Asian American evangelical churches and parachurch organizations have taken the lead on opposing same-sex marriage and other issues associated with the Christian right. For example, Korean American clergy in California actively mobilized their congregations in support of the 2000 CDSRA antigay ballot proposition by purchasing ads in the Korean ethnic press and distributing petitions among worshippers at Sunday services (Lee 2000). Religious organizations that encourage the denial of rights to gays and lesbians or support patriarchal gender norms may encourage more political participation, but may also promote intolerance in ways that threaten some groups' democratic participation. As might be expected, political mobilization is deeply entwined with religious ideology, sometimes toward inegalitarian or intolerant ends. This is not to say that participation in religious organizations is a threat to democracy.

Many religious organizations adopt an inclusive approach to minorities and newcomers. Some provide a much-needed voice for immigrant and worker rights (Wong 2006). The work that these religious organizations are doing to further the participation and representation of marginalized groups in the United States deserves support and should be commended. We also do not mean to imply that evangelicalism, conservative ideology, and Republican partisanship are undemocratic in and of themselves. The political participation associated with these orientations contributes to democracy. Many would argue that expressing one's political viewpoints, including opposition to same-sex marriage, and mobilizing around the issues one cares about are rights that must exist in a democratic society. But if some religious beliefs and practices also lead individuals to advocate policies that abridge the equality and full participation of others in American life, the democratic value of religion must be reevaluated and constantly scrutinized.

Furthermore, a fuller profile of Asian American immigrant life that takes seriously the link between religion and political participation may prove useful for social justice work more traditionally defined. While those operating from a progressive social justice frame often readily recognize that issues involving race, gender, and sexual orientation are interrelated, if not inextricably linked, these same workers might need to consider that others who do not hold the same view may still be useful allies when it comes to particular causes. More specifically, this study as well as others (Jeung 2005) suggests that Asian American community organizers may be able to gain the support of immigrant evangelicals when it comes to issues of immigration rights or race, but not when it comes to certain legal rights for women (e.g., abortion) and for gays and lesbians (e.g., civil union). Ideological divisions within the Asian American community and among immigrant-rights advocates highlight the analytic utility of a standpoint theory of social justice (Hondagneu-Sotelo, this volume).

In this critical spirit, our own study raises new questions—ones that we would like to propose for future research. These include (1) What is the specific content of the conservative ideology that Asian American evangelical church-goers claim to uphold? (2) How do the experiences and worldview of non–Judeo Christian Asian Americans substantively shape their political orientations? (3) Is the relationship between religious affiliation and attendance at religious institutions similar or different across racial groups?

Too often scholars who study the relationship between religion and political participation treat religion as a monolithic category devoid of substantive content. Doing so leads to simplistic assumptions about the role of religion in the political lives of individuals and groups. Focusing more closely on the substantive nature of religious commitments and how those commitments affect political ideology leads to a more complex understanding of the role that religion plays in a diverse democratic society.

This said, for those who engage in social justice work in the Asian American community from a progressive standpoint, Asian American evangelicals and their more conservative outlook cannot and should not be simply dismissed. As we have seen in our analysis, these Asian Americans are definitely more conservative than the general Asian American population. However, they are still more liberal vs. conservative, Democrat vs. Republican, than Americans as a whole, which again points to a possible avenue of future research: exactly why are Asian American evangelical Christians more leftward leaning than their non–Asian American brethren?

Here the work of Asian American panethnic churches may offer a clue: with a clear focus on issues such as racial reconciliation, this constituency obviously draws heavily from their experience as racial minorities and their parents' own immigrant history. The conservative Asian American faithful may constitute potential coalition partners around issues of race and immigration spear-headed by social justice advocates, but may prove less willing to support a social justice agenda that includes other marginalized communities. As such, progressive activists and scholars might ask how such moral sympathies can be stretched to include gay and lesbian and other marginalized concerns. How can differences in political outlook be theologically and practically bridged? (Or can they?) And for the current moment: How might those committed to social justice for immigrants build coalitions, or, in Christian terms, begin to break bread, with the evangelicals in our midst on those issues individuals most likely and surprisingly agree?

NOTES

1. Alumkal (2003, 171) also emphasizes the complexity of the gender norms fostered within evangelical churches, commenting that "rather than making a simple movement from relatively patriarchal to relatively egalitarian gender norms, the individuals in this study maintained a substantial (though far from absolute) commitment to gender hierarchy. . . . However, like other American evangelicals, the individuals in

this study were not insulated from the influence of norms of gender egalitarianism manifest in some sectors of the broader American society."

2. Carnes and Yang (2004, 8) also acknowledge this.

3. The PNAAPS includes a total of 1,218 adults of Chinese, Korean, Vietnamese, Japanese, Filipino, and South Asian descent residing in the Los Angeles, New York, Honolulu, San Francisco, and Chicago metropolitan areas. These metropolitan areas are the major areas of concentration for Asian Americans in the United States. The telephone survey took place between November 16, 2000, and January 28, 2001. Respondents were randomly selected using random-digit dialing at targeted Asian zip code densities and listed-surname frames. Selection probability for each ethnic sample is approximate to the size of the 1990 Census figures for the ethnic population in each metropolitan area. The ethnic quota, however, is close to the 2000 results because of the oversampling of certain ethnic populations. The sample consists of 308 Chinese, 168 Korean, 137 Vietnamese, 198 Japanese, 266 Filipino, and 141 South Asians. When possible, the respondents were interviewed in their preferred language (English, Mandarin Chinese, Cantonese, Korean, or Vietnamese). Respondents of Japanese, Filipino, and South Asian descent were interviewed in English. The survey methodology and limitations are described in greater detail in Lien, Conway, and Wong (2004).

4. The strong correlation between national origin and religious affiliation means that it is difficult to conduct multivariate analyses that include variables for *both* national-origin group and religion due to colinearity problems.

5. Mark Noll (2001, 22) argues that "new leaders and new concerns have created a more pluralistic evangelicalism than has ever existed in American history." Similarly, Michael Emerson and Christian Smith (2001, 3) describe evangelicals as "a mosaic socially, politically, economically, and regionally," though "they share the defining features of the evangelicalism movement."

6. However, the differences in participation between those who attend religious services frequently and those who do not attend services frequently are only statistically significant for voter registration among immigrants and participation in nonvoting activities among immigrants.

4

Finding Places in the Nation

Immigrant and Indigenous Muslims
in America

KAREN LEONARD

Linking religion to issues of social justice for immigrants seems to rest on two assumptions: first, that immigrants are seeking social justice, and, second, that religion helps integrate immigrants into the nation and achieve social justice. Most of the immigrants thus envisioned are undocumented or poor, and most of the religious movements reaching out to them that have been studied are Christian. Muslim immigrants in the United States, however, do not conform to this pattern. Muslim immigrants are one of two major groups of American Muslims, the other being indigenous African American Muslims. Despite their very different histories, these two groups were trying to move closer together at the end of the twentieth century (Leonard 2004). However, after the terrorist attacks of September 11, 2001, immigrant Muslims and African American Muslims find themselves moving further apart. Race, always of crucial concern to African Americans, has become crucial to immigrant Muslims, but in a new way, as many immigrant Muslims develop the idea that they are being racialized as Muslims. The two groups are also diverging on issues of law and social justice. As scholars in the two groups attempt to reconcile Islamic and American law, it is African American Muslim legal scholars who are seeking more radical rein-terpretations of Islamic law in America, although the two major thrusts under way are again very different from each other, one highlighting the needs of poor black Americans and the other of women. It is middle- and upper-class immigrant Muslims who are mastering and using American law for their own security and protection, turning from concerns of social conservatism to civil rights, justice, and freedom of speech.

Furthermore, in tracing the converging and diverging histories of indigenous and immigrant Muslims, one finds that these two groups of American Muslims have changed positions on the issue of integration into the nation in

fascinating ways, ways that have different implications for issues of social justice. While major early African American Muslim movements encouraged members to seek separation from the American nation and to look for social justice
in Asiatic origins and the Islamic religion, early immigrant movements encouraged their members to be simultaneously American and members of an international Islamic *umma*, envisioning American leadership of that international
umma. Now, leading African American Muslims stress their Americanness, con-
trasting themselves to immigrants whose cultural baggage constrains their full
citizenship, yet they invoke the pluralist legal traditions of the umma to allow
for contextualized interpretations of Islamic law tailored to the needs of oppressed
blacks and/or women in America. The immigrants, in turn, stress their status as
American citizens and seem to be emphasizing the universal principles of
Islamic law and its areas of agreement with generalized American notions of
social justice.

To establish these points, some historical review is needed. Indigenous
African American Muslims were arguably the first in the United States to mobilize on the basis of the religion of Islam, and they did so in the early twentieth
century, seeking to attain social justice by building new and separate religious
and socioeconomic communities as best they could. African Americans moving
north in the late nineteenth and early twentieth centuries were not only trying
to establish themselves economically but were looking for alternatives to white
and Christian domination. They created new and syncretic religions, several
strongly oriented toward Islam. Of the two early movements to Islam, the Moorish
Science Temple (1913) and the Nation of Islam (1930), the first counseled loyalty
to the nation, but the second and more powerful movement explicitly encouraged members to reject citizenship and duties like voting and service in the military. Although in both cases contact with early Arab Muslim immigrants seems
to have furnished some of the impetus and provided some of the content of
these movements, there was little significant interaction between indigenous
African American Muslims and Muslim immigrants. The arrival of a few dedicated Ahmadiyya missionaries from British India in the 1920s did give both
movements access to the Ahmadi English language translation of the Koran and
some of the Old World teachings (Allen 1998; Curtis 2002; Nuruddin 1998).
These and other African American Muslim movements, based in poor inner-
city communities, battled crime, drugs, and poverty by building economic self-
sufficiency and offering new spiritual resources.

The second group to mobilize on the basis of Islam in North America was
that of Arab Muslim first- and second-generation immigrants in the 1950s and
1960s. Many had come, along with larger numbers of Christian Arabs, in the late
nineteenth century; others were foreign students. Earlier, Arab Muslims had
mobilized on the basis of national origin, of Arabic culture, together with Arab
Christians. They, too, found that American notions of race initially complicated

their citizenship, but early decisions that Arabs were Asiatic and therefore could not be citizens were reversed and they were classified as Caucasian and white (Joseph 1999). The Arab Muslim leaders of these early movements (the Federation of Islamic Associations, the Muslim Students' Association, the Islamic Circle of North America) mobilized to maintain and transmit their religion in North America, in Canada as well as the United States; their focus was inward, on members of their families and communities.

It was only after 1965, when the Immigration and Naturalization Act of that year spurred the immigration to the United States of increasing numbers of Muslims from all over the world, particularly from South Asia, that American Muslims began to form political coalitions on the basis of religion and encourage participation in national politics. South Asian Muslims, a strikingly well-educated group of new immigrant professionals, now constituted a third major group of American Muslims. These new Muslim immigrants arrived after the 1923 decision to bar Asian Indians from citizenship as nonwhites had been set aside by the Luce-Celler bill of 1948 (Leonard 2002b), and they and other post-1965 Muslim immigrants gradually moved to become U.S. citizens. Muslim national political coalitions sprang up in the 1980s and 1990s (American Muslim Alliance, American Muslim Council, Muslim Public Affairs Council, Council on American-Islamic Relations). Arab and South Asian leaders made efforts to involve some African American Muslim groups in these coalitions. The renamed Nation of Islam, led by Warith Deen Mohamed, son of Elijah Muhammad, who died in 1975, was moving close to mainstream Sunni beliefs and practices, and Warith Deen Mohamed participated in some coalition activities, notably as a member of the Islamic Society of North America's governing council. At the turn of the twentieth century, although statistics are disputed, African American Muslims constituted from 30 to 42 percent of the American Muslim community, while Arabs constituted from 12 to 33 percent and South Asians from 24 to 29 percent (Leonard 2003). The three major groups of American Muslims were working on converging constructions of race, religion, and the nation and on converging religious and political trajectories in the late-twentieth-century United States (Leonard 2004). Still, their focus was not on social justice but on maintaining and furthering Islam, and the immigrant alliances with African American Muslims were weak.

However, the traumatic attacks of September 11, 2001, on the Pentagon and the World Trade Center disrupted this process of convergence. Nomination of American Muslim spokespersons by mainstream politicians and the media moved beyond the national coalition Muslim leaders and widened the range of representatives of Islam and Muslims in the United States. After 9/11, all major Muslim national organizations have reflected a growing and more open recognition of differences among Muslims. The open recognition of diversity and the broader range of religious and political actors seems healthy and is drawing all

Muslims into closer engagement with the nation, yet it is clear that diverging ideas of law and social justice within the American Muslim community are dividing immigrant and indigenous Muslims.

American Muslims were thinking about their place in the nation and in the world before 9/11 with great optimism (Khan 1998), an optimism that character-ized Muslim organizational efforts in the 1990s. These national religious and political coalitions were and are led by immigrants, most of them Western-educated professional men. Not scholars of Islamic law and civilization, these leaders made their own literalist, often rather puritanical and conservative, interpretations of the core Islamic texts and talked confidently not only about representing Islam in America but also about leading the umma or international Muslim community. At the same time, however, in their separate organizations and coalitions they were building and in the surveys they were taking (e.g., Bagby, Perl, and Froehle 2001), they were defining the Muslim community in certain ways, drawing bound-aries that kept out those they considered marginal: Ahmadis (a sect declared legally non-Muslim in Pakistan in 1974), Nizari Ismailis (followers of the Aga Khan), Sufis (followers of mystical paths in Islam), and the Nation of Islam (Louis Farrakhan's split-off from Elijah and Warith Deen Mohammed's early Nation). The national leaders had no significant challengers in the 1990s, and they did have tremendous optimism and forward momentum. In fact, the national Muslim coalition, AMPCC, supported the Bush/Cheney ticket in 2000 and urged Muslims to vote Republican (their primary consideration was the Israel/Palestine issue). African American Muslims were minor players in these national political coalition efforts.

Then, after 9/11, these self-appointed national leaders were challenged and often set aside while President Bush, other reigning politicians, and the media looked for Muslim leaders who were less insistently negative about American foreign policy, more willing to criticize Islamic extremism, and more sympathetic or "American" in appearance and accent. They found such "more congenial" leaders among those marginalized by the American Muslim political organizations. They found Sufis, Nizari Ismailis, African American men and white women con-verts, and academics, scholars of Islamic law and civilization (Leonard 2002a). Newly in the spotlight were people like Sheikh Hamza Yusuf (Sufi and Islamic law teacher), Ali Asani (a Nizari Ismaili and Harvard professor), Khaled Abou El Fadl (UCLA professor of Islamic law), Shaykh Hisham Kabbani (controversial leader of a transglobal Sufi order); Ingrid Mattson (a white woman convert and Islamic Society of North America officer); and Siraj Wahaj (a powerful African American Sunni orator and imam of a mosque in Brooklyn). These new spokes-people ably represented and defended Islam to the American public. Warith Deen Mohammed, leader of the Muslim American Society, the largest African American Muslim community, spoke primarily to his own people and empha-sized being American, blending in. His group, basically the Nation of Islam he took over after his father Elijah Muhammad's death in 1975, had been renamed several times: in the 1990s it was the Muslim American Society, with Mohammed saying that Islam came first; his emphasis was on orienting his community toward Sunni Islam. After 9/11, W. D. Mohammed changed the name again, to American Society of Muslims, putting America first, he said.

African American Muslim efforts to seize the initiative and regroup after 9/11 have widened the split between immigrants and indigenous Muslims. While several immigrant Arab and South Asian Muslim groups have tried to merge after 9/11 (the American Muslim Alliance and American Muslim Council attempted a merger, as did the Islamic Circle of North America and the Muslim American Society, the former a Pakistani-dominated religious group and the latter an Arab-led group that had appropriated Warith Deen Mohammed's name for his community), African American Muslims have experienced further divisions, both from immigrant Muslims and within their own ranks. On the one hand, an observer says (Rouse 2003, 219), "the events of 9/11 freed the African American community from the shadows of the immigrant Muslim community. . . . one brother mentioned . . . how nice it has been to speak at interfaith meetings . . . as an authority on Islam." A member of Warith Deen Mohamed's community told me that the American Society of Muslims felt its American roots now entitled it to a greater leadership role. She argued that African American Muslims are well suited for interfaith activities; their Christian backgrounds have remained relevant after conversion, since Islam includes Abraham, Jesus, and others in its line of prophets before Muhammad. On the other hand, there is some evidence of decline of African American Islam. Ihsan Bagby's survey of mosques in the Detroit area mentions the possibly declining fortunes of African American mosques; this survey also showed that African American Muslims are least likely to follow classical schools of law and heavily favor contextual approaches (2004). The latter point brings issues of social justice to the fore.

But organizational changes among African American Muslims bring issues of social justice even more strongly to the fore. Leaving aside the puzzling and unresolved current state of Warith Deen Mohammed's community (in August of 2003, Mohammed unexpectedly stepped down from the leadership of his community and did not install a successor to lead this community of some one thousand imams and mosques), there has been the very significant founding of a new African American–led split-off group from the immigrant-led Sunni Muslim groups. MANA, the Muslim Alliance of North America, justifies the split-off by talking about social justice. Powerful African American Sunni Muslims were involved in planning this since 1999, with Jamil Al-Amin (the former H. Rap Brown) in Atlanta and Imams Siraj Wahaj and Talib Abdur-Rashid in New York; they conferred with other indigenous leaders, including Shaykh Hamza Yusuf. After Jamil Al-Amin's arrest in 2000, MANA was formally inaugurated in February of 2001. Its head is Siraj Wahaj, Sunni imam of the Al-Taqwa mosque in

Brooklyn and a very charismatic speaker; other leaders include Ihsan Bagby, long a key insider in the Islamic Society of North America, and imams in Cleveland, Detroit, Ann Arbor, New Haven, and North Carolina.

These indigenous almost entirely African American Muslim MANA leaders have turned away from the national immigrant-led organizations because of their failure to work for social justice for African Americans. They argue that the national organizations do not reflect the concerns of indigenous Muslims, they focus on overseas agendas, and they are trying to become part of the dominant or white mainstream culture. The leaders of MANA are also alienated from Warith Deen Mohammed's community, charging it with ignoring the problems facing black Americans, talking about Arabic and traditional Islam, and trying to join the American middle class. MANA goals call for maintaining a critical stance toward American society, and they define "indigenous" as "anyone who is native to America, thus including second generation immigrants" (http://www.mananet.org/about.asp). The fall 2003 issue of *Grassroots*, MANA's journal, features stories on particular African American Muslim congregations and activities like an annual Islamic Riyaadah or sports activities day in Cleveland and an Islamic Family Reunion and Hip Hop Conference in Atlanta.

This African American Muslim separatist initiative is also reflected in academic battles. As a respected African American Muslim scholar of Islamic law, Sherman Jackson has publicly attacked Khaled Abou El Fadl, the latter professor of Islamic law at the University of California in Los Angeles and now part of a newly emergent progressive Muslim group of academics. Jackson (2003) claims Abou El Fadl (2001, 2003) and other immigrant intellectuals are buying into white America's claims to false universalisms and are overlooking the justifiably different African American interpretations of Islam and African American needs for social justice. Jackson calls for different versions of Islam tailored to constituencies strongly marked by race, class, and histories within the nation. He accuses immigrant Muslims like Abou El Fadl of being "American Muslim romantics" who try to appease the dominant culture by presenting an acceptable "universal" and progressive version of Islam; he sees them as presenting only a part, a specifically Middle Eastern "East's truth", as the whole in order to preempt views that lie outside the boundaries of their imagination or experience (Jackson 2003, 116). Asserting that the Prophet Muhammad was sent for all peoples, at all times and in all places, and that there are not only New and Old World realities but also different realities within the New World, Jackson sees Islam's pluralistic legal traditions as enabling interpretative communities to adapt Islam to their circumstances. Jackson would use Islamic legal traditions to justify polygyny (to ease black women's poverty), Islamic punishments for adultery (when it destroys and impoverishes black families), violence (in the face of the overwhelming and unjust state power exercised by Israel against the Palestinians), and affirmative action (rather than reliance on Islam's commitment to equality). If American Islam is to be truly pluralistic, he writes, "it will have to be bold and vigilant in its refusal to ignore or jettison any of these histories and experiences in favor of appeals to a false universal, no matter how chic, power-ful, or expedient the latter may be (Jackson 2003, 132)." Jackson (2005) makes a powerful case for Blackamerican Islam (his phrase) and against white and immigrant elitism as he grounds African American Islam firmly in American, not Middle Eastern, religious history.

Jackson is making the same point being made by the mosque-based imams who founded MANA. His turn against Abou El Fadl, a highly trained *fiqh*, or juris-prudence specialist, is a turn against others like him who represent an important strand of cosmopolitan Islam in the West. This strand could be called progressive or liberal (Kurzman 1998), sometimes even feminist in ideological orientation, and it has become high profile after 9/11. The range of spokespeople here is broad, including not only Sunni Muslims but also Nizari Ismailis and other Shias; it con-spicuously includes Muslim women who are immigrants, African American, and Euro-American, some of them Sufis. A recent book, *Progressive Muslims* (Safi 2003), exemplifies this strand and its cosmopolitan base in America. The fifteen contrib-utors are almost all now teaching in the United States, but many are immigrants, and their academic degrees come from all over the world. Four are American con-verts, two of them African American women. The new Union of Progressive Mus-lims (fall 2004) and the Web site, Muslimwakeup.com, go well beyond the book's agenda in terms of sexuality and gender issues.

A major component of this emerging progressive Islam in America is the gender jihad (Webb 2000); but here, too, there are divisions emerging not only along immigrant/indigenous lines but also along lines of social justice. Like women in other religions in the United States (Braude 1997), Muslim women play key roles. An early researcher (Elkholy 1966) argued that in the early decades among Arab Muslims the energy and activity of women was key to establishing major mosques in Detroit and Toledo, and American Muslims are beginning to recognize that early history and the key role of Muslim women today. The Muslim feminists writing about Islamic law and jurisprudence include indigenous and immigrant Muslim women. Amina Wadud (1999), an African American Muslim and an Islamic Studies professor, is a leading thinker here, calling for a radical and continual rethinking of the Koran and hadith, asserting that much now con-sidered divine and immutable sharia or law is the result of a long, male-dominated intellectual process. Another African American Muslim and a Sufi, Gwendolyn Zoharah Simmons writes of the growing number of Muslim women scholars and activists "seeking to separate Islam, the religion, from culture, tradition, and social mores. . . . at times bringing to the foreground the interpretations of earlier sects or groups in Islam who were labeled heterodox and their views dismissed" (Sim-mons 2000). The gender jihad, then, works across denominational boundaries, too, one of the few movements in American Islam to do so (and thus participate in the blurring of denomination boundaries now characteristic of American Christianity [Wuthnow 1988]). A 2004 march on a mosque by six Muslim women (Arabs, South Asians, and an African American) attracted media attention (Goodstein 2004). Since then, in an even more widely reported event, Amina Wadud gave the sermon and led men and women in Islamic prayer in a New York City setting on March 18, 2005. An incident leading up to her prominent role in this innovation involved apparent attacks on her by Arab Muslims while at a Toronto speaking engagement. However, Jackson would classify feminist reinterpreters of Islam, including Amina Wadud and other African American scholars, as moving to placate white mainstream America as part of the progressive movement he sees co-opted by immigrant intellectuals impervious to the needs of African American Muslims.

Issues of social justice in the wake of 9/11 have forced immigrant Muslims to see themselves as newly racialized on the basis of their religion. The national Islamic and Muslim political organizations have been pushed into new and different paths in the American political landscape after 9/11. Joining in two significant trends in the religious sphere of American life, the formation of "special purpose religious coalitions across denominational lines" and the growing importance of religion in American civic life (Wuthnow 1988), Muslim political organizations and coalitions were and are clearly participating in both, taking stances on highly divisive public issues and contributing to America's expanding but increasingly politicized civil religion (Khan 2002). Previously, American Muslim political organizations were more conspicuous on the conservative end of the political spectrum, with Muslim groups at both local and national levels talking about Muslim family values, American immorality, and issues like homosexuality, marriage, and divorce. But now the liberal end of the political spectrum is being embraced as American Muslims, along with others, emphasize civil rights, justice, and the freedom of speech and assembly.

Some of the national Muslim organizations are also moving along the lines of the academic progressives. One of them, the Muslim Public Affairs Council, or MPAC, made progressive Islamic thought the theme of its 2003 convention in Long Beach and invited some of the academics in the Progressive Muslims volume to speak; MPAC has also published an issue of its journal, *The Minaret*, focused on progressive Islam and Muslims and advocating moves in that direction. The third annual convention of MPAC was held in December, 2003; the January 2004 *Minaret* issue title was "Progressive Muslim Thought: A Window to the Future." MPAC also started a National Grassroots Campaign to Fight Terrorism, enlisting mosques and working with the FBI and other law authorities, in July 2004. Even the more religiously oriented and conservative Islamic Society of North America, or ISNA, in its journal, *Islamic Horizons*, started a three-part series on its own history, with a focus on the role of Muslim women in nurturing the Muslim Student Association and its development into ISNA

(May/June 2003), and the July/August 2004 issue focuses on civil rights. This growing liberal, moderate, or progressive movement wherever it manifests itself is under attack from immigrant Muslim conservatives.

Even immigrant Muslim conservatives, however, tend to support interfaith and civil rights activities, activities now prominently engaged in by all of the American Muslim national coalition groups. There is much discussion of the new racialization of immigrant Muslims (although it is often traced back to political events in the Middle East and Iran and their repercussions in the United States). The older American racism against African Americans is not brought into these discussions, but new initiatives are taken to reach out to civil and human rights groups and to Japanese Americans, who came forward to support American Muslims after 9/11. Indignant articles about discrimination on the basis of names, of *hijab*-wearing, of Arab or Muslim appearance, are produced and reproduced, and alliances with Sikhs from India (whose turbans provoked harassment and even murder in two cases after 9/11) and others are vigorously pursued. The focus is, again, on fellow immigrants even more than fellow Muslims, an emphasis that may change as younger, American-based Muslims of immigrant ancestry move to leadership positions.

The stances of immigrant Muslims and indigenous African American Muslims on integration into the nation have changed. Despite the highly negative impact of 9/11, it can be argued that there has been an opening up of the political arena to American Muslims and among American Muslims after 9/11, accompanied by a growing realism or openness on the part of Muslims about differences among Muslims. Yet the new organizational efforts and also the new and diverging interpretations of Islamic law reflect sharp differences of national origin, race, and class in America. Immigrant Muslims are taking up issues of civil rights and social justice concerned with the war on terror but not concerned with race relations in the United States; they are leaving that to African American Muslims, whose spokespeople and organizations are now emphasizing race relations above relations with immigrant Muslims. African American Muslims are now strongly claiming their American roots, no longer arguing for separatism from America but from immigrant or Old World Islam and from immigrant Muslim leadership. Immigrant Muslims are no longer talking about the international umma or emphasizing connections to Muslims outside the United States; indeed, most groups have moved to disassociate from donors and influences beyond U.S. borders. They now emphasize their citizenship in the United States and accommodations of Islamic and American law that will grant them justice and liberty within the framework of the nation. Both groups are increasingly engaged in American society and politics despite their differences, more engaged than was historically true for either the immigrant or indigenous Muslim communities.

5

Faith-Based, Multiethnic Tenant Organizing

The Oak Park Story

RUSSELL JEUNG

On a bright San Francisco morning in the fall of 2000, an unlikely group emerged laughing from an ornate skyscraper.[1] Among the three dozen assembled were undocumented residents from Mexico, a European American minister, Cambodian refugees, and a Taiwanese American city planner. They had just won almost one million dollars from their landlord in one of the largest legal settlements of its kind (DeFao 2000). In addition to winning monetary damages for forty-four households, the group's victory transformed the complex into brand new apartments that are held permanently at affordable rents. Overcoming obstacles of race and class, the Oak Park Tenants Association is a model of faith-based, multiethnic community organizing.

This housing victory was unlikely because it involved primarily Latinos, some of whom avoid the government for documentation reasons, and Cambodians, who had been tortured by their government (Counts 1999a; Ochs and Payes 2003). Linguistic isolation prevented them from understanding the American legal system or fully integrating into this society (Bolivar et al. 2002). And because the tenants were on public assistance or worked as day laborers, they could not afford other housing if they were to be forced out. Despite these fears and structural barriers, the tenants organized against substandard living conditions that threatened their health and safety. Remarkably, these two ethnic groups joined together as a tenants association and remained united throughout the three-year struggle. The anomalous success of their efforts demonstrates the need for communities to build upon both the ethnic and religious social capital of low-income communities. Similarly, this case study demonstrates how faith-based organizers required both kinds of capital to bond the tenants and bridge them to outside resources.

Theories of Social Capital and Community Organizing

Both social movement research and community organizing literature assert the social capital is a necessary factor for group mobilization. Robert Putnam's *Bowling Alone: The Collapse and Revival of American Community* distinguishes two dimensions of social capital. According to Putnam, "social capital refers to connections among individuals—social networks and the norms of reciprocity and trustworthiness that arise from them" (Putnam 2000, 19). This capital may be "bridging" and encompass people across social cleavages, or it may be "bonding" and reinforce exclusive identities. For example, religious institutions may bridge Latinos and Asians as they attend a Catholic church and connect them to job opportunities offered by other parishioners. On the other hand, a Buddhist temple may merely bond those who are Thai because of the language and rituals employed. For those in low-income communities, social capital is especially important because they have less access to human capital (education) and physical capital compared to other communities.

Richard Wood (2002) applies these concepts about social capital in his comparison of race-based and faith-based community organizing. He argues that multiracial groups have restricted access to social capital in that racial groups usually have little trust and interaction with one another. Consequently, organizers of multiracial organizations expend considerable efforts building trust among racial groups. Faith-based organizers, on the other hand, can draw upon networks established within congregations. More significantly, religion offers both a rich symbolic culture (songs, scriptures) and structural information channels to mobilize members (Greeley 1997; WOOD 1997). As a result, faith-based community organizing groups serve as better bridging institutions than race-based ones.

Faith-Based Organizing of Immigrants

Similarly, Mark Warren observes the difficulty in organizing these largely immigrant communities. He explains, "We simply do not have very many institutions in which Americans from different racial groups cooperate with each other" (Warren 2001, 27). He suggests that networks of faith-based organizations offer space where multiethnic groups can cooperate and participate in politics. Organizers in these faith-based, immigrant networks have utilized four key principles that they have found to be successful. First, they apply the "Iron Rule" that organizers should not do for others what they can do for themselves. Instead, they aim to develop local leadership and organizational capacity so that groups themselves can voice and lobby for their concerns.

Second, immigrants organize around issues of self-interest that tend to be broad based. Mary Ochs and Mayron Payes observe that recent newcomers "will not find their new living conditions in the U.S something to organize about," but will address issues when they "experience extreme discrimination or victimization" (Ochs and Payes 2003, 20). Both community organizations and unions now acknowledge that immigrant organizing should be done in and out of the workplace and should be holistic in concerns (Louie 1992; Wong 1994).

Third, faith-based organizers recognize that ethnic faith-based institutions offer great networking opportunities. Unfortunately, community activists have ignored these temples and congregations for a variety of reasons (Yoo 1999). However, the faith communities offer immigrants safe places to voice their fears and issues. These indigenous organizations often operate like large, extended families and can turn out numbers at direct action events (Bolivar et al. 2002).[2]

Lastly, organizing immigrants requires an understanding of the group's history and traditions, as well as their community strengths (Gutierrez et al. 1996). Besides building upon family and religious networks, organizations can mobilize through ethnic markets and media. To agitate groups to action, organizers have learned they must earn the right to meddle by building personal relationship and valuing the group's traditions (Noden 2002).

These understandings of social capital and the principles of faith-based organizing have arisen from case studies of successful organizing networks. Organizers work with multiple organizations that usually share the same general faith. In contrast, this case study of Oak Park involves immigrants coming from Buddhist, Catholic, and evangelical Protestant backgrounds. Furthermore, the tenants did not belong to preexisting formal organizations. In fact, the Cambodians and Latinos living in this apartment complex had occasional conflicts with one another as a result of language barriers and mistrust. The organizers at Oak Park, therefore, needed to establish both trusting relationships and a new organization in order to mobilize successfully.

Participatory Action Research Methods

This study is the result of participatory action research over twelve years. As a Chinese American sociologist, I moved into Oak Park in 1992 to learn about the adjustment of Southeast Asian families to low-income, urban settings. I entered this field site through introductions by staff of Harbor House, a Christian ministry in the neighborhood. As my roommate and I developed relationships with our neighbors, youth and parents asked for assistance in their education and in dealing with government agencies. I quickly realized that I could not study these families as an objective outsider. Instead, they became like extended family members to me as they welcomed me to their homes, fed me, and protected me in various situations. As a fellow Asian American, I did not want only to document the lives of Cambodian Americans, but also to empower my community.

Subsequently, other Christians volunteering with Harbor House and I became actively engaged with our neighbors around issues affecting immigrants.

Our organizing efforts around the housing conditions at Oak Park came after six years of building relationships and trust. Four years after winning this legal settlement in 2000, I have interviewed 25 percent of the households who participated in the case with the help of Spanish and Khmer translators. To do so, we did utilize social capital within the local ethnic groups as well as the resources of our faith-based group.

Oak Park Apartments: History and Demographics

Oak Park Apartments originally was a fifty-six-unit apartment complex in the San Antonio/Fruitvale district of Oakland, California. The one-bedroom apartments all faced a central courtyard, which filled with scores of children after school. With an average family size of more than six persons, Oak Park children had to sleep in the living rooms. In fact, the complex was well known for being an overcrowded tenement for recently arrived refugees.[3]

Oak Park's neighborhood is an exemplar of an impoverished, underclass barrio. According to the 2000 U.S. Census, the community was 52 percent Hispanic, 25 percent Asian, 16 percent African American, 3 percent white, and 1 percent Native American or Pacific Islander. Children and youth dominate the streets, with 36 percent of the population under eighteen. Locked out of job markets because of language and immigration status, 51 percent of those over sixteen were not employed, and 54 percent received some type of public assistance. One-third of the families in the neighborhood were below the poverty level and 62 percent had not completed high school.

Those living at Oak Park were even worse off than their neighbors. The Cambodians, who arrived in the mid-1980s, had gone through the genocidal killing fields of the Pol Pot regime and still suffer greatly from posttraumatic stress syndrome. One forty-four-year-old woman, Sarah Prum, shared her experiences about this time: "I was about fifteen years old when the Khmer Rouge came into Cambodia, and they took both my mom and dad and killed them. My oldest sister had a nephew who was about a year old. They tossed him up and had him fall onto a rifle bayonet. Later, life at the work camp was very hard. We had no food. A half-cup of rice had to be shared between about thirty people. I dug up for potatoes in the fields for food to eat. We worked at early sunrise . . . from five in the morning to midnight."[4] The ravages of war and the refugee experience created such dislocation that few could concentrate to learn English and gain meaningful employment.

The Latino families also moved to Oak Park for the low rents. By the mid-1990s, 45 percent of Oak Park households were Cambodian, 45 percent were Latino, and the rest included Chinese Americans, African Americans, European

Americans, and Native Americans. The Latinos, many of them undocumented, had to survive on day labor work. Francisco Martinez described the hardships of moving to Oakland in order to support his family:

> We brought [our oldest daughter] here at three months, when she was very small. And we crossed [the border]. . . My God, how one dares to do things! We crossed hugging her and running. I tried to bring her by getting her a passport, but I couldn't because, well, it was not possible. And I did not have enough money to do that. So, I tried to cross the border.
>
> That first year was stressful because when you arrive in a new place, it's difficult. You have to learn how to get a job—someone has to teach you the streets, how to go on the major streets to look for your jobs.

Because of their undocumented status, families could only find temporary work without benefits. Latinos and Cambodians banded with co-ethnics at Oak Park for mutual support in adjustment, job information, and local resources offered by the government and nonprofits. Sitha Le, a mother of five, whose husband had left, explained why she moved to Oak Park: "At Oak Park I saw a lot of Cambodian people, and I liked living near to other Cambodian people. If I have a problem, I can go to talk to them, get some advice or suggestions for what I can do to solve a problem. If we're sick, we can help to take care of each other. I didn't really know anyone here before I moved here, but it was easy to get to know them, and I became friends with the people here." Similarly, Mexican families encouraged other family members to rent at Oak Park so that they could look out for one another, and to have close access to bilingual educational and health resources.

While these two ethnic groups lived side-by-side at Oak Park, they rarely interacted with one another because of language differences. Even the children remain segregated as the local school tracked them into different bilingual programs. The older youth maintained friendships along racial lines and gang affiliations. Periodically, contentious interactions would escalate into racialized conflicts. Because individuals could not distinguish the members of another group, they tended to blame an entire group for problems rather than seeking to hold an individual responsible. Mrs. Le complained about the ethnic conflict and perception of out-group homogeneity: "We've had some problems with other members living in Oak Park from different ethnic groups. Some people have accused my kids of stealing their things, a computer laptop, and they called the police. I was very afraid."

Another group came to Oak Park in the 1990s, but religious faith connected them rather than ethnic bonds. In the late 1980s, a nonprofit organization, Harbor House, began offering English as a Second Language (ESL) tutoring at Oak Park as part of its Christian ministry to refugees. When Daniel Schmitz arrived in 1989 to start a cleaning business that employed refugees, Harbor House had already developed trust with the tenants. As another Harbor House volunteer,

I moved to Oak Park in 1992 to do participant observation research with Southeast Asian youth (Jeung 2002). As we got to know our neighbors, they began to ask for assistance, so Schmitz and I began a tutoring program, ESL classes, and a mentorship group for boys. Other college graduates interested in doing urban ministry came to volunteer, and by 1997 evangelical Christians rented five Oak Park units. Soon independent from Harbor House and loosely organized as Oak Park Ministries (OPM), this collection of whites, Latinos, and Chinese Americans brought in other volunteers to run the programs.

Carlos Flores, a second-generation Latino who was raised in the Assemblies of God church, learned about doing urban ministry from John Perkins, a founder of the Christian Community Development Association. Perkins teaches that urban ministry requires three R's: the relocation of Christians to low-income areas, reconciliation between racial groups, and redistribution of wealth and resources. Flores explained that he wanted to join a group doing such a ministry. Furthermore, he found the spiritual community of believers pivotal to his activism:

> My main reason I moved into Oak Park was that I saw what God was already doing there and wanted to become a part of it. The community drew me—seeing how people shared their life together. It wasn't just people moving in to do cool things, but I had a sense that it was driven by God.
>
> By deciding to live here, I am making this neighborhood now my community. This is the place where I'm going to work out my salvation, the context where I want to live out my daily faith walk with God and to love others. We're working out what it means for my neighbors to follow God, and for myself to follow God.

Oak Park's Housing Conditions

During the 1990s, two individuals owned this complex and held it under as a corporate entity, Oak Park Apartments. The first Cambodians who moved there in 1984 could not recall the landlords ever making any capital improvements or repairs to the building. Mr. Schmitz attempted to make some needed repairs when he worked as the on-site manager in 1997, but he eventually quit because of the lack of maintenance funds. He observed: "Our building takes in $25,000 per month, and I was only given $150 a month for repairs. What I saw in this building, and in other buildings they own, was active, calculated neglect—not just passive neglect. They would find out about dangerous situations and make it seem like they were repaired" (Counts 1999).

In the winter of 1997–98, El Nino rains flooded the Oak Park courtyard, backed up the sewers, and leaked through the roof. Gabrielle Alvarez, wife of Francisco Martinez, remembers how sewage ruined their entire apartment: "Around 1998 all the filth started coming out of the bathroom. We went to do the wash and when we returned, the whole hallway, everything was full of water! At that time I didn't have the money to just go somewhere else to sleep with my kids. And it was worse when it dried. A smell lingered that no one could stomach. It took two days to clean up, but the smell lasted more than a week." As those on the bottom floor were flooded, those on the second floor had to put out thirty-gallon garbage cans to collect the rainwater leaking through the ceiling. Dara Pheng, a sixty-nine-year-old grandmother receiving a Section 8 housing waiver, suffered the worst: "I lived on the second floor and the roof leaked a lot. It leaked so much, all over the place! Parts of the roof fell into the house. My bedroom wasn't leaking with rain, but the walls were kind of moldy. I had maggots in my home—it was like rice everywhere."

The landlords also failed to manage and maintain the property properly. Trash littered the building, the complex lacked fire extinguishers, and extermination service was a rarity. Mice and roaches overran the complex. Gabrielle Alvarez joked about the situation: "We couldn't stand the cockroaches. Honestly, one went into Mario's ear! He got sick twice, and he came out of the hospital. The second time he came out, a cockroach went into his ear. We were almost going to take him right back to the hospital! In the hospital they asked us where we lived and how the situation was in our apartment. They said we should move." Although the tenants complained about the lack of security at Oak Park and about the housing conditions, the management did not respond. Dara Pheng expressed her anger over the negligence: "I called the manager and asked him about fixing the leaking, but he never fixed it. I wasn't well during all the raining and leaking. I got rashes and things all over my back and body. I made complaints, but he looked at it and said the problems were minor and didn't fix anything."

Inside apartments, mold blackened entire walls as the rains brought about damp conditions. The environmental conditions created by the mold and roaches led to extremely high asthma rates at Oak Park. That year, at least eight households had to make emergency room visits because of asthma attacks. Later, when we tested six children from three different households, all had mold spores found in their bloodstream. Unfortunately, because of their lack of income, the families had to endure these conditions as their children became sick.

OPM members living at Oak Park suffered through the same conditions. A three-by-five-foot piece of the ceiling, under the weight of gallons of rainwater, fell onto one woman's bed. During a shower, another tenant's hand went through the rotted bathroom wall when he tried to brace himself against it. By the end of 1997, OPM members began to take more decisive actions.

Bonds of Tenant Solidarity: Building Upon Ethnic Social Capital

To organize their fellow tenants at Oak Park, OPM members drew upon the respective ethnic bonds of the Cambodians and Latinos. Along with calling upon the trust and respect that they had earned from their neighbors, they were able to form the Oak Park Tenants Association to take a collective stand. By helping tenants recognize their common concerns, they helped establish the group identity of the tenants association.

As stated earlier, both the ethnic communities possessed extended familial networks within Oak Park. Francisco Martinez and Gabrielle Alvarez vocally supported the lawsuit and facilitated organizing through their relationships with others at Oak Park. Gabrielle Alvarez was close to her next-door neighbors, who would cook and sell tamales together. Francisco Martinez developed friendships with men of other Spanish-speaking households and assisted them in getting work.[5] These personal ties later would provide the trust necessary to work together in suing the landlord.

In addition, the ESL classes encouraged further face-to-face interaction and group activity, especially among the Cambodian tenants. At the twice-a-week ESL classes, mothers would share stories of their past and their daily concerns. The year following the stabbing of the Mexican tenant, these Cambodians decided to continue their New Year festivities but invited Latino participation in a community potluck. Over three hundred persons celebrated together that year. Salsa music followed tunes of traditional Khmer folkdances, with the Macarena being played every third song. Sarah Prum brightened when she recalled, "I liked the feasts and potlucks we had. Everyone would gather together and everyone would cook food to eat together. We had special cultural dances."

The ESL classes also facilitated collective action among the Cambodians. When the U.S. Congress introduced welfare reform along with the Republican "Contract with America," the Cambodians became alarmed that their sole means of subsistence would be cut because they were noncitizens. During the ESL classes, tenants learned of legislative updates and wrote letters to legislators. OPM members, who considered this scapegoating of immigrants as unjust, actively lobbied against the reform and supported their neighbors' struggle. OPM member Alice Wu, a second-generation Taiwanese American, explained her concern for immigrants:

> Immigrants have a special vulnerability, not knowing the laws of the land, and being seen as foreigners. I think I have compassion for this vulnerability partly because my own parents were immigrants, and I know there were times that they were taken advantage of in this new land.
>
> I think God also has a special affinity for immigrants, especially for refugees from war, and understands the longing they feel for a home that is comfortable. We should be "groaning inwardly as we wait eagerly" (Rom 8:23) for the hope of our redemption. I believe God has more in store for us, for our immigrant neighbors, for our imperfect world, and I do groan inwardly along with my neighbors as we believe God is not yet done.

When the legislation passed, the ESL classes became citizenship classes so that the students could continue to receive needed benefits. This early organizing effort helped the Cambodians recognize their common plight as ethnic minorities in the United States.

Because the tenants were accustomed to meeting in the apartments of OPM members for party planning, ESL classes, or potlucks, they did not hesitate to attend meetings regarding Oak Park's living conditions. In the first tenants' meeting with Oak Park management in December 1997, representatives identified their most serious issues: leaking roofs, sewage problems, security, and infestation. The management claimed that plans were under way to renovate the buildings, but the meeting devolved into a shouting match, and even greater mistrust of the landlord resulted. With the failure of mediation, OPM members then investigated the possibility of a lawsuit to bring the building up to code. Through church contacts at the Alameda County Legal Assistance Center, we met with a private housing attorney who agreed to take the case on retainer.

While the five OPM households could have sued their landlord on their own, the attorney recommended that securing other plaintiffs with egregious complaints would bolster the case. OPM then met with each household individually, asking them about the damages caused by rain and mold and informing them of their housing rights. The families were clearly hesitant to resist the landlord. Like her fellow tenants, Sitha Le was uninformed of her rights and fearful of government or landlord retaliation: "I didn't know my rights or the process of suing. I was living in Oak Park and thought it was wrong to complain and make reports on the bad conditions the landlord made us to live in. I was afraid to join the lawsuit because I didn't really know what would happen, and I was afraid of getting into any controversy because I was on welfare." Alvarez expressed similar concerns: "I was scared at first, thinking they might throw us out on the street. I first thought we shouldn't get involved because they'll kick us out and we'd have to look for another apartment. Other places say you can't have kids, or this and that, a lot of requirements. They also ask for large deposits, and we couldn't afford such changes."

When the prospects of organizing a large number of tenants seemed unlikely, the landlords paradoxically assisted us by raising the rents. This final straw outraged the tenants, who could not afford higher rents given their fixed incomes. The Cambodian grandmothers, especially, felt free to vent their wrath toward the landlord. Touch Chen, another senior citizen on Section 8, summarized the tenants' feelings: "I joined the lawsuit because the landlord wouldn't fix anything and the conditions were so bad in the apartments. We have rodents everywhere, there was mold in the walls, and the ceiling was leaking. And so we all got together to join this lawsuit because we were angry that the landlord didn't care and nothing was being fixed."

Once a few other tenants agreed to sue, OPM called larger group meetings. These group meetings especially capitalized on the close ties of the ethnic groups. For Khmer translation, we obtained the free services of Suon In, a leader at the Cambodian Buddhist Temple and staff person for Asian Community Mental Health Services. His involvement at the temple made a recognized and trusted partner in the organizing effort. Carlos Flores, one of the OPM members, worked as a community organizer for another nonprofit and used his language skills to facilitate the Spanish-speaking meeting. He explained his approach toward organizing: "People have a desire to make things better for themselves, to make things that are unjust just. But a lot of times, people don't know how to do so even though they see something is really wrong. Organizing brings a broader perspective of the wider, systemic injustices. God really wants justice to happen, so organizing people for justice on earth brings hope to people and a wider perspective. And that's related to my faith in the gospel."

Each person interviewed answered that they participated in the lawsuit because they saw their co-ethnics also suing. Believing that the situation could not get much worse, Juan Avila threw his lot in with the group: "I saw that everyone was joining. Daniel had told me that there was an option. If we win, good. And if we don't, we don't. So that's why we joined in the suit—we weren't sure if we were going to win or not. But then I told him, well, just put us down, we're with you, whatever happens, happens." Likewise, Sophal Chan, a grandfather with two children who each had their own apartments at Oak Park, decided to join once he saw the group unity: "I heard people talking about the lawsuit and that's how I knew about it. I heard everybody talking about it. After talking with a lot of people and my wife, and seeing everyone joining the lawsuit, I decided to join too." The family networks, the face-to-face communication, and the easy access to one another served as ethnic social capital that facilitated a group identity and collective action. Using bilingual leaders to lead meetings and garnering the support of the elders were two culturally sensitive methods to mobilize this ethnic social capital.

The personal relationships that OPM organizers had formed with their fellow tenants were another form of bonding social capital. Having attended their marriages and funerals, tutored their children, and acted as their English teachers, OPM members built particularly strong ties with the Cambodians. We traded on this earned respect to gather the tenants to group meetings and secure a hearing. The younger tenants decided to sue based on rational choices and their confidence in the organizers. Ra Chhom explained: "When Russell and everyone talked with us, told us the process, and gave us all the information, we decided to join the lawsuit. Yes, I thought it was a good idea. Since Russell and everyone were helping with it, we felt they knew what they were doing and felt confident about joining the lawsuit. We weren't afraid." On the other hand, the older tenants made their decisions mostly on the basis of their loyalty to the OPM members.

Sam Kong joked: "I trusted Russell and everyone so I signed the papers. If we lost and I got evicted I would go live with Russell! He loves the Cambodians, kids and all. We can all go live in a big house together. I joined to support Russell, Dan, and the others." For him, joining the lawsuit was an act of reciprocity to repay OPM members for their work in the community. While we thought we acted to empower him, we later learned that Kong was doing us a favor.

The family ties and close interactions promoted ethnic social capital, but they also led to ethnic divisions. To overcome mistrust and segregation, OPM attempted to forge a group identity as tenants. Large trilingual group meetings, held in our cramped living room, brought the ethnic groups together. In these sessions, Martinez recognized that the tenants shared the same issues: "For my part, when we joined the lawsuit nobody knew if we were going to win or not. What helped us was when we all got together. You know the saying; 'There is strength in numbers'? In these apartments there are many tenants. If we all have the same problems, like with the electricity coming and going, and we come together, we can do anything."

Moreover, Kong commented on the similar material conditions that the ethnic groups faced: "We are all people in the same situation going through the same things, and we just need to help each other and work together. It doesn't matter to me what race someone is, as long as we are together and working together." Meanwhile, OPM organizers recognized that the Cambodians and Latinos were being exploited precisely because they were low-income tenants who were unlikely to complain. Given this exploitation, "their outcries for social justice overcame their ethnic boundaries," commented OPM member Alice Wu. "I think the Tenants Association overcame ethnic barriers because the residents saw we were all having the same problems and were in this together, and they knew that we [the organizers] were there to help. They also trusted us because we played with and tutored their kids, both Cambodian and Mexican kids. So I think the kids were a big part of bridging the trust gaps, even as they helped to bridge the language gaps by translating for their parents."

With high amounts of trust and reciprocity, forty-four of the fifty-six households at Oak Park joined the lawsuit by February 1998, much to the surprise of the attorney. In total, we had 197 plaintiffs in our case, almost all of whom were noncitizen, limited English-speaking, and low-income immigrants.

Sustaining the Lawsuit: Bridging Social Capital

Once we initiated the lawsuit, our landlords did not bring the building up to code as expected but allowed the building to fall into even greater disrepair. They apparently tried to delay court hearings and outlast the tenants, who began to move away over time for various reasons. To bring more pressure to bear on our landlords, OPM members and our attorney strategized to gain city government support and garner media attention. The active involvement of these two institutions bolstered the tenants' morale. As symbolic cues, their actions became important for the cognitive liberation of the tenants, who saw that their efforts could be successful (McAdam 1982).

The lawsuit required the documentation of the housing violations at Oak Park by city code inspectors. Because previous inspectors had not been thorough, I contacted district council member Ignacio De La Fuente. I had worked as an assistant to another city council member, and my relationships with the city officials proved quite helpful. De La Fuente's new assistant, Libby Schaaf, took on the Oak Park case as one of her top assignments. With their influence, a comprehensive team of health, building, fire, and police inspectors visited Oak Park in April 1999 and cited the landlords with forty-three code violations. In addition to levying fines, they placed a $50,000 lien on the property. Avila observed the effect of official city involvement: "When the government came, we thought this was for real, and that maybe we were going to win. When the person came from the city and told us that all of this was wrong, he said we would win the case. And when a person like that comes here it's not just to visit. He said there were many irregularities here: there are dead rats; there are lots of things that are not right. This gave me encouragement because I saw him when he was saying all of this." Unfortunately, the inspectors also declared Oak Park Apartments as substandard, which threatened the community's survival, as we feared being relocated.

OPM members believe that their faith practices and beliefs sustained them during this difficult period. The group met weekly to study the Bible, as well as to share and pray about their different ministries. Carlos Flores recalls that "there were times during the lawsuit that were very distressing, that we let down all the people. It was really scary, the possibility that people would be displaced and the community would break up. OPM meetings helped challenge my faith and grow. Most encouraging was listening to people sharing about the different ministries—how different kids changed or made decisions to follow God—and being able to pray about those things. If one person was feeling down, others would pick them up. Sticking together through everything was really positive."

In June 1999 the landlords claimed corporate bankruptcy and the building went into federal receivership (Counts 1999). The tenants association discussed mass relocation to other sites as a likely event. More vacant units became boarded so that Oak Park looked increasingly like an abandoned slum. In October 1999, Section 8 officials gave thirty-day notices to the grandmothers Pheng and Chen because Oak Park failed to pass their inspections.

These events would have broken the tenants association if not for continued media attention. In October 1999, reporters gathered again at Oak Park to hear that De La Fuente's Decent Housing Task Force had named it as one of the city's seven worst slums (DeFao 1999).[6] The press, both mainstream and ethnic, helped the tenants feel that they were not alone in their cause. Sarah Prum stated: "News about the lawsuit with Oak Park was even on the news in Long Beach. People I know there called and asked me what was going on and asked me what I was doing on the news." This attention further strengthened the tenants' ethnic social capital in that they felt they became celebrities in their own communities. Gabrielle Alvarez exclaimed: "I went to Mexico, and a cousin of mine said, 'I know that woman!' She saw me here in Oakland on TV. The same with my mom, she said she saw me on the news. We became famous because of our situation, to try to better it."

Fortunately, in July 2000 the City Attorney's Office developed a creditors' plan in which the City of Oakland, Fannie Mae, and the tenants would jointly take over Oak Park through bankruptcy proceedings. This concerted strategy brought the landlord back to the negotiating table. The tenants agreed to settle their case only on the condition that Oak Park be sold, be brought up to code, and made permanent, affordable housing.

Finally, almost four years after the initial organizing efforts, the Oak Park Tenants Association achieved their housing victory. We received $950,000 in damages and gained permanent, affordable housing. The tenants learned invaluable lessons about their rights and their abilities to effect change. Juan Avila encouraged others to organize in similar ways: "I learned that united, there is strength and you can do more things. If we hadn't joined together, nothing would have happened. My brother-in-law lives in apartments that are all messed up. I would tell him to unite. And they've even seen us on TV there. But they lack a lawyer and a person that helps them organize. The conditions are bad but they don't organize. They need some sort of union."

The bridging social capital that the OPM members brought to the Oak Park Tenants Association was invaluable. Because of their own religious faith, they remained committed to loving their neighbors and to seeking social justice. Their networks with attorneys, government officials, media, and nonprofit organizations proved significant in each step of the organizing process. Not only did they bridge the Oak Park Tenants Association to outside resources, but they also facilitated communication between Cambodian and Latino families. Since the lawsuit, Oak Park families continue to join together to do youth organizing, intergenerational family events, and, of course, for parties.

Conclusion

The victory of the Oak Park Tenants Association illustrates key lessons for organizing immigrant communities. In contrast to Putnam's thesis that Americans demonstrate declining social capital, newcomers to the United States possess much ethnic social capital that becomes intensified through the immigration process. The strong familial ties and close, face-to-face interaction of these communities facilitates mass mobilization. While faith-based organizers stress utilizing preexisting ethnic organizations, the Oak Park experience indicates that new multiethnic organizations can be established when groups are in close proximity and share common agendas.

Religious groups, such as OPM, may bring bridging social capital to these marginalized communities. OPM members developed long-term relationships over a period of years with their neighbors so that they could bridge the Cambodian tenants with the Latinos. While secular tenant organizers might build trusting relationships in order to secure winnable victories, OPM organizers established relationships in order to follow God, to build community, and to love their neighbors. The group's corporate faith practices encouraged them to persevere as tenants at Oak Park. Even when the building was condemned and no legal settlement seemed foreseeable, these evangelical Christians stood by their neighbors. As Pastor Dan Schmitz has written, "Contextualizing the gospel, I think, means taking care of people's physical needs, seeing the love of Jesus in very practical terms. That's really the focus of our ministry—it's being obedient, expecting God to work in our midst without presupposing what that looks like" (Schmitz 2001). Importantly, OPM itself was a multiethnic group, and other tenants could identify with them along ethnic and racial lines. They then called on the trust and friendships that had been established to invite households to attend tenant association meetings and to participate in the lawsuit.

The bridging capital of OPM members also connected the community with outside resources. By working with a leader from the Cambodian Buddhist temple, OPM secured even further credibility with the refugees. Visits by government officials and the media encouraged the tenants and reinforced their sense of efficacy. Contacts with and assistance from these entities were instrumental in forcing the landlord to settle.

This bridging capital helped our neighbors forge identities as not only Cambodian or Mexican but also as immigrant tenants with rights. Along with winning the lawsuit and helping Oakland establish a Decent Housing Month, the Oak Park tenants gained a new sense of power. Ra Chhom reflected, "The main thing I've learned, that I can hold on to, is that I have rights. If I am in a living situation where I'm renting a place with bad conditions, I have rights. And I can take action and not just allow what is happening to continue. If our lives or our families' health are at risk or something, then we can do something about that." In the same way, even the faith-based organizers learned something about faith and hope. Alice Wu Cardona concludes: "I learned that God really is above all other powers, and that He truly is a God of justice! I hadn't expected much from our lawsuit, but it seemed the faithful thing to do at the time, having exhausted all other reasonable avenues to make Oak Park decently habitable. I think before the lawsuit, I had some vague idea of God's justice coming into play in the last days. But the Oak Park lawsuit showed me that God can and will bring about justice in the here and now, for the poor and the voiceless, for people that He loves."

NOTES

1. The author wishes to acknowledge Carlos Flores and Rebecca Chhom for their interviewing and translating assistance, as well as Joan Jeung, Matthew Jeung, Daniel Schmitz, Shauna Olson Hong, and Alice Wu Cardona for their support on this project.

2. Organizers have learned that Southeast Asians have not been responsive to door-knocking recruitment techniques. On the other hand, they have been able to tap into preexisting organizations to help Cambodians engage politically (Hoyt 2002; Noden 2002).

3. To highlight the negative environmental impacts of these new populations, the *San Francisco Chronicle* published photographs of Oak Park that showed idle Mien women with babies on their backs and toddlers at their feet (Gilliam 1989).

4. Pseudonyms of some tenants are used to protect my respondents' anonymity and confidentiality.

5. Similarly, many Cambodian tenants brought their relatives to live there, and at least four marriages were arranged among Oak Park families.

6. I was one of the tenant representatives on the task force that included property owners and city officials.

6

Bringing Mexican Immigrants into American Faith-Based Social Justice and Civic Cultures

JOSEPH M. PALACIOS

Since the mid-1960s, immigrants to the United States have entered a social and political world with a legacy from the civil rights movements of African Americans and Latinos, farmworkers, women, and others that opened up American political culture to previously excluded citizens. Immigrants enter a world where, at least legally, there is an assumption of a liberal democracy that guarantees equality, opportunity, freedom of religion for all and voting rights based on citizen rights and obligations. But most immigrants come into the United States as precitizens and must wait to be fully naturalized as American citizens in order to fully participate in American political life, particularly participation in party politics and voting.

However, as "precitizens" immigrants can participate in the life and activities of an extensive American civil society and its associations, primarily through religious and cultural organizations that reinforce the immigrants' previous home affiliations. In this sense the American version of an immigrant's religious or cultural association can serve both as a bridge to American public life and a haven for one's already established social life. Some scholars make a case that immigrants bring a cultural citizenship with them to their new homeland that can provide a sense of community and support for them (Flores and Benmayor 1997; Kymlicka 1995; Rosaldo 2003). While I can concur that immigrants bring cultural capital to their new homeland, to emphasize cultural capital over actual citizenship rights and obligations distorts the basis for actual civil and human rights that immigrants should rightly experience and hope for. I will argue that religious and cultural associations in the United States can assist immigrants in developing a sociological imagination that can help the immigrant move private concerns, or what C. Wright Mills called "woes," to public solutions (Mills 1959)—as well as their cultural capital—in order to help immigrants enter public life, facilitate legal citizenship, and become fully part of the American community (Dagger 1997; Lloyd and Thomas 1998; Taylor and Gutmann 1994).

I argue that American citizenship is more than a legal status; participation and membership in American public culture provides a sense of personal agency and responsibility, particularly in the social and political cultures, that creates a cultural system reinforcing the values and practices of American liberal democracy. But this is no easy matter in an American public life that has become fragile due to the decreasing participation of citizens in civil society and elections (Putnam 2000). Thus, longstanding citizens are often not good role models for immigrants eager to take advantage of new opportunities in a fragile American political culture.

Tackling this problem has been a primary goal of faith-based community organizers inspired by the political philosophy of the late Saul Alinsky, who developed the American community organizing model in the working-class neighborhoods of Chicago. What I will refer to as the "Alinsky method" is an elegantly simple concept and methodology that privileges one-on-one relationships as the foundation of democratic society (Alinsky 1989). Through neighbors knowing neighbors, a community can discover what its interests are, its public issues (Skerry 1993). The Alinsky method is reflective of Alexis de Tocqueville's observation that the best of American civil society was based on self-interest rightly understood (Tocqueville 1995). Tocqueville observed that the first institution in American public life was religion, because it is the first association people join, and that only in the United States was there a flourishing of true religious freedom. He observed that Americans were capable of being both American and religiously affiliated without government interference in religion or religious interference with government. Thus, Americans could be Catholic, Jewish, Episcopalian, Quaker, etc., within a religiously pluralistic society. Furthermore, Americans chose their religious affiliation and operated their religious institutions with a high degree of lay involvement in the same democratic spirit that they formed their town councils. Even Roman Catholics exhibited this democratic spirit in the early 1800s before the Vatican intervened in the mid-1800s to correct the heresy of Americanism (McGreevy 2003). It is important to understand this interconnection between religious participation and American civil society. For Tocqueville, religion provided the spirit and values for American public life, particularly since early Americans were the first political community to establish the principle of religious liberty and many of the colonists came to the New World escaping religious persecution. Indeed, over the course of almost two centuries Americans had developed a Judeo-Christian ethos that imbued the political culture—often acting as a conservative force but also as a prophetic corrective to social and political injustices. The abolitionist movement, women's suffrage, the labor movement, the

civil rights movement, the farmworkers movement, and many other social movements were inspired by religious activists to change law and the political culture
(Guerrero 1987; Herberg 1983; Morris 1984).

Immigrants of the post–civil rights era bring with them stories of various
types of oppression, repression, poverty, and struggle that reflect prior generations of immigrants. They like prior immigrants turn to religious institutions as
a first institution that bring them into a new associational life that they must
choose. They become members of a religious congregation and are asked to support the congregation through their financial and material contributions and
most importantly through a hands-on participation as they join the congregational model of American religion (Ahlstrom 1972; Ammerman et al. 1997).
While there may be a strong cultural or ethnic impulse to participate, neverthe-
less there is a social shift to a congregation. This never becomes more apparent
than when an immigrant is recruited to join a congregation—parish, synagogue,
temple, mosque, etc.—or must make a decision on which congregation to join
(Dolan 1987). It is my argument that this first step into American religious life
begins a process of moving the immigrant into precitizen activities within religious structures that act as schools for public life and actual citizenship. As
schools they are formators (i.e., teachers/formers of character) of a political
ethos—a political habitus—providing practical skills, habits, and virtues for
public life (Seligman 1992; Verba, Schlozman, and Brady 1995).

Development of the Faith-Based Community Organizing Model

While participation in a religious congregation may seem very mundane, I think
it is the most significant entry point for an immigrant to participate in American civil society and public life, since religious institutions themselves are considered part of American civil society and give the precitizen a social location
for worship, education, culture, ethnic identity, social welfare, recreation, and
friendship. In the 1980s Alinsky-inspired community organizers from the Pacific
Institute for Community Organizing (PICO) realized that religious congregations
were the most reliable and effective social structures to organize neighborhoods
and communities, particularly with the decline of labor unions, PTAs, and social
clubs.[1] They also noticed that immigrants were joining congregations in changing urban neighborhoods—very often revitalizing dying congregations.

At the beginning these organizers saw congregations as being ready-made
recruitment pools for citywide community organizations. But by the mid-1980s
PICO organizers began to rethink the role of the congregation in community
organizing as more than a recruitment source. Many pastors and lay leaders
resented their congregations being used simply for recruitment and wanted a
greater voice on the role of religion in a community organization. The PICO leadership both at national and local levels began to reflect upon the tremendous

resource of values, culture, and associational life that congregations carried to sustain membership enthusiasm and loyalty—particularly the role of Catholic social justice teaching and black liberal Protestant biblical justice could play in relationship with the Alinsky method.

The concept of faith-based community organizing emerged from this reflective process by PICO organizers. They rediscovered Tocqueville's emphasis on religion as a first institution and realized that the religious cultural system could generate an ongoing spirit and structure for community organizing, particularly with immigrants and working-class people who trust religious institutions and participate in them. Both the community organization and the religious congregation could assist each other and realize common values and goals in ways that energize both in a synergistic rather than symbiotic relationship.

It was my privilege to be a participant-observer of the Oakland Community Organizations (OCO), PICO's community organization in Oakland, California. From 1996 to 2001 I was a member of Saint Anthony Catholic Parish and participated in community organizing. I also served as the Spanish-speaking supply priest for a multigenerational Latino community. Founded in 1881, Saint Anthony's is the second oldest parish in the Oakland diocese. The San Antonio District of the city of Oakland comprises about 35,000 people, of whom approximately 70 percent are Hispanic, 10 percent black, 10 percent Asian, and 10 percent white. However, in the immediate neighborhood of Saint Anthony's Parish the population is largely immigrated from Mexico, Vietnam, and Cambodia. I chose to study Saint Anthony's because of its multigenerational Latino community and its history of having Mexican American pastors. However, in 1996 a Vietnamese pastor was appointed and brought with him a rapidly growing Vietnamese presence that by 2001 eclipsed the Latino community. I was a witness to all of these changes, and the research location became a much more interesting research site.

My primary reason for choosing this district to observe was that it had one of the oldest and continuous community organizing efforts in the United States, particularly in the West. As well, community organizing is the largest social justice phenomenon in the United States, involving more than one to three million people (Warren 2001). The San Antonio and the Fruitvale districts were the first neighborhoods to form the Oakland Community Organizations in 1973 as a network of local organizing committees. In the first few years the organizing was neighborhood centered and utilized local churches to recruit members and provide meeting space. The early organizers were two California Jesuit priests who had been trained in Chicago and wanted to create an organization similar to Alinsky's Woodlawn in Chicago. The old-timers of Saint Anthony's local organizing committee told me that in these early days, the late 1970s, they wereconcerned with the proliferation of liquor stores and prostitution in their community, especially along the two main boulevards of the district. By the 1980s the liquor store issue was replaced by crack cocaine houses in the middle of the neighborhoods and the violence that came along with drug dealing.

Oakland Community Organizations, founded in 1977, has been highly successful in training local lay people in the Alinsky method. The fundamental premise of the method is that when community members discover their common self-interest they can work in a concerted effort to achieve that interest. Thus, self-interest becomes the common interest—the common good. For Alinsky and his followers in Oakland the problem in the United States is that poor people, the working classes, immigrants, and minorities are often not organized in a way that allow their self-interests to emerge. Middle-class, upper-middle-class, and wealthy citizens are organized in many ways through involvement in politics, business, and professional associations, and through a variety of other networks where their self-interests become institutionalized. The mission is to organize the interests of disempowered people into an associational life and civic institution that can represent their interests.

At every Saint Anthony's and citywide meeting a credential is read to start the meeting that reflects the power of the organization: "Oakland Community Organizations is an organization of 35,000 families in the City of Oakland in 32 churches. . . ."[2] Over the years it has become the largest civic organization in Oakland and can claim for itself a successful track record of victories. As one of the lay founders states: "Those were simple beginnings, the issues were less complex and local—stop signs, stray dogs, run down properties—but the seed was planted, the soil was right, and it was bound to grow. As we began working together as groups to resolve issues, first in our own neighborhood, then with others who had identified similar problems, we were, and still are, constantly challenged to move beyond, to stretch our horizons, and to develop leadership qualities we didn't even know we had!" These victories resulted from a strategy of mediating the self-interests of the members of the local organization and the institutional structures of urban life, such as the police and fire departments, city council, school board, zoning boards, the Catholic Diocese of Oakland and other religious bodies, the business sector, and philanthropic foundations. This strategy is a leveraging mechanism that places the organization between the people as citizens with interests and the institutional players of a community. Thus, the local and citywide organizations define the problems that emerge from one-on-ones (the basic method of neighbor interviewing neighbor to gather information on local needs and issues), which then become the basis for connecting the constituency to the institutional structures with the goal of effecting long-term institutional change in the existing institutional structures. The goal in a victory is that all the players win: the constituency gets a problem solved and the institutional players can claim that they are not only doing their job but also working on behalf of the grassroots. The organization is not interested in running programs or building new institutions. Rather, it wishes the existing structures to work for the people they are intended to serve. The one-on-ones keep the organization always current on the issues, so that once an issue is won the organization can easily move to another issue.

Faith-Based Community Organizing as a Social Justice Cultural System

At Saint Anthony's and other Catholic parishes the appropriation of sacred symbols and the scriptures for social purposes was a common integrative process for faith-based community organizing. Indeed, the almost unconscious American instinct to do this was a key reason that PICO moved from a neighborhood-based community organizing model to a faith-based model in the early 1990s.[3] PICO provides its affiliate citywide organizing committees professional community organizers and offers national training institutes for empowering local lay and clergy leadership.[4] PICO's long-term executive director, John Baumann, expressed to me the fundamental drive of the organization: "In its own way, PICO too, is a family—a place where people can find their own true voice. It is a place where all people are treated as individuals deserving of respect and love. And, like a family, PICO looks out for its own. We are all filled with anger when we see conditions that foster fear, hatred, and despair. We are moved to justice to make the world right for our family. And we realize that the power to change the world rests in our capacity to unite as family, as community, and as children of God." In this sense faith-based community organizing draws upon a pragmatic approach of getting new members from religious congregations and the theoretical desire to integrate religious culture, social justice teaching, and the scriptures into the life of community organizing as a way of providing ongoing meaning for the disciple citizens.

In January 1997 I was invited to attend the national leadership training held each January in Ponchatoula, Louisiana.[5] During the five days of intensive training of leaders from throughout the United States I was able to observe the classic organizing tools and behaviors that unify all of PICO's local units and citywide community organizing efforts. In his study of PICO and OCO Richard Wood discusses these tools and behaviors within the framework of a Geertzian cultural system as a set of practices, beliefs, and ethos that become culturally tailored in the black and Latino communities (Wood 2002). In addition, the skills developed by PICO and other Alinsky-type civic organizations have a primary cultural orientation toward American civic culture that has a normative orientation toward incorporating its members into American civil society, and the organization has set the foundational cultural milieu for religious social justice teaching and implementation at the local level.

The normative orientation of PICO can be seen in its educative mission to empower its members to effect grassroots change in American public spaces, such as school boards, city halls, police departments, and governmental bureaucracies. In this sense PICO training in civic participation is a school for the behaviors necessary for active members of civil society, what Alinsky himself called "popular education"—that is, education and mutual understanding among various groups in order to gain a "new appreciation and definition of social issues"(Alinsky 1989, 155). PICO training as a school for popular education represents what David Lloyd and Paul Thomas see as a cultural education in public life in the Gramscian sense of nurturing organic intellectuals for a newly constituted ethical state: "The school, in other words most effectively permits the transfer of the subject from the private domain of the family into the public world of the political, not by teaching civics but by representing representation" (Lloyd and Thomas 1998, 20).

The educative mission for PICO is located in public meeting spaces in which people gather as participants in the public and in democratic practices of civil society—of "representing representation." More specifically, PICO training assists its practitioners in learning fundamental roles of trust. As Adam Seligman notes regarding the difficulty of talking about trust without reverting to an essentialism of attitudes: "Roles here are used as a heuristic device, as a type of analytical shorthand the better to grasp the structurally conditioned nature of trust and remove it from all philosophical abstraction or theological justification" (Seligman 1992, 8).

The primary behaviors of PICO, the repertoire of civic behaviors as skills or social capital, as noted by Richard Wood include the following:

- *One-on-Ones*: The primary process for relationship-building that initiates the organizational web work of trust wherein each member is important through the identification of the issues related to one's self-interest in the grassroots development of trusting relationships and common values and interests.
- *Prayer*: The exteriorizing of beliefs in the public forum in order to create a culture of belief.
- *Credentials*: A process at every PICO gathering in which a leader reviews the organizational identity, its membership status, and its own self-identity vis-à-vis other power relationships in the community.
- *Research*: The process of systematically evaluating one-on-ones to determine issues for the organization to develop and execute with the cooperation of other organizations, elected officials, academics, other professionals, and government bureaucrats.
- *Action*: The specific activity of creating a target to effect research—that is, holding the target accountable through the gathering of a mass meeting that can be organized at various levels: local, areawide, citywide, interorganizationally, regionally, or statewide.

- *Accountability*: The development of a challenging process for organizational discipline as both an internal activity of the organization and an outside activity of holding a target accountable.
- *Negotiations*: Usually a behind-the-scenes process of lay leaders and organizers meeting with targets to forge agreements prior to an action so that agreements can be ratified at the action.
- *Evaluations*: At the end of every meeting of a local organization committee research meeting, or action an evaluation is made by the leaders and organizers present in order to hold accountable the various participants of the event and to improve communication and critical reflection among the leadership. (Wood 2002)

On the day-to-day level of local organizing, the PICO model employs a standard methodology of conducting a meeting or action that becomes a fixed cultural ritual or repertoire. The rules of order for a meeting are not taken for granted because they are viewed as constitutive of the democratic process. By experiencing the democratic process at meetings, the participants learn democratic values and skills as a new kind of discourse that will integrate with the social teaching of the Catholic church—particularly the key doctrinal elements of participation and association that are fundamental to achieving more abstract doctrinal elements such as the dignity of the human person and solidarity. The methodology of a one-hour meeting includes a call to order, prayer, organizational credentials (the citywide organization is identified, along with how many congregations and families are involved, and the mission of the organization is stated), opening remarks, discussion of agenda items, discussion of action items, polling of commitments to do one-on-ones, closing remarks, and closing prayer. Newcomers are folded into the organization by involvement in the practices of civic participation as habits of the organization that facilitate a well-organized and effective process. Newcomers are not given overviews of organizational philosophy as an ideological formation. Through the one-on-one a newcomer is given the experience of being able to articulate one's self-interest with a willing listener who also shares his or her interests (Palacios 2004).

Thus, the cultural system of practices, beliefs, and ethos is put into effect as a training, a school for civic participation through bottom-up, experiential processes of civic participation and insertion into public life through the practice of the precitizen skills, habits, and language of American civic culture.[6] These practices serve as an ideal-typic model for civic participation functioning across various lines of cultural, religious, community, political, and ideological variance among its members and local units and provides for an experiential solidarity among the various members—solidarity as organizing principle, as well as solidarity in relationships or public friendships—in political and social settings. Furthermore, this cultural system functions as an American model of civic participation that is normatively embedded in the public life of democracy (Putnam, Leonardi, and Nanetti 1993).

Case Study: U.S. Civic Life Utilizing the PICO Model
of Civic Participation

My primary observation of Oakland Community Organizations was at fourteen monthly Saint Anthony meetings. The local unit followed the standard meeting format as outlined earlier. In the meetings, attendees dealt with citywide issues related to classroom size reduction in the Oakland Public School District and the development of homework centers in the neighborhoods. Information gathered at the meetings for these issues was moved forward in research meetings attended by key leaders and the organizers. This led to negotiations with school officials prior to a citywide action held March 1996.

At that March citywide action over two thousand members gathered at the Oakland Convention Center to gain commitments from both the City of Oakland and the Oakland School Board to fund classroom size reduction and the proposed homework centers. At this highly charged, multicultural event, which began with music from two gospel choirs and one Latino music group, the organization was able to gain commitments from officials from the city and the school district to fund the two projects. The slogan "For the Children!" was repeatedly used by the dynamic leaders of the meeting to evoke a high-energy rally. Each time an official committed him or herself to the projects the audience would break out into wild applause and shout "For the children!" or "¡Para los niños!" The meeting began at 6:30 P.M. and promptly ended on time at 8:00 P.M. The grand ballroom of the Convention Center was filled to capacity, and I sensed that the people around me thought the rally was highly successful.

Oakland Community Organizations' citywide actions illustrate the multicultural alliance of the primarily ethnically or racially oriented congregational units. Whites, Latinos, and blacks bring distinctively culturally based repertoires to the citywide actions. The culture from below moves up to form a larger, more cohesive cultural ensemble. At the larger actions the organization incorporates the cultural practices that work best for the particular cultural groups in the context of a multicultural event.

Saint Anthony Parish is organized in its parish associations and its local unit to allow for the life of separate ethnic enclaves to operate in one parish plant—an organizational model that has become the de facto post–Vatican II American parish model to handle various language and cultural needs (Leege and Germillion 1984; Morris 1997). For example, when one walks into the modern post–Vatican II church building one encounters a multitude of ethnoreligious images conveying the interests of the Latinos, Filipinos, whites, blacks, and Vietnamese that make up the parish. Each of the four Sunday masses caters to a specific ethnic group in the parish: the 8:00 A.M. Mass in English with traditional music oriented toward the remaining whites and blacks in the parish; the 9:30 A.M. Mass in Spanish with Mexican-oriented hymns; the 11:00 A.M. Mass in Vietnamese with traditional Vietnamese music; and the 12:30 P.M. Mass in English with a Filipino choir that sings contemporary American church music. During the liturgical year the Latino and Vietnamese communities, the dominant enclaves in the parish, might display for various periods of time their specific ethnoreligious customs, such as an elaborate Virgin of Guadalupe shrine in mid-December and the special altar for the Vietnamese New Year. During the major liturgical seasons such as Advent and Easter it is not uncommon to find banners in English, Spanish, and Vietnamese. In one wing of the church there are three different images of Mary, each catering to Vietnamese, Mexican, and Filipino Marian customs. It appears as if there are competing cultures vying for space. Judging by the fresh flowers placed at these various shrines every week, there seems to be regular devotional activity around these cultural-religious practices.

Oakland Community Organizations has relied on Saint Anthony's to produce key Mexican American leaders for the citywide organization. Because of the cleavage caused in the Latino community with the appointment of the Vietnamese pastor several of the key leaders dropped out from the parish unit and continued their activity in citywide research meetings and actions. In the initial months of my observation the attendance at the monthly meetings was small, usually four to eight women. However, whenever there was a call for Saint Anthony's presence at a citywide action, the parish could generate from 100 to 250 parishioners to attend because of prior victories affecting the neighborhood—primarily eliminating drug houses and limiting liquor stores.

In the spring of 1996 two new members, a Mexican-born male, Manuel, and a Mexican American female, Silvia, were recruited by the local organizer. They helped bring a new vitality to the group. By the fall of 1996 the local organizing committee and the organizer began to strategically recruit new members, since it was clear that many of the old activists had changed parishes. That fall one of the old activists, Carolyn, a white female who speaks fluent Spanish and who is very Mexican in culture and style, returned. The local members made a decision to utilize the liturgical year of 1996–97 to begin a process of parish renewal in the Latino community by holding parishwide meetings on Sunday mornings following the Spanish Mass. It should be noted that the pastor did not attend meetings until 1999. However, he faithfully paid the parish dues to the city organization, which help pay the salary of the local organizer, and the organizer kept him informed of his activities in the parish. I also met with the pastor on a monthly basis to keep him aware of my ongoing research and activities in the parish.[7] He never impeded the organization's activity, but when he got involved in the organization in 1999 I noticed that he brought new energy into the meetings, especially by introducing multilingual music to get the people motivated.

Scott, the lead organizer, and I had observed that on Sunday mornings following the Spanish Mass many parents escorted their children to the Catholic school for religious instruction held from 11 A.M. to 12 P.M. every Sunday during the school year. Many parents waited in the gymnasium during this time. Scott suggested that we might target these parents as potential new members. With this idea the members decided to offer an Advent retreat entitled "On the Road to Tepeyac," signifying the idea that Mexicans are *Guadalupanas* on a continuous journey of faith. The idea was to connect themes of neighborhood social justice issues with the religious practices associated in the Mexican community with Advent (four Sundays preceding Christmas), Our Lady of Guadalupe (December 12), and Christmas.

"The Road to Tepeyac" theme for the meetings was an attempt to integrate the liturgical cycle, the social justice image of Our Lady of Guadalupe that has developed in the United States, and the legitimation of social concerns vis-à-vis common religious symbols and impulses of the Mexican immigrants. This type of integration is quite common in American pastoral practice and planning based on a pragmatically oriented pastoral life driven by the practical question: "How do we get more people to our meetings?" The use of saints and feast days by Catholic pastoral workers for various social objectives, particularly in immigrant communities, is common in U.S. Catholic history (Dolan 1992; Matovina and Riebe-Estrella 2002; Morris 1997). The appropriation of Our Lady of Guadalupe for social purposes in the United States is a significant development in the evolution of the meaning of the apparition (Deck 1989; Deck, Tarango, and Matovina 1995; Elizondo 1997; Guerrero 1987; Rodriguez 1994). According to Virgilio Elizondo, the leading theologian of the social Guadalupe, "the real miracle seems to be in the hearts of the people. Mary, as Mother, gave a meaning to the people's lives and granted them the strength and courage to undertake over and over again, what, humanly speaking, seemed impossible: for the illiterate, the powerless, the poor, and the oppressed to rise up against the powerful to bring about justice" (Elizondo 1981, 112). This kind of social justice theological reflection is not at all common in Mexico, even though Mexican national identity has been historically driven by the Guadalupe story—particularly in the image of Father Hidalgo, the founding father of modern Mexico who led the country into independence under the banner of Guadalupe and the red, green, and yellow flag of the new nation-state on September 16, 1810.[8] Thus the appropriation of Guadalupe for faith-based community organizing objectives would be part of the ordinary construction of a social justice cultural milieu for Mexicans in the United States. This has been borne out in the way the U.S. Hispanic church has used Guadalupe as a symbol of social liberation for the national Encuentro processes of 1972, 1977, 1985, and 2000, conducted by the bishops' office for Hispanic affairs.[9]

It is important to note that the Mexican immigrants who have come to the United States since the 1980s are primarily what Mexican sociologist Roger

Bartra calls *urbano-campesinos*, who come from the semi-urban farm laborers inhabiting much of the periphery of Mexican cities that have developed since the 1970s restructuring of the agricultural sector (Bartra 1980). Mexican migrants in both Mexico and the United States are largely semiliterate, working-class people who must seek any kind of wage labor to sustain themselves and their families. Unlike their agrarian predecessors they are often unsettled, on the move, and do not have stakes in local community life and culture. They developed low levels of cultural, social, and political capital. In my ethnographic work among these *urbano-campesinos* in Guadalajara, Jalisco, Mexico, and Oakland and Los Angeles, I have noticed that initially they do not participate in local civic life or parish activities as members but as consumers of local festivals, activities, and religious services. In Mexico, Catholics just go to Mass; there is no such thing as registering to become a member of a parish or congregation. Thus when they come to the United States they do not know that they need to register to become members of a local parish, use envelopes for their financial contributions, and take home and read a Sunday bulletin with all of the activities of the parish. If they have children, they do not know that they should join a local Parent-Teacher Association and volunteer time. They are like blank slates when it comes to participatory civic or religious life and need to be introduced to the practices of local associational and institutional life. However, once introduced to the rudiments of public life many migrants quickly learn the civic and religious cultures and become active participants (Camp 2001).

Over the course of eighteen months I participated in eight consultation processes with Mexican immigrants held in the Catholic school gymnasium. I was able to witness a continuum of behaviors related to civic participation: entering the meeting room, signing in, putting on a name tag, finding a place to locate oneself, talking to a new person, participating in a variety of consultative and democratic processes (expressing one's opinion, casting a vote, volunteering for an activity), socializing with one's peers, being helpful, etc. Even helping to set up chairs and take them down was learned and replicated. These behaviors may appear to be very commonplace in American civic life, but for the Mexican immigrant *urbano-campesinos* in Oakland these behaviors were not natural but something to be acquired, developed, and passed on to other newcomer immigrants.

At the beginning of the process the participants were brought into the public meeting space through personal invitation by the outside leaders. Around twenty people came to the first meetings—including eight old-timers from the local organizing committee. Toward the middle of the initiative the immigrants were inviting their friends and family members to join the effort, so that by the end of the process there were up to sixty people at the Sunday meetings. From the more than fifty new immigrants came six new leaders who would bring new energy to the educational agenda that was the focus of organizing in the years ahead. These noncitizen leaders would be at the forefront of the creation of charter schools and small schools within existing schools, as well as school bond initiatives, through the acquisition of precitizen skills and commitment to the principles of faith in action.

The introduction of skilled civic participants—that is, other Mexican Americans involved in other parts of the parish—helped introduce the immigrants to other more social aspects of civic participation: chatting with one's peers, enjoying refreshments together, and being helpful in setting up and taking down chairs and tables, preparing refreshments, and cleaning up. These old-timers modeled social skills for the newcomers, who, at least in this situation, were uncertain, oblivious, or nervous about such social behaviors.[10]

Over time the parents adapted themselves to joining in, participating, and enjoying a certain style of public meeting. Not only had they learned the primary skills for civic participation, they had also learned to become citizens together, seeing each other as peers and becoming involved with each other's opinions, values, and commitments, even though they were not legal citizens. They began to see and experience that they themselves can effect change in their localities. They began to realize that the meetings they were attending were giving them skills and voice that they could apply to the situation in the parish and in the community, as evidenced in the incremental changes that the Latino laity are making in the parish and community. As well, many began to see the limitations of their noncitizen status in not being able to vote.

Bringing Immigrants into American Civic Life

While working for two years (1987–89) with another Alinsky neighborhood and congregation-based model in Los Angeles, it was my experience that without the faith-based integrative process the rank-and-file activists lost their commitment and enthusiasm once their social objectives had been met. Often they resented their parish being used by the organizing committee simply to get people to a citywide action. PICO's faith-based process allows for an ongoing reintegration of social issues, parish pastoral cycles and processes, and leadership development. The faith-based model helps balance the pragmatism of the Alinsky community organizing model with renewing processes drawn from the liturgy, religious education, and cultural practices.

All throughout the education campaign (1996–2000) the professional community organizers, particularly Scott, worked with the local leaders (priests, nuns, pastors, and lay men and women) to find ways to integrate their motto of "faith in action"—the integration of social justice principles and processes—with the social issues of the community. Scott was very concerned that the faith dimension needed to be institutionalized in the ongoing processes of PICO national training and local issue formation and processes. In early 1999 he invited me to help him offer the first articulated faith component into national leadership training held for primarily immigrant Spanish-speaking leaders in Oakland, California. Scott had been introduced to the biblical reflection process of "See, Judge, Act" (Ver, Juzgar, y Actuar) of the European Catholic Action Movement that became very popular in the Latin American *comunidades de base* through a course on multicultural ministry that he took at the Franciscan School of Theology in Berkeley during the summer of 1998. The process is very easy to teach: oral recitation of a scripture passage, time to reflect on it, and sharing of what it means in everyday life. At the national training we utilized a group dynamic of poster making. Scott asked the participants to take a social issue that they were working on in their local unit and utilize the scripture reading of the loaves and fish (Matt. 15:32–39) to illustrate the issue. Once the process was explained, the participants working in small groups quickly went to work using poster paper and colored markers to complete the task. At the completion of the posters each small group leader explained to the entire assembly what the poster signified. Every group made an application of a scriptural principle to the social issue chosen.

Scott continued to make this kind of faith-based contribution at the local meetings and in planning large citywide actions. As a practicing Jew he had taken to heart the concepts of biblical justice that he learned at a PICO trainers' meeting in 1998, which was the first attempt for PICO to institutionalize faith-based social justice concepts, albeit Catholic ones, in the ecumenical organization. For Scott the idea of right relationships was intimately associated with how one-on-ones should be conducted and how local solidarity should be constructed. Indeed, wins for PICO should be on the principles of biblical justice. As an organizer Scott realized that the techniques of "see, judge, act" and other games and processes were important tools to use at meetings in order to convey these principles and experience them in the educational process itself. I noticed a subtle but significant change in the citywide organization as the faith-based dimensions were more integrated into the organizational culture—particularly, more articulated faith-testimony and faith-principle dimensions. For example, at an Oakland City Council meeting that activists attended in 1999 in order to lend city support to the building of a supermarket in West Oakland, one of the professional organizers—a black liberal Protestant pastor—speaking before the council actually spoke about food in such a way that left one councilmember later in the meeting articulating that access to good food is a fundamental human right. Two years prior, the issue would have been framed by local leaders in terms of equal access to food and would have appealed to the emotions of the council members with testimonies of senior citizens taken advantage of by the high cost and inferior quality of food sold at the small corner liquor-grocery stores in the neighborhood.

Within the professional group of community organizers I had noticed over the course of three years a melding of Catholic social teaching, black liberal

Protestant biblical justice emphases, and a general Christian spiritual emphasis on common prayer and discernment. In interviews with these organizers I realized that they themselves saw their work as a social justice vocation and that they, as well as their membership, wanted more from community organizing. They wanted spiritual meaning in their own lives. One Latina feminist organizer in her mid-twenties who was not personally involved in institutional religion, although she had gone to Catholic schools, said, "Through organizing we're doing God's work." She felt quite comfortable finding scriptural passages to use at her local organizing committee meetings and told me that one of her favorite sections of the Bible is the Exodus story of Moses and Pharaoh. She had used this text to help her LOC see the need for research on an issue—that "to let my people go" requires necessary footwork to prepare for the journey.

Since 1997 the PICO national organization has spent time working with pastors to develop a more articulated faith-based organizational culture. According to the national PICO leaders I interviewed, Protestant pastors do not have difficulty understanding and using the principles of biblical justice and the principles of Catholic social justice teaching (e.g., solidarity as an organizing principle, dignity of the human person, human rights, association, participation, the right to organize, the dignity of human work, etc.) as the ideational foundation of PICO's evolving faith-based culture. And Catholic priests and women religious learn how to express the biblical foundations of their faith in a more emotive way through the influence of the black Protestant pastors whose homiletic and prayer style often utilize the call-response technique that brings people into the emotions, as well as the content, of the scripture texts. My understanding of this technique is that it brings the scriptures back to their origins in the oral tradition: the scriptures convey stories of people's real lives. I thought it remarkable that Latino immigrants easily connected with the black cultural repertoire, which was an easier move into the American civic culture than the white cultural repertoire with its procedural emphasis. This suggests that black cultural practices can serve as a bridge for Mexican immigrants to enter the practices and values of the larger so-called white American political culture.[11]

At a citywide action the dynamism of scripture and testimonies of real people often become integrated into a common message. During the campaign for homework centers, a passage from Joshua, chapter 6, on the siege of Jericho, conveyed that the power of the people would prevail over the forces of resistance to changes in the Oakland Public School System: the people would march around the walls of the school district headquarters (Jericho) until the walls fell. At these actions a mural of the walls of Jericho was placed behind the speakers' tables so that the membership could visualize their faith in action. And during the course of the meeting the leader, a black man in his sixties who at the time was the chair of the citywide steering committee, would let out a rallying cry: "For the children! ¡Para los niños!" Everyone would respond: "For the children!

¡Para los niños!" Over the course of a one-hour rally this cry sounded like a clarion call for political battle. And the politicians and school board members in attendance could certainly feel the emotive power of the membership.

Furthermore, the religious dimension of social justice in these public settings comes across as a natural ecumenism of black spirituality, Catholic social justice teaching, and multicultural expressions such as Latino use of Our Lady of Guadalupe, Posadas, Stations of the Cross, and commemoration of the lives of Archbishop Oscar Romero and the martyrs of El Salvador. All of these cultural dimensions contribute to a rearticulation of American civic life through civil religion. These facets of the PICO faith-based organizing model have emerged in an evolutionary way of integrating pragmatic organizing styles to achieve sociopolitical wins, recruitment and retention of members, accountability to the religious congregations and other funders, and the internal development of the professional organizers. In building their community organizing model the PICO leadership did not have a strategic plan on how to incorporate faith dimensions into neighborhood and congregation-based models. However, they knew that many of their affiliate pastors and some of the most active laity wanted more from the organization as a religiously inspired type of social justice program.

This basic impulse is driving the ongoing evolution of PICO faith-based community organizing, particularly in its more recent outreach to immigrants and through their ethnic congregations.[12] As PICO has entered the second millennium it continues to focus on a pragmatic issues and results-oriented strategy of delivering social justice through participation in democracy. Immigrants are drawn into neighborhood issues of jobs, security, education, health care, and social services through their local congregations. The local organizing committees continue to introduce newcomers to precitizen skills learned through the Alinsky method, democratic practices, and faith-based evaluation processes. Their own cultural expressions are preserved but brought into a multicultural public life of shared practices and values, into self-interest rightly understood. Mexican immigrants become Americans through participatory democracy and help reweave the fabric of the American community; thus, in the end, they actually help reintroduce to longstanding citizens the arts of citizen participation (Pacific Institute for Community Organizations 1997).

NOTES

1. There are three key Alinsky-inspired community organizing structures in the United States: the Industrial Areas Foundation (IAF), founded by Alinsky; PICO; and the Gamaliel Foundation.

2. In 2005 Oakland Community Organizations had grown to forty congregations representing more than forty thousand people in the City of Oakland.

3. Actually, PICO grew out of Oakland Community Organizations' foundations as the first organizing committee in the PICO network.

4. In 2001 PICO had eighty-five affiliate organizing committees in fifteen states. In 2005 it had more than one thousand member institutions representing one million families in 150 cities and seventeen states. PICO is one of the largest community-based efforts in the United States.

5. National training of key lay leaders are held yearly in January in Ponchatoula, Louisiana, and in July in Los Altos, California. These leaders are identified and recruited by local professional organizers with the help of pastors and other leaders. The tuition and transportation costs are provided by the local congregation and LOC.

6. I employ a dynamic cultural model that understands the synergistic relationship among practices, institutions, and language (discourse, symbols). See Swidler (1986).

7. As an ordained Roman Catholic priest I made myself available to celebrate the 9:30 A.M. Mass in Spanish, and to officiate at Spanish-language weddings and Quinceañeras.

8. In discussions with priests and lay pastoral workers in Mexico I found that the idea of using Guadalupe as a social justice icon was odd. Indeed, I could find no written theological or pastoral works related to Guadalupe social interpretation. Guadalupe scholarship is confined to historical works on the apparition itself or in devotional materials. For Mexican Catholics, Guadalupe is part of a religiocultural construction that is set in the permanent ritual and cultural processes attached to the feast of Guadalupe on December 12 and the devotions carried on both publicly and privately, such as pilgrimages by dioceses to the Mexico City shrine. Deviation from these processes has been rare. Only since the 1990s has there been artistic deviation of the reproduction of the Guadalupe image in Mexico, mostly articulated by feminist painters who have drawn on the basic elements of the image to relate Guadalupe to ordinary life and feminist self-projections. However, ordinary Mexicans both in the United States and Mexico would find these interpretations offensive because an artist is changing the set image.

9. For histories of these Encuentro processes, see the office of Hispanic Affairs of the United States Catholic Conference online at http://www.nccbuscc.org/hispanicaffairs/history.htm.

10. I did not interview these neophytes, therefore I do not know what they were thinking. After observing this group for over a year I believe that these social behaviors are not natural behaviors in such a public space. One might think that these people have social skills in other parts of their lives, such as home and work. However, in observing this group's behavior in the church space I believe that the Mexican *urbano-campesino* in the United States goes to the public spaces of church and halls without expectation to socialize. Rather, church is a place to pray; the gym is a place to wait for one's children. In the second phase of this research I intend to do in-depth interviews of a sample of this immigrant group.

11. Toward the end of my study in 2001 I noticed the inclusion of Vietnamese and Cambodian immigrants in OCO activities, particularly after Saint Anthony's Vietnamese pastor became visibly supportive of OCO activities. They mirrored the Latino immigrant enthusiasm for the black cultural repertoire, especially the use of gospel music and the call-response method of speakers.

12. In 2004 PICO instituted its New Voices campaign, stating, "Through civic education and leadership development PICO federations are equipping immigrants to participate in public life and take on leadership positions in the community. PICO is working for fair treatment of immigrants in all areas of society and for solutions to problems with the current immigration system" (http://www.piconetwork.org/issues_immigration.asp, accessed January 5, 2005).

PART III

Faith, Fear, and Fronteras

Challenges at the U.S.-Mexico Border

7

The Church vs. the State

Borders, Migrants, and Human Rights

JACQUELINE MARIA HAGAN

Contemporary nation-states increasingly exercise their rights as sovereign nations to determine who crosses their borders. In recent years, the United States and Mexico have embraced this right by taking unprecedented steps to restrict the entry of unauthorized migrants by beefing up police activities along the border, strategies that have dire human consequences for journeying migrants. The U.S. campaign, which is officially known as "Prevention through Deterrence" was initiated in the early 1990s, in response to the failure of the Immigration Reform and Control Act of 1986 to curtail undocumented migration. Under the Prevention through Deterrence campaign, resources devoted to the border increased dramatically as agents and new technology were funneled to the area at the cost of roughly $2 billion a year. Much of the new technology and manpower is concentrated along historical urban crossing areas, such as San Diego, El Paso, and Brownsville.[1] The new campaign prevents migrants from crossing in these well-established corridors and deters them to more remote rural areas where they are exposed to greater dangers and risk of death. The mortality bill resulting from these strategies is staggering. Since 1992—the year the campaign was initiated—more than three thousand migrants have died trying to cross the U.S.-Mexico border, which translates into at least one migrant death per day.[2]

The Mexican government launched its campaign, "Plan Sur," in 2001 to curtail Central American migration into southern Mexico. Hoping to gain amnesty for Mexican residents in the United States and under pressure from Bush to extend the U.S.-Mexico border farther south, the Mexican government deployed troops to the southern states of Chiapas and Oaxaca to conduct border patrols and install checkpoints along well-established crossing corridors.[3] The strategy and subsequent human consequences mirrors events on the U.S.-Mexico border, which is not surprising given that the Mexican campaign is largely based on the Prevention through Deterrence model. To avoid the checkpoints in southern

Mexico, which are located near towns and villages, Central American migrants take more risky routes in remote areas, where they fall prey to violent gangs, the most notorious of which is the Mara Salvatrucha.[4] Migrants crossing into Mexico face rape, murder, robbery, injury from train wheels, shakedowns from government officials, and abandonment in the forests. When I interviewed Father Flor Maria Rigoni, a young Scalabrini priest and director of a migrant shelter in Tapachula, Mexico, he described Chiapas—the southern state of Mexico—as a "cemetery without a cross." In 2000, 120 migrants died at or near the 600-mile Guatemalan-Mexico border. By 2001, less than a year later, this number had almost tripled to 355. The most recent figures indicate another increase: in 2003, Mexican authorities reported 371 migrant crossing deaths near the 600-mile-long Mexican-Guatemalan border.[5]

These governmental policies have come under increased scrutiny and criticism by Catholic and Protestant churches, religious leaders, and interfaith coalitions throughout Central America, Mexico, and U.S. border areas. Recognizing that contemporary Latin American immigration to the United States is part of a larger phenomenon associated with the globalization of labor, religious leaders and interfaith coalitions throughout the region increasingly convey the message that the current U.S. immigration system is broken and in need of reform. The consequences of the current system, religious leaders argue, are morally unacceptable—the exploitation of migrant labor and the abuse and death of migrants who seek to enter. These conditions—they argue—threaten the basic human dignity and rights of the migrant. Thus, although both Protestant and Catholic churches recognize that sovereign nations have the right to control its borders, they do not condone such a right when it violates the human rights and human dignity of a migrant, regardless of legal status. Thus, increasingly the church calls for policies that do not abuse or exploit migrants, place them in danger, violate their due process, or detain them indefinitely. To protect the migrants from violation of their rights, religious leaders propose that churches become more involved in creating a just and humane border environment, including providing humanitarian services for journeying migrants.

Triggered in part by the U.S. Sanctuary movement of the 1980s—a religious-based movement that provided Sanctuary to growing numbers of Central Americans fleeing political turmoil in their homelands—and later fueled by recent large-scale immigration of poor Latin Americans to the United States in the context of the militarization of the U.S.-Mexico border, a growing body of literature has developed that focuses on how Protestant and Catholic churches, religious organizations, and communities mobilize around the rights of migrants, especially at their arrival in the United States.[6] I would like to extend the discussion to include Mexico and Central America and shift the focus from advocacy of migrant rights per se to the ways in which religious leaders, groups, coalitions, and institutions at local, national, and international levels are responding, both privately and publicly, to the everyday needs of undocumented migrants in transit. Of concern is how religious leaders in communities of origin and in transit countries serve the religious, spiritual, psychological, and practical needs of undocumented migrants as they prepare to leave their home communities and on their journey north. This is a primary battlefield on which the rights of migrants are played out but one that the literature on migration and social justice rarely addresses. The discussion takes place in the context of more restrictive state policies, which run counter to the official or unofficial positions of the church.

Research Design and Study Sample

The data for this chapter come from a larger project on religion and migration that explores the ways in which migrants have access to and draw upon religious resources—as a form of cultural capital—during various stages of the migration process, including decision making, preparation, the journey, and the arrival. The larger project, which is being prepared for a book, was based on an initial case study of a transnational Maya community (Hagan 2003, 2004). In addition to interviews with migrants and religious leaders, the project has also involved fieldwork and interviews at roughly twenty sacred places and Catholic shrines where migrants stop to pray either before leaving their home communities, during their journey north, or on return visits to their home communities to give thanks.

I designed the larger project to explore how migrants interpret and create everyday religious practices to derive meaning for the decision to migrate, and to seek spiritual guidance and protection during the process of international travel. I administered a religion and migration survey to 312 recently arrived Mexican, Guatemalan, Salvadoran, and Honduran immigrants: Catholics and Protestants, women and men, frequent and rare churchgoers, legal and undocumented. The respondents were interviewed in 2001 and 2002 in religious and nonreligious settings in Houston, Texas. The diversified sample was designed to provide data on the various ways in which different subpopulations express or engage in religious rituals and practices related to the migration experience.

The migrant survey was complemented with close to one hundred face-to-face interviews with Catholic and Protestant religious leaders in the United States, Mexico, Guatemala, El Salvador, Costa Rica, and Honduras. The interviews were conducted with a cardinal, several bishops, and numerous church ministers, along with directors or staff of migrant shelters that provide religious counsel and humanitarian and legal assistance to journeying migrants. These programs, which are often referred to by the Catholic church as "transit," as opposed to traditional "settlement," programs for migrants, have become increasingly visible in Mexico in recent years, as well as among other religious orders, such as the Presbyterian church along both sides of the U.S.-Mexico border, the Mary-knoll houses in Mexico, and, most notably, the Scalabrini in Mexico and Central America.

In this chapter I draw primarily from interviews with religious leaders and faith-based coalitions to examine the institutional dimension of religion in the migration process. My concern is with describing the ways in which churches and religious leaders—at local, national, and binational levels—have responded to the growing humanitarian, material, and spiritual needs of undocumented migrants.

The Role of Local Clergy in Migrant Sending Communities

Responses to the needs and rights of undocumented journeying migrants begin in their home communities, where migrants turn to trusted clergy for spiritual and psychological counsel before embarking on their journey. Burdened by myriad financial, emotional, and psychological concerns, prospective migrants often turn to the spiritual anchors of their communities for guidance and comfort. In the sample of 312 migrants, close to two-thirds of the migrants—Protestants and Catholics alike—turned to religious icons for divine intervention and trusted religious leaders for counsel. Present-day migrants request more advice and guidance than in the past, according to ministers, because of increased personal and financial hazards involved in an undocumented journey. As one young evangelical minister in the Guatemalan highland Department of Totonicapan explained, "Because the investment is so high, the risk so much, and crossing the borders implies uncertainty, the majority of those in our community who make this voyage are focused on seeking divine intervention in their undertaking." He continued, "Moreover, the poverty in this area is so great that people have no other alternative but to seek out God's miracles, regardless of the outcome."

The functions of the local clergy in migrant-sending areas are threefold.[7] First, many prospective migrants rely on local clergy to provide for the spiritual and psychological needs of the family left behind. As Pastor Chuc, an independent evangelical minister from the Guatemalan highlands explained, "It is common for the whole family to come to pray before a migrant departs. It is understood in this final prayer and time of counsel that the family will be cared for by me and the migrant's brothers in my ministry."

Second, many clergy, especially young ministers who keep up with events beyond their communities and are socially progressive, provide important sources of information to prospective migrants. From these trusted clerics, migrants learn about the dangers of crossing international borders and, in some cases, are directed to alternative and safer routes than they would otherwise adopt. In a Catholic Church and adjoining shelter in Altar, Mexico—the staging ground for the seventy-five-mile-long deadly migrant trail north to Arizona—a young priest provides educational classes on the dangers of crossing and the legal rights of migrants for prospective migrants. Catholic priests and lay workers involve themselves far more in providing information to potential migrants than do their Protestant counterparts, a difference that relates to the more transnational character of the Catholic church in the Americas, which transmits information across a network of parishes.

Local clergy also provide religious and moral sanction for the migration, a type of spiritual travel permit that in many poor and marginalized communities has enormous symbolic value.[8] So powerful are its psychological benefits that in the mind of a migrant it may in fact exceed the value of a visa or passport issued by the state. According to the local vicar at the infamous shrine of the Black Christ in Esquipulas, Guatemala, approximately forty to fifty departing and journeying migrants visit the shrine each day. Some are journeying migrants who stop primarily for material assistance, such as a hot meal and a fresh change of clothes. Many, however, are departing migrants who make the pilgrimage to Esquipulas to gather up the spiritual strength necessary to endure the hardships of the journey north. "They come to be blessed," explained the attending priest. "Some pass by the feet of El Cristo and pray, but most go to the confessionary or the atrium where we bless them. At these blessings, which are often group blessings, we anoint them with holy water, pray together for their safety, and counsel them on the family they are leaving behind." He explained, "The blessings are very important to them. Sometimes, if time allows, they also share the Eucharist with us, but since many who stop here are not practicing Catholics, all they really want is a final blessing to protect them before they go on their way."

The degree to which clergy sanction the migration varies by religion. Most ministers of small evangelical Pentecostal churches or independent ministries in Central America reluctantly endorse the migration of their members. Recognizing the devastating effects migration could have on family left behind, and also the financial loss to an independent church itself, many evangelical pastors first attempt to discourage the migration of their members before granting approval and providing a blessing. In contrast, most Catholic priests, while counseling the potential migrant on the consequences of family separation, rarely discourage the migration itself, recognizing that the need to migrate to feed and provide for one's family is a fundamental right.

Often the local diocese or judicatory cooperates with local clergy in providing for the religious and psychological needs of the departing migrants. In the religious Mexican state of Jalisco and the Salvadoran state of San Miguel, for example, the area bishops celebrate the annual Day of the Migrant. In the diocese of Tegucigalpa, Honduras, this celebration is performed by the cardinal of the country. In parishes in established migrant-sending communities throughout Mexico, further rituals have been institutionalized to commemorate the domestic or international migrants, including the Day of the Emigrant and Day of the Absent Sons (Fitzgerald 2005).

Religious Organizations and Responses to Journeying Migrants

The struggles mount once an undocumented migrant departs the journey. Trusted coyotes protect some. However, many migrants, especially those who cannot afford the services of a coyote to accompany them the entire journey, must travel some, if not most, of the entire distance alone or with friends and family and without protection.

For these migrants, the problems and hardships they encounter are enormous. Among the undocumented migrants interviewed for this study, 78 percent experienced a problem on the journey, ranging from robberies to exposure to extreme physical elements to physical or sexual assault to injuries. Central American migrants experienced more problems than their Mexican counterparts, which is not surprising given that the former migrant group is forced to travel a greater distance and cross at least two international borders.

In recent years, in response to the increasing dangers associated with undocumented migration to the United States from Latin America, a growing number of churches and religious organizations have come to the assistance of the journeying migrant—some national, some international. Many undocumented migrants interviewed, especially those from Central America, credit a Scalabrini-run safe house with helping them during their journey. Since its creation in 1886, this Italian Catholic congregation remains the only religious group in the world whose sole mission is pastoral care for migrants and immigrants. The congregation has a global presence, with approximately six hundred priests in more than twenty countries. Originally, the Scalabrini attended to the needs of immigrants in countries in which Italians had settled, but since about the 1960s the congregation's focus has broadened to include all migrants and immigrants worldwide. In most host countries, including the United States, the charge of the Saint Charles Missionaries of the Scalabrini Congregation is to assist in the settlement of migrants and their families and services are largely legal and educational. In Guatemala and Mexico, however, its mission is unique. It provides pastoral and humanitarian care for the journeying migrants and resettlement provisions for the returned migrant who has been deported home.

To that end, the Scalabrini Congregation has established a network of migrant shelters, called Casas del Migrante (migrant houses) that are situated along the most dangerous crossing corridors along the Guatemala-Mexico and Mexico-U.S. borders. The transit shelters provide humanitarian, educational, and psychological services and support. In addition to giving food, shelter, and clothing, the Scalabrini missionaries educate the migrant on the dangers awaiting them on the journey north and their rights as undocumented migrants. If requested, religious counsel or a blessing is provided. Religious services are held but migrants are not required to attend. The first Scalabrini shelter was established in 1987 in Tijuana, at that time a major crossing location for Latin American Mexican migrants. Indeed, in the late 1980s an attending priest of the Casa in Tijuana erected a makeshift altar alongside the highway that divides Mexico from the United States, and held masses for would-be nightly crossers. In more recent years, as flows have been redirected to other areas of the border, the Saint Charles Missionaries have responded by erecting shelters in these more dangerous crossing locations along the Guatemala-Mexico and U.S.-Mexico border areas.

The Scalabrini also work closely with local Mexican and Guatemalan Dioceses and the Mexican National Episcopal Conference. The Scalabrini, in conjunction with local dioceses of migrant-sending areas throughout Mexico and Central America, for example, have produced a migrant prayer book *(Devocionario del Migrante)* that priests provide to prospective migrants to accompany them on the trip. The pocket-size fifty-six-page devotional contains numerous prayers for the migrant to recite on the journey north, each of which reflects the concerns of the journeying migrant. For example, there are prayers to care for family left behind, others to help the migrant find work, and still others to substitute for a religious service missed while traveling north. These devotionals are published with support of local dioceses and distributed at churches in migrant-sending communities and at transit shelters in Mexico and Central America. The Scalabrini also publish a weekly magazine, *Migrante*, which is distributed to dioceses throughout the Americas, but especially to those located in migrant-sending areas in Central America and Mexico. In addition to providing an abundance of information on migration trends and issues in the region, *Migrante* publishes repeated messages encouraging more involvement in migration matters by local priests in migrant-sending, receiving, and transit areas.

The growing need for transit shelters and provisions for journeying migrants has not gone unnoticed by Catholic bishops in Mexico and the United States. In recent years and in direct response to the escalation of border enforcement activities along the Mexico-U.S. border, the Catholic church in both Mexico and the United States has become increasingly vocal and explicit in its position concerning the right to migrate and its opposition to the current U.S. immigration system. In 2003, the Catholic Bishops of Mexico and the United States, who collectively shepherd more than 150 million Catholics, published the first-ever joint pastoral letter on migration, entitled "Stranger No Longer: Together on the Journey of Hope."[9] The letter calls for immigration reform in a number of areas that directly challenge the immigration policies of both the Mexican and U.S. governments.[10] Among the many proposals discussed in the document are those that directly question the consequences of current enforcement policies for the rights and dignity of journeying migrants. Because of the escalated dangers and abuses facing contemporary migrants as they make their way north, the letter further proposes that the Catholic church provide ministers to accompany, protect, and counsel migrants on their journey.

Informally known as the Tex-Mex bishops, a subgroup of U.S. and Mexican bishops accompanied by a host of religious workers from both sides of the border convened the Fourth Annual Binational Workshop on Pastoral Services for Migrants, held in Mexico City during the September 7, 2003, national celebration of the Day of the Migrant. Roughly seventy religious leaders and local priests attended this conference, which was sponsored by the Mexican Episcopal Commission for the Pastoral Care of Human Mobility, the U.S. Conference of Bishops, and the Vatican, all of which promote or direct transit programs. Chief among the issues raised and discussed at the conference were ways to improve and coordinate transit programs and services for journeying migrants and promote social justice along the international borders that migrants must cross.

For many undocumented migrants, the most dangerous stretch of the journey is crossing the U.S.-Mexico border, where the current U.S. enforcement campaign redirects migrants from well-established urban crossing points to remote corridors where migrants are at the mercy of physical elements. One of the most popular and also deadliest crossing points is located in the desert areas southwest of Tucson. Altar, Sonora, a small Mexican town in the Sonora Desert, is a staging point for thousands of migrants headed across the Mexico-Arizona border. The seventy-five-mile migrant trail across this desert claims hundreds of deaths each year.

Numerous local, regional, and binational religious coalitions have organized around the issue of migrant deaths along the treacherous trail. Churches on both sides of the border are united under a series of organizations to assist migrants. The organizations have grown in size and scope over the years and are now referred to under the umbrella term of a social- and faith-based movement. Some of the movement's architects are from the Presbyterian Church USA and include a number of leaders who can trace their concerns for migrant rights back to the days of the Sanctuary movement, which flourished in the Tucson area in the 1980s. In 2000, in response to a marked escalation of migrant deaths in the area, a cowboy clergyman, Robin Hoover, founded Humane Borders, a binational religious coalition established to "create a just and more humane border environment."[11] Responding to the escalation of migrant deaths along the Mexico-Arizona border resulting from U.S. enforcement strategies that deflect migrants from established urban crossing areas to more remote and dangerous routes, Humane Borders places water stations near well-traveled paths across southern Arizona. By 2003, they had erected thirty-one water stations along the U.S. side of the migrant trail and had dispensed more than fifty thousand gallons of water. Their members include thirty-three Protestant and Catholic churches in Mexico and Arizona, along with a host of human rights organizations.

But water stations were not enough to make a dent in the number of migrant deaths. In 2003, John Fife, a leading Presbyterian minister in Tucson and cofounder (along with Jim Corbett) of the 1980s U.S. Sanctuary movement, established the Good Samaritan, a coalition of Quakers, Jews, Methodists, Catholics, and Presbyterians that regularly tour the deadly desert in four-wheel-drive vehicles equipped with water, food, and first-aid supplies. If they find a migrant in distress they will transport him or her to a hospital.

In the spring of 2004, a broader effort developed to work for justice along the border and provide sustained 24/7 humanitarian relief for journeying migrants. The campaign is entitled "No More Deaths," and its members include a diverse binational coalition of individuals, faith communities, and human rights grass-roots organizers. The movement established a campaign to limit more deaths and challenge U.S. enforcement policy. Central to the campaign is the biblically inspired "Ark of the Covenant" strategy, which includes placing moveable desert camps in the desert. In the summer months, the camps are manned round the clock by volunteers from churches throughout the United States. The desert camps provide water, food, clothing, and medical assistance for journeying migrants. Developed by Jim Corbett during the U.S. Sanctuary movement, volunteers employ what Corbett referred to as a civil initiative as opposed to civil disobedience protocol and adhere to lawful actions.[12] From 2004 to early 2005, members avoided any confrontation with government officials, although their efforts were closely monitored by Border Patrol. Things took a dramatic turn on July 9, 2005, when U.S. Border Patrol stopped a vehicle occupied by several unauthorized migrants and two No More Death volunteers. The two volunteers were arrested and later charged with transporting migrants. The two volunteers are scheduled to go on trial April 2006 (Innes 2005).

Discussion

In recent decades the church has become increasingly active in its provision to journeying migrants and its opposition to the militarization of the southern border of Mexico and the United States. In migrant-sending communities throughout Central America and Mexico, local clergy have incorporated migrant counseling into the general services they provide to their ministries. Transit shelters in Central America have also been established to provide material, humanitarian, and spiritual services for journeying migrants. In some areas, especially the U.S side of the Arizona-Mexico border, the growing opposition to the state and subsequent activities of church-based groups and religious leaders are reminiscent of the Sanctuary movement of the 1980s. The migrant conditions and movement goals are different today than they were twenty years ago. As Reverend Fife explained, "The context of migration changed in the 1990s and so has the migrant needs. The context today is not political, as it was in the 1980s, but economic and related to NAFTA, globalization, that is, issues of economic inequalities for migrants today are paramount, e.g. right to cross, work, receive medical treatment. We are trying interim efforts such as humanitarian assistance to migrants, like that provided by Humane Borders. However, if militarization of the border continues and escalates and migrants continue to die, we may have no choice but to organize into a movement, one that might ultimately lead to sanctuary."[13]

Migrants continued to die along the Mexico-Arizona border in record numbers in 2002 and 2003 and Fife's words proved prescient. By 2004, the No More Deaths movement was founded. For the moment its goal is the development of a more humane border policy and social justice for migrants. The emergence of this interfaith movement along the U.S.-Mexico border suggests that a battle between the state and the church is well under way. It should prove interesting in the near future to see how the state responds to the church's spiritual and humanitarian strategies along the border and how effective the church's mobilization efforts are in changing U.S. border policy and ultimately ensuring safe passage for journeying migrants.

NOTES

1. For a comprehensive overview of the militarization of the U.S.-Mexico border, see Dunn (1996) and Andreas (2000).

2. There is a burgeoning literature on the increasing dangers associated with contemporary undocumented travel from Latin America. Eschbach, Hagan and Rodriguez (2003) document deaths incurred to migrants while trying to cross the heavily guarded U.S.-Mexico border. Grayson (2003) and Menjivar (2000) focus on the dangers experienced by Central American migrants on the journey north. Urrutia-Rojas and Rodriguez (1997) focus on the particular perils confronting young unaccompanied migrants: Hagan and Rodriguez (2004) and Rodriguez (2002) provide preliminary comparisons of the comparative risks of Central Americans and Mexicans. Chavez (1992) writes about the undocumented experience in general, including the perilous journey.

3. See Flynn (2002).

4. The Mara Salvatrucha are often compared to their notorious northern counterparts in Los Angeles—the Crips and the Bloods. The gang is considered a product of the civil war in El Salvador. Many displaced youth fled to Los Angeles during the crisis; among the displaced, some founded the Mara Salvatrucha. Some members were later deported from the United States. They have since established a visible presence along the El Salvador-U.S. migrant trail where they prey on migrants as they hide in concealed train compartments or jump off the trains as they approach checkpoints.

5. See Grayson (2003).

6. See, for example, Coutin (1993); Casanova (1994); Warren and Wood (2001); Wood (2002); and Hondagneu-Sotelo et al. (2004).

7. For a more comprehensive discussion of the role of local clergy in the preparation stage of the migration process, see Hagan (forthcoming b).

8. Hagan (forthcoming b).

9. U.S. Conference of Catholic Bishops (2003).

10. Some of the other proposals discussed in the document are increased opportunities for family-based immigration; a broad legalization program for undocumented migrants residing in the United States; a new temporary guest program for foreign workers living in the United States, and due process for migrants and asylum seekers.

11. See their mission statement at http://www.humaneborders.org/.

12. See http://www.nomoredeaths.org/ContactUs.html.

13. Interview with author, June 13, 2002.

8

Serving Christ in the Borderlands

Faith Workers Respond to Border Violence

CECILIA MENJÍVAR

Religious congregations have been involved in providing multiple forms of assistance to immigrants for a long time. Not only are immigrants already familiar with the churches they come to join, but the churches and their congregations are perhaps some of the most supportive and welcoming institutions, particularly for immigrants who face extremely difficult circumstances. Many churches and congregations offer newcomers material and financial support, as well as legal counsel, access to medical care and housing, a lobby for less stringent immigration policies, and a welcome from the nonimmigrant coreligionists. To reach out to newcomers, churches conduct services in the languages of the immigrants and incorporate popular religious practices that are culturally essential for immigrants. Immigrants also create new religious spaces, new churches and congregations, and bring new expressions of the faith to long-established churches. Thus, in efforts to become relevant to newcomers, established churches and their congregations do not remain static. Responding to the needs of the new flock, churches themselves are changing and new ones are being created, so that in the interaction between new immigrants and the receiving society's religious spaces transformation occurs both ways (Menjívar 2003).

In previous work I have examined the spaces that churches provide for immigrants to remain connected to their communities of origin (Menjívar 1999), the kinds of assistance that the church and congregations provide and what it means for the immigrants (Menjívar 1999, 2001, 2003), and national and ethnic differences in the meaning immigrants attach to such assistance (Menjívar 2001). In general, this work has focused on the immigrants and the central place of religious congregations in their settlement. The focus of this piece is not the place of the congregations' assistance from the point of view of the immigrants, but on how faith workers respond to the conditions immigrants face.[1] Specifically, I focus on how they respond to border violence, drawing on social justice teachings as well as on the link between their work, scripture, and definitions of the context within which they respond. In doing so, I engage discussions at the intersection of religion, politics, and immigration law.

A few definitions are in order before I embark on this discussion. From the angle I approach this examination, the "border" is not only the physical border, though it is central in this analysis, but also the legal and social borders derived from exclusionary immigration policies. Gloria Anzaldúa (1987, 25) referred to the Mexico-US border as an "open wound where the Third world grates against the first and bleeds ... the lifeblood of two worlds merging to form a third country—a border culture." However, Anzaldúa's image of the borderlands also has been used to refer to other, metaphorical borders, those created by systems of stratification such as class, race, ethnicity, and gender. Thus, I will also use this concept to refer to the borders created by exclusionary immigration policies and militarized border strategies that marginalize immigrants socially, economically, and politically. From the standpoint of the faith workers, these borders represent unique sites to express their socially and politically engaged interpretations of scripture as challenges to be overcome and transcended.

I must also explain my use of the concept of violence. In this work, violence is a multifaceted concept that does not refer solely to the willful infliction of physical pain or injury or even mental anguish, but also to the deprivation of services to maintain mental and physical health and to the warlike atmosphere created by militarized border policies. Thus, from this angle, faith workers respond to violence that takes place at the physical border but also in other borders; that is, to the kind of violence produced by broader structural forces that generate and exacerbate other forms of violence. The workers' responses are fundamentally linked to social justice teachings; they view their actions as advancing social change with a focus on the marginalized and excluded.

The responses I examine are those of faith workers of different denominations who live and work in Tucson, Arizona. This context provides an important site to examine how faith workers galvanize a moral voice to respond to immigration and border policies. Arizona has become the focus of numerous initiatives that endanger the lives of immigrants in multiple ways. First, the implementation of border policies that push undocumented border crossing to more rugged and dangerous terrain has directly contributed to an increase in human rights abuses and deaths (Eschbach, Hagan, and Rodriguez 1999). The militarization of the border resulting from the Border Patrol's different operations in California and Texas, Operation Safeguard in Nogales, Arizona, in 1994, as well as the more recent escalation after 2001, has created a climate where direct physical violence endangers the lives of immigrants. As a result of border militarization, the change in migration patterns (e.g., alternate border-crossing points, where almost half the deaths since 1995 have occurred) has made this region a type of ground zero (Massey 2003). The Border Patrol's militarized response to a border perceived out of control has unleashed actions that threaten the physical well-being of immigrants and nonimmigrants alike, and brutalize the public in general (Kil and Menjívar, forthcoming).

Second, in addition to anti-immigrant legislation at the federal level (e.g., the Illegal Immigration Reform and Responsibility Act of 1996), Arizona recently implemented a new law that severely restricts immigrants' access to social services and further criminalizes their presence. Originally called Proposition 200, Protect Arizona Now, or Arizona Taxpayer and Citizen Protection Act, this initiative was approved by voters on November 2, 2004, and enacted into law on December 22, 2004.[2] This new law is supposed to help stem the flow of undocumented immigration to Arizona; instead, it makes even more vulnerable the immigrants who are already living in the state. Also, at the time of this writing there are several bills pending in the Arizona legislature that would place even more restrictions on what undocumented immigrants can do. These laws threaten the existence of immigrants, as they push them further away from society's benefits into more marginalized and clandestine lives. Both militarized border initiatives and new immigration laws make up an aggressive system of exclusion and marginalization, expressed in multiple forms of violence against immigrants at the physical border and in the environment in which they now live. It is this multifaceted violence to which faith workers respond. Thus, examined from this angle, violence is not the result of individuals' choices alone, but, more important, it is the product of inequalities institutionalized in legal systems and justified through a host of frameworks, such as ideology and history (Bourgois 2001). This multifaceted concept of violence captures the consequences of militarized border policies and of exclusionary immigration laws that provide a context within which faith workers carry out their mission.

I examine how faith workers interpret this context and how, from a stand that relates scripture and biblical teachings to the conditions immigrants face, they respond by advocating a clear political stance. I focus on the work of two interdenominational organizations with roots in the Sanctuary movement that operate in Tucson. There are many contemporary instances in which religion is moving beyond the confines of worship, spirituality, and ritual "to challenge and inform public morality" (Hondagneu-Sotelo et al. 2004), which Casanova (1994) has referred to as the "deprivatization of religion" or the "set of beliefs that link theology to public affairs," and that Guth and his colleagues (1997) define as social theology. In the cases I examine here, the work that faith workers carry out is clearly informed by these frameworks. According to Robin Hoover, the director of one of the organizations on which I focus, "Theology is the source of motivation for many . . . and what is more important than theology is social theology, that is, the connection between theology and matters of public policy" (Hoover 2004). In some instances, faith workers also make explicit the links between their work and central tenets of liberation theology, which is yet another way by which Latin-American religious traditions infuse change in U.S. churches and congregations' worldviews.

Structuring Border Violence

Images of immigrants as invaders and the use of war metaphors at the border create ideological victims and enemies that justify war strategies (Kil and Menjívar, forthcoming). As the War on Drugs was coupled with enforcement efforts against undocumented immigration, state officials have shown an increasing penchant for using war terms when discussing border issues (Huspek 2001). Using war rhetoric and deploying low-intensity conflict methods to enforce border policies increase the social and racial polarization, and encourages a climate of abuse and violence toward undocumented immigrants and those who racially or ethnically resemble them (U.S. Commission on Civil Rights 1997). As Leo Chavez (2001, 223) notes, the "invasion metaphor evokes a sense of crisis related to an attack on the sovereign territory of the nation." And Peter Andreas (2000) observes that loss-of-control arguments serve as powerful narratives that obscure the ways in which government practices themselves create the very conditions that generate calls for and justify increased state authority. Thus, repressive forces in themselves become legitimized responses to social forces perceived to be acting against the interests of the state and, thus, in need of control.

The militarization of the southern U.S. border has created an atmosphere of warlike characteristics that has contributed to a wide range of civil and human rights abuses. U.S. immigration authorities use a range of bellicose tactics and technology, such as infrared detectors, electronic sensors, infrared radar, helicopters, closed circuit television monitoring, and even fence barriers to contain the flow. Interestingly, the deployment of these strategies has been carried out with the intent of creating a warlike atmosphere through fear-inducing tactics in the civilian population. Dunn (1996) notes that the low-intensity conflict (LIC) doctrine that the INS implemented in the border region was originally conceived of as a U.S. tactic to subdue guerilla warfare in developing countries. LIC involves various levels of military involvement with Border Patrol duties, from loaning high-tech equipment to authorizing military personnel to arrest and search, to confiscating civilians and/or their possessions for border-enforcement purposes.[3] In addition, immigration authorities have been intent on building physical barriers along the border with collaboration from the military. In 1990 the U.S. Navy Sea Bees built a ten-foot-high wall of corrugated steel between San Diego and Tijuana with floodlights to illuminate it during the night (Dunn 1996). Recently the Border Patrol proposed the building of a new twenty-mile fence approximately sixty feet north of the existing fence that separates Douglas, Arizona, and Naco, Mexico, so as to concentrate their patrolling in the space in between ("Colocarán otra barrera" 2005).

Not surprisingly, these tactics have directly contributed to an increase in immigrant deaths, by pushing the flow to more rugged and dangerous rural terrain and by encouraging more dangerous strategies to cross. The actual number of deaths due to stiffer border policies is unknown, since no official attempt has been made to record them systematically (Eschbach, Hagan, and Rodriguez 1999). However, social scientists and human rights groups estimate that more than two thousand people have died in the desert on the U.S. side since a count began in 1994 (Massey 2003). In the first days of January 2005 alone there were over twenty deaths reported in the Tucson region (Villa 2005). And Robin Hoover (2004) estimates that there is an average of at least one death per day, but that these estimates only include those deaths on the U.S. side of the border. Oftentimes those apprehended are medically distressed and when deported go to die in Mexico or their countries of origin. These deaths are not factored in the estimates.

This situation has prompted coyotes (smugglers) to adopt more aggressive tactics to conduct their businesses, often extorting, robbing, raping, and assaulting their own compatriots in order to compete in the perverse market of human smuggling. The economic costs of crossing have also escalated substantially. Nowadays it is not unusual for smugglers to charge $1,000–1,500 a person for taking them across the border (Gonzalez 2003). In many ways, the coyotes' actions exemplify instances of everyday violence, in which the socially vulnerable inflict violence onto those closest to them, actions that mirror the state's legitimized violence. However, instead of public attention focusing on how border policies have created this phenomenon, the moral panic over coyote activities generally spotlights on the greed of the smugglers (Associated Press 2003b; Holthouse and Scioscia 2000); describes their tactics as similar to those of drug smuggling (Gonzalez 2003; Billeaud 2003); likens their activities to a modern form of slavery (Fiscus 2003); accuses them of abusing migrants in the desert (Riley 2003); and blames them for unsolved murders of undocumented migrants (Carroll 2003). Noteworthy, very little or no attention centers on the immigration and drug policies that have created the conditions in which human smuggling has proliferated.

The Border Patrol is not alone in deploying sophisticated military technology; vigilante groups also feel they need to contribute to stem the flow. These groups do not see themselves as violating the law; instead, they see themselves as helping the efforts for enforcement and border control. Thus, vigilante groups imitate the government's policy and rhetoric of militarization and, thus, also patrol the border region armed with hi-tech equipment and warlike strategies. Since Arizona has been the center of recent Border Patrol operations, vigilante groups have moved from California and Texas into Arizona to be near their perceived ground zero (Kil and Menjívar, forthcoming). Several have adopted names very similar to those of state agencies in charge of implementing border control policies. For instance, the American Border Patrol moved operations from California (where this organization was called Voices of Citizens Together/American Patrol and recognized by the Alabama-based Southern Poverty Law Center as a hate group) and began operations in 2002 with a focus on high-tech detection equipment installed along the border (Hammer-Tomizuka and Allen 2002). Recently, American Border Patrol conducted its first test flight of a radio-controlled, miniature spy plane called "border hawk" (Associated Press 2003a). Some of these groups, like Ranch Rescue, describe themselves as an "armed volunteer organization" interested in protecting private landowner's property rights from "criminal trespassers." This group circulated a flier in Arizona calling for recruits to "hunt" immigrants and "to help keep trespassers from destroying private property" (Rotstein, cited in Kil and Menjivar, forthcoming). Members are openly armed and "operate on public lands, patrol routes leading to water stations [set up by humanitarian groups to aid immigrants] and have volunteers apply for concealed weapons permits" (Associated Press 2002). There are other, less organized but equally eager, vigilantes who mimic the government's military border paradigm in rhetoric and strategy, that contribute to an atmosphere of violence and racial hate.[4] More recently, there has been a nationwide effort called the Minuteman Project that has recruited volunteers, particularly people with law enforcement and military backgrounds, from all states and Canada to "protect the country against a 40-year invasion" and to "help the Border Patrol in 'spotting'—with the aid of binoculars, telescopes, night vision scopes—intruders entering the U.S. illegally." Their web ad features an "I Want You" Uncle Sam image and reads: "Are YOU interested in spending up to 30 days along the Arizona border as part of a blocking force against entry into the U.S. by illegal aliens early next spring?" (http://minutemanproject.com/). As of this writing, they are holding their mission (April 1–30, 2005) on a stretch of the border near Tombstone, Arizona. The Southern Poverty Center, which tracks hate groups, monitored this project closely because it sparked great interest in neo-Nazi Web sites (Carroll 2005).

Methods and Data

The data used in this piece come from interviews conducted with faith workers in Tucson in 2004 and 2005. One of my assistants and I visited BorderLinks and Humane Borders on different occasions. We interviewed the director and codirector of both organizations, as well as two staff members at Humane Borders, and the academic coordinator of BorderLinks. The interviews lasted approximately one hour and took place in the offices; these were conversations about interpretations of the faith workers' activities but did not expand on their own individual histories and backgrounds. These interviews include Colombian-born Luzdy Stucky, codirector of BorderLinks; Jerry Gill, its academic coordinator and board member, who is a member of the Presbyterian Church and holds a Ph.D. in theology; Robin Hoover, director of Humane Borders and pastor of the First Christian Church in Tucson, who holds a Ph.D. in Political Science; Sister Elizabeth Ohmann, a Franciscan nun whose order makes it possible for her to donate at least half of her time to Humane Borders; and Sue Goodman, the administrative coordinator at Humane Borders.[5]

In addition to these five individuals, we spoke with volunteers from both organizations. We also collected written material, pamphlets, and visual documentation from both organizations and a good amount of information through their websites. A third source of data was the educational trips that my assistant and I took on separate occasions with BorderLinks to Sasabe, Mexico, and to Agua Prieta, Mexico. The trips provided key supplementary information through group discussions, excursions, observations, and presentations on both sides of the border.

Faith Workers Respond

How do faith workers see and respond to border violence? Certainly not all workers interpret the situation in Arizona in the same way or respond to it in a homogeneous fashion. Religious groups to the right of the political spectrum tend to agree with the strategies that the U.S. government has implemented at the border and with the new immigration law in Arizona. Sometimes they do not publicly agree, but nonetheless would not openly engage in opposing such strategies. For instance, when I initiated this research we contacted a much broader range of Christian denominations so as to make sure that we were not including only those we knew were engaged in opposing the government's formal strategies. Among other congregations, we contacted the Mormon Church of Latter-Day Saints (LDS) due to its strong presence in Arizona. The LDS Public Relations office in Mesa, Arizona, informed us that they do not do any organized immigration work as a church because of legal liabilities; they would rather not sponsor activities that are perceived to be against the law. However, they mentioned, individual members can engage in helping immigrants if they chose to do so.

Thus, the focus in this chapter is on faith workers in interdenominational groups that do engage in activities that speak up against immigration law and border strategies and take a clear political stance on the issue. Robin Hoover (1998) examines how and why some denominations are active in a particular public policy area and others are not, and why some denominations create organizations to work in public policy, whereas others do not. His research points to the presence of social theology as influencing the presence, size, and scope of the activities of religiously affiliated organizations working in the area of immigration. The cases I examine here certainly draw on a set of theological beliefs infused with social justice teachings to do and interpret their work, and uniformly view their actions as responding to a higher calling, above government-sponsored strategies. "My only judge and the only one I need to respond to is God, and God is on our side," the Catholic nun in Tucson said when asked if she was concerned about how immigration officials might interpret her work with undocumented immigrants. Importantly, although the groups on which I focus can all be located to the left of the political spectrum, I cannot capture all the possible combinations of social theology, politics, and the law; however, those I examine here vividly expose these intersections.

BorderLinks is one of the organizations on which I focus. The Tucson-based organization was created in 1987, with origins in the Sanctuary movement.[6] BorderLinks aims to be a truly binational organization with facilities on both sides of the border, with staff in roughly equal numbers from the two countries, and with bicultural programs and bilingual board meetings. Its staff includes program and trip coordinators, administrators, house managers, a fundraising and an academic coordinator, and three codirectors. It also has a board of directors, which includes faculty from different universities, as well as prominent leaders in Tucson, including key figures in the Sanctuary movement. The number of volunteers varies from none to ten at a time. Their operating budget comes from donations as well as from the fees participants pay for the educational programs. Within this overall framework, there is one heavily unidirectional mission: to be an educational resource, to raise the consciousness and awareness of U.S. citizens about the economic, social, and religious realities of the border and the effects of U.S. policies on its southern neighbors (Gill 2004). BorderLinks' various educational programs are designed not only to make U.S. participants keenly aware of the great inequalities that exist at the border, but also to make them cognizant of increasing trends of inequality in the United States. As Rick Ufford-Chase, its founder and international director and elected moderator of the Presbyterian church, notes, "Christians who come to learn from the border are pushed hard to examine their faith. . . . The challenge is to squarely face the contradictions that exist for North American Christians who are benefiting from a system that depends on the deepening poverty of factory workers all over the world. An honest reading of the Bible in that context makes most of us squirm" (http://www.borderlinks.org).

BorderLinks organizes trips to visit border towns on both sides (in which one of my assistants and I participated in on separate occasions), some of which are weeks, or even a semester, long. The trips usually start with presentations in the Tucson office, where a member of a participating church gives a brief presentation. In the trip I joined to Sasabe, a Catholic nun who works at Casa de la Misericordia (also BorderLinks-run) located in Nogales, Mexico, gave us a brief introduction and accompanied us during part of the trip.[7] Trips also include meetings with U.S. immigration officers at the border and with Mexican officials on the other side, meals at the homes of Mexican families, and visits to local markets and maquila assembly plants in Nogales. Trips that last several days also include readings and reflections of biblical passages, linking Christ's teachings to the lives of contemporary migrants and poor residents of border towns. The specific focus on border inequities allows for discussions of similar issues on both sides of the border; thus, through focusing on life south of the border, participants also gain a critical awareness of their own country as well. As its academic coordinator and board member points out, "BorderLinks aims at a pedagogy of the oppressor'" (Gill 2004, 4). These educational trips allow participants to examine the macrostructural forces that shape contemporary migratory flows. Through discussions of NAFTA, the militarization of the border, U.S. policies in Central America in the 1980s, and the elimination of the ejido system in Mexico, participants gain a unique understanding of how these policies have affected the lives of the poor who live south and north of the border and have compelled them to migrate, as well as the border itself. Gill (2004, 16) notes, "All these difficulties are focused powerfully on the border, and this renders it a crucial and excellent place to carry on an educational enterprise aimed at raising the consciousness, as well as the conscience, of those of us living in affluent North America."

Humane Borders, created in 2000, is another interdenominational group that operates in Tucson, placing water tanks in the desert; its president, Robin Hoover, is also the pastor of the First Christian Church (Disciples of Christ) in Tucson. This organization came out of BorderLinks and, as such, has had a strong interfaith approach from the very beginning. The Reverend Phil Anderson, a Lutheran pastor, was a catalyst for its creation, as were Rick Ufford-Chase of BorderLinks, the Reverend John Fife of Southside Presbyterian Church and a founder of the Sanctuary movement, Amy Schubitz and Marianna Neil of the Southside Presbyterian Church (also Sanctuary workers), and David Perkins from the Pima (Quaker) Friends Meeting. Sister Elizabeth Ohmann, a Franciscan Catholic nun and one of its founders, explains how it was formed:

> We need[ed] to sit down and reflect on these [migrant] deaths and then see what we [could] do about the whole situation. So Perkins came over to BorderLinks to talk about this; he talked to Rick and then Rick called me in because they said we need to think about this from a theological point of view and then work on the action for it and the three of us thought about it for a while and decided it was a situation way too big for three people. So Dave asked if we would consider . . . Dave is Quaker, Rick is Presbyterian, and I'm Catholic, and so Dave asked if we would consider doing this according to the Quaker method, which means you write up a query and pass it out and people think about it and then we come together for a meeting. Rick and I are both familiar with that because we use it for certain things, so we said fine. . . . Each of us thought of ten people whom we thought might be interested and invited them to come to a meeting the following Sunday afternoon and invite anyone they wanted to bring along. That Sunday afternoon sixty people showed up, which totally blew our

minds and just that in itself told us this is a really important question and that there are a lot of people concerned and a lot of people wanting to do something but not knowing what. So then ninety-six people sat down and discussed this question and came up with a conclusion. There were four people and one of those was Robin Hoover, who thought of the organizational part of Humane Borders and that evening came up with the name of Humane Borders, so he reported to us at the following meeting . . . that we consider the birth of Humane Borders."

Humane Borders is comprised of about thirty-four organizations that include congregations, denominational agencies, human rights organizations, legal assistance organizations, and businesses located in Mexico, Arizona, California, Texas, and Minnesota. Its staff includes a president, vice president, secretary, and treasurer. Their budget comprises donations from the local government of Pima County, from churches (including the water to fill the tanks, which comes from the First Church of Christ), and from individuals. In contrast to BorderLinks, Humane Borders does provide direct humanitarian assistance to migrants who are found in distress in the Arizona desert. Humane Borders also advocates for a nonmilitarized border and for legal work opportunities for migrants as well as for legitimate economic opportunities for migrants in their countries of origin.

One of its main goals is to reduce the number of migrant deaths in the desert, principally through the deployment of seventy fifty-five-gallon water stations (a few are only serviced during the summer months and some of them are not in operation during the winter months because the federal permits require the organization to take them down) that they have set up and maintained since March 2001. According to the organization's records, in fiscal year 2004, they dispensed more than 25,000 gallons of water, relying on the work of approximately 100 volunteers to service the water stations. Most volunteers live in the area, but often they come from far away, as the case of a youth group from New Hampshire that donated one week of voluntary work. Water is replenished every seven days in the summer and every ten days in the winter, with about six stations requiring daily maintenance. A tall flagpole marks these water stations so that migrants can spot them from afar in the desert. Humane Borders operates the water stations with permits negotiated with the National Park Service, U.S. Fish and Wildlife, the Bureau of Land Management, Pima County, and the Border Patrol. The Border Patrol allows its operations, and has been largely cooperative, provided that no volunteers ever aid undocumented workers in their trips by providing them a ride or by extending help that is not deemed strictly humanitarian. However, initially the Border Patrol was not convinced that this was a good idea. Sister Elizabeth explains:

We met with Border Patrol first. Robin met with the chief several times, and then Robin said to him he would like to have more of us, so that the chief realize that this was not just his opinion, that there are others of the same opinion and that we are working together on this. And the chief in turn said, "If you want to bring more, fine, then I will also bring more." So the day we had the meeting thirteen of us went and the chief had invited all the [Border Patrol] supervisors from southern Arizona to come to the meeting and that made about twenty-five to thirty agents. It's rather intimidating walking into a room with twenty-five to thirty agents all in uniforms and guns and all. . . . The chief asked each one of us if we would just give our opinions as to why we wanted to do this. In the beginning he kept saying, bad idea, very bad idea, don't do it because it's going to be going against all kinds of laws, and we kept saying we have a duty to our neighbors. We call it based on our faith, and sometimes faith laws are stronger than other laws for us so we need to do this. And at the end of that meeting we came to an agreement. We want to keep communication open because we don't want to start an underground railroad. We don't want to do something that is not open; we want people to know about it. It was a handshake agreement and the Border Patrol promised they would not use our water stations as bait stations to catch immigrants. And we promised them that we would get water, food, and first-aid types of medicine because we are medical people. . . . we may not transport immigrants, we promised we would not do that."[8]

Humane Borders keeps communication open with all interested parties. Thus, while engaging in critical discourse and condemning what happens at the border as immoral, the organization's decisions and actions have been public, open, transparent, and within the bounds of the law. As the administrative coordinator pointed out, "I would like to be clear. Our work is different from that of other organizations that do similar things to what we do. We work within the framework of the Border Patrol. If they tell us not to transport, then we are OK."[9]

During a visit to Humane Borders headquarters in Tucson I had the opportunity to see the water containers they use to dispense water. However, one of the containers, with one-quarter-inch walls, was perforated at different points. The guide explained that this particular container was not the only one that had been vandalized, as there had been several ruined water containers and thus volunteers need to check for these in addition to servicing the water stations. No one knows exactly who might vandalize the tanks or if it is the work of wild animals in the desert.

Humane Borders' president was well aware of criticism of their work.[10] He noted: "There are people that say that we are making it easier for terrorists to come in here and I just tell them that my work just follows on justice, it is justice, law, and morals." Indeed, at the office of Humane Borders they keep a thick binder that they have labeled "hate mail." They showed me some emails that come from different states and even from other parts of the world, including Australia. The Catholic nun who works there and the administrative coordinator explained that this correspondence comes from people who believe that having water available gives the immigrants false hope (that they can get through the desert without any problems), or from those who believe that by providing water they contribute to harboring undocumented immigrants. When asked if he felt they were encouraging law-breaking by making it safer to illegally enter the United States from Mexico, as many critics argue, Hoover responded, "It's immoral to use the desert as part of a deterrent system" (Sailer 2003). And there are also other critics who believe that these workers are "interpreting religion wrongly."

There are a few other faith-based groups in Tucson, such as the Samaritans, a group of volunteers that patrols the desert to find and assist immigrants in distress. This group is strongly backed by Rev. John Fife's Southside Presbyterian Church, the birthplace of the Sanctuary movement. Another active group is No More Deaths, which also organizes actively to oppose immigration policy and to create a more humane environment for migrants. Members of BorderLinks and Humane Borders participate in these efforts as well; Rick Ufford-Chase is also a founding member of No More Deaths. In addition, members of these organizations also participate in protests, marches, and demonstrations to oppose unjust border policies. And the Ministerios de María (Ministries of Mary), a Latino group, has organized a "journey of prayer" and a "white ribbon" campaign to respond to the Minutemen project. As well, there are several secular organizations based in Tucson, such as the Coalición de Derechos Humanos (Human Rights Coalition) and Alianza Indígena sin Fronteras (Indigenous Alliance without Borders) that also work on behalf of the migrants.

Border Theology

Rick Ufford-Chase of BorderLinks observes that "the border gives us insight into the divisions that exist in all of our communities across North and Latin America. It highlights both the opportunities and dangers of a world growing rapidly smaller as our economics render national boundaries meaningless. It demands of all of us that we redefine the boundaries of our churches and communities to embrace our brothers and sisters wherever they are. The border can help us understand what it means to be fully 'church'" (http://www.borderlinks.org). And Jerry H. Gill, the BorderLinks board member and academic coordinator, wrote in *Border Theology*, "I have come to conclusion that the concept of borders is at the heart of our political, economic, and spiritual lives as human beings on this planet (Gill 2003, 1)."

Many faith workers, regardless of their denomination, often referred to borders—metaphorically and physically—in their discussions of the link between scripture and the work they do for immigrants. For instance, according to these workers, Christ did not only cross physical or social boundaries on earth, but did so at a mystical level as well. In Gill's view, the idea of the Incarnation itself is directly related to a "divine border crossing" (Gill 2003, 10). He notes, "At yet a deeper level we can recognize that Jesus was an 'undocumented alien' in a cosmic sense as well. According to the Christian notion of Incarnation, he initially crossed the boundary between the transcendent dimension of reality and the natural dimension in which humans dwell. As John has it, 'The Word became flesh and dwelt among us . . . and we beheld his glory . . . full of grace and truth . . . He came unto his own and his own received him not.' Or as Paul expresses it, 'He humbled himself and became even a servant' to those he came to minister . . . God would seem to dwell 'at the border' and invites those who seek to be faithful to do likewise" (Gill 2003, 5–6). From this view, through the act of crossing borders—physically and metaphorically—one responds to God's message.

For Gill as well as for other active members of the organization, their work helps to eliminate borders, not only by standing up against increasingly militarized border policies but also by working to eradicate extreme inequality, which in their view creates multiple borders. And this is a guiding principle in their work. Thus, Gill (2003, 112–13) writes: "If God calls us to cross borders and break down barriers, it is not a call to a vague or impossible mission . . . national boundaries do provide especially fertile ground for borderland reflection and witness in the 21st Century." And when asked if the work he did was in conflict with the law, as many critics of these interfaith groups argue, none of them viewed their work as conflicting with the law, as they interpret their actions as responding to a higher calling. Instead, they view individuals as having the right to migrate, to cross borders, even if it goes against the laws created by humans. In their eyes, seeking better opportunities and safety was a right above the laws created on earth, a right given by God. Sister Elizabeth, for instance, said, "I believe that God lies above civil law in certain situations and so I would tend towards that."

Several workers had specific comments about violence or defined the context in which they work as particularly violent for immigrants and nonimmigrants alike. And such violence, in their view, was related to immigration laws. For instance, in the eyes of the president of Humane Borders, Proposition 200 would be particularly deleterious for immigrants; if passed (we interviewed him before it became law in Arizona), it would generate even more of the multipronged kind of violence that they work to eradicate. In his words: "I think Prop 200 itself is flat evil, it's a pernicious kind of a law and I'm hoping that the courts will throw all of this, but the problem is that the success of it is already creating a copycat in other regions of this country."

The Teachings that Inform Their Work

All the faith workers were quick to use scripture and biblical passages to support their interpretations, explanations of the work they do, and the reason why they see it as their obligation to help immigrants in need and to advocate for humane border policies. For Sister Elizabeth, the main grounding for the work she does is the Bible itself. In her words:

> Well, for one thing, I'm Christian, I'm Catholic, I'm a religious, and I'm a Franciscan, and Franciscans tend to work with the poorest of people and tend to help those who others are somewhat afraid to help, or go into situations that are somewhat risk-taking. Another point is the fact that the Bible is one of my favorite books and have studied it and there are many passages in the Bible that tend toward this way of life. So I've chosen it as my way of life, I mean I follow that as a Christian, as a follower of Christ. I have vows for life to do that. Give a cup of water in my name, as Jesus said, and that's what we have decided to use as our motto [for Humane Borders] because the majority of the deaths in the desert are by dehydration, and what other remedy for dehydration than water? So we give a cup of water in the name of Christ.

Several faith workers said that they see their work as being directly informed by liberation theology. Gill, the academic coordinator of BorderLinks, for instance, noted that the objective of the educational trips is that experiences of life at the border and in Mexico will lead to reflection, "and reflection will lead to action. It is based on the process focused in the motto 'praxis as reflective action: see, reflect, act,' derived from Paulo Freire" (Gill 2004, 32). He explains that two sources for the educational philosophy that drives BorderLinks are "Liberation theologian Gustavo Gutiérrez, who urged those who wish to learn about life and serve those in need to stay close to the lives and struggles of the poor . . . and the actual reflection opportunities in BorderLinks seminars are borrowed in large part from the ideas of Paulo Freire's *Pedagogy of the Oppressed*" (Gill 2003, 99).

Others were very well aware of the multiple philosophies that guide their common work. Gill noted, "We are what we call faith. We interpret that very softly; we have no requirements or doctrinal beliefs or anything like that. What we believe in is justice, social justice, as it applies specifically to the border and to immigration and all of that. We are not political, even though it is pretty obvious that we have a point of view." Similarly, Luzdy Stucky, a Mennonite and codirector of BorderLinks, mentioned the importance of nonviolence teachings in her own life and work. "Growing up in Colombia there was a lot of political violence and I became very aware of teachings that are mostly based on the theology of peace and nonviolence, following the message of nonviolence that Jesus taught us." And Robin Hoover explained that even though most of the people who are inspired to do the work they do on behalf of the immigrants draw from social justice teachings, not everyone uses the same reference points or approach to guide their work. He explained,

> If you ask, as I have done, in formal research some Unitarian over here,
> why are you over here sticking water in front of these migrants, sticking

up for them? They'll cite human rights, civil rights, decency, some sort of issue of the world neighborhoodness or something like hospitality. If you stick the microphone in front of Lutherans, Quakers, Seventh-Day Adventists, well they'll say God told me to do this, you know. So you can have people operating from entirely different ethical reference systems, be they religious philosophical, ideological, whatever, but who engage in exactly the same behavior of doing the same thing for different reasons.

He mentioned that even though there may be conflicts among the different groups over strategy or interpretation, ultimately they end up doing the same thing because, above all, they are Christians first. He recalled the case of a Cuban man who had been in prison in his country for nearly a decade and hated everything that had to do with Communism. "So when he found that he needed to be serving Nicaraguans who were Communists coming to the United States in the eighties early nineties, he was, you know, just, he had to do a whole lot of soul searching because he did not want to help these people until he finally realized that he was a Christian first. They were Communists, but he had an understanding as a Christian first and as an American second." Similarly, Gill observed:

We are all Christian, although occasionally we get a Jewish person or a Buddhist. We have a lot of people who aren't anything, but most of the support comes from Catholics and Presbyterians. And one of the original Sanctuary guys was a Quaker, and Quaker churches have been involved, but lots of others, Lutheran, Methodist too. So we tend to be kind of quasi . . . in fact, our founder and director, Rick Chase, who may have taken you in your trip, he often did those ASU trips on the big bus. He was elected moderator in the Presbyterian church. . . . So we have Presbyterian ties. Most of my life I've been Presbyterian. In a couple of places I have worshiped in the Catholic community because there were no Presbyterian churches in the area. . . . That's not as important to me as the Christian faith is. This, to me, is very, very important. Catholics have a tradition as social workers for a long time, Quakers as peace church, and a lot of people like that, but the Sanctuary movement triggered a whole bunch of stuff in this country and other denominations too. So I see it as absolutely essential. You help the poor, you help the needy, you help the marginalized, that's what the gospel is about . . . regardless of your specific denomination.

They felt strongly about the link between their work on behalf of the immigrants and scripture. In our conversations I pointed out that there are people who criticize them for "interpreting scripture wrongly." Jerry Gill commented, "What is there to interpret? It's right there in the Bible. . . . The Lord said, free the poor, let the captive go, and he goes through this whole social justice thing.

Never once He says, believe in me as your personal savior, you know, any of that stuff. That's the gospel, his gospel is social justice. How can you interpret that? It's clear, it's right there, it's pretty amazing."

They also compared Christ and immigrants in various ways; they often mentioned that migrants personify Christ, using specific passages from the New Testament to interpret the lives of contemporary migrants. For instance, Jerry Gill states in his book *Border Theology*:

> In unguarded terms I am arguing that in several senses Jesus is portrayed in the Gospel accounts as having been an "undocumented alien" during his sojourn here on earth. Not only did he cross many borders through-out his ministry, such as those between Judea and Samaria, Galilee and Jerusalem, and Israel and various Canaanite communities, but he was always something of an "outsider" in relation to his own relatives, neigh-bors, and even his own disciples. . . . God came among us as an "undocu-mented alien," taking up the causes of those who are oppressed. Can we do any less? (Gill 2003, 5–6)

Along these lines, some mentioned that as children of God, or as personifying Jesus himself, migrants had a fundamental right to migrate in search for a bet-ter life, and the reasons why they migrate are not purely individual but are linked to broader structural forces. In Rick Ufford-Chase's view, "The most suc-cessful way to resolve our border and immigration crisis is to create economic opportunities that will allow people to stay in their countries of origin. But that will never be accomplished with a trade policy that regards smaller nations as nothing more than a cheap labor supply. It is not morally defensible to create a global economy without accepting the responsibility of building a global com-munity" (Ufford-Chase 2004).

Discussion/Conclusion

The faith workers' responses to border violence that I examine here are clearly based on socially engaged readings of scripture and Bible passages. Their actions are based on social justice principles, such as dignity of the person, according to which all human beings are sacred and made in the image and like-ness of God; rights and responsibilities of individuals, which calls for individuals' fundamental right to life, food, shelter, health care, education, and employment; promotion of peace and disarmament, according to which peace is not only the absence of war, but also involves mutual respect and collaboration between peoples and nations; and the right people have to productive work and fair wages, safe working conditions, and to participate in decisions that affect them in the workplace. At the root of the workers' actions is one of the fundamental principles of social justice teachings of the Christian faith—that is, the duty to side with the poor and to create a just society, and the obligation of the more fortunate to put their own resources and abilities to the service of others. Accordingly, the poor and marginalized have the most urgent moral claim on the conscience of the nation. Based on these principles, Christ's teachings are not to be restricted to spirituality alone but also include adopting a political stance to guide one's work. Consequently, faith workers in this study believe that they are called to question public policy decisions that affect the poor, and to articulate that the deprivation and powerlessness of the poor wounds the whole community.

Basing their actions on these basic principles, they oppose border militarization policies as well as immigration laws that brutalize the lives of immigrants. Importantly, however, these workers do not interpret the context in which they work or even their responses and approaches in the same fashion. Also, although they draw from social teachings of the Christian faith, they focus on different aspects and interpret them in slightly different ways. This point is important, as not all those who work in interfaith organizations on the left (or on the right, for that matter) interpret teachings and biblical readings in exactly the same manner. These workers' experiences, interpretations, and life work are grounded in multiple identities and positions, and thus their interpretations will not be homogeneous. In the end they do similar work, engage in similar ways of organizing, oppose violent structures, and dedicate their lives to pursuing justice and creating a just society. And through these actions they live their faith.

NOTES

1. I use the term "faith workers" to refer to the volunteers and staff who work in the organizations I examine here. Initially, I had referred to members of these organizations as "religious workers," but in subsequent conversations with them they explained that "faith workers" was a more appropriate term. As a Catholic nun explained, "When we say faith people working in this we mean people who are trying to live the faith they profess, the faith system they have." And Jerry Gil, from Border-Links, commented about the term "faith," "Yeah, that's the term we used, but then George Bush started throwing that term around and people suggested that we should change. Well, really, I couldn't come up with anything . . . And I write my stuff mostly from a theological point of view . . . so how about religious social activist?" I opted for faith workers, but with the caveat that this term did not come up without lengthy discussion. Also, I would like to acknowledge the research assistance of Joshua Whistler.

2. This law requires proof of eligibility to receive social services such as retirement, welfare, health, disability, public or assisted housing, postsecondary education, food assistance, unemployment, or similar benefits that are provided with appropriated funds of state or local governments. (It was already against the law to receive these benefits without proof of eligibility.) This law also requires state and local workers to report immigration violations to federal authorities in writing. Failure to do so or to

not withhold benefits from individuals who fail to provide proof of eligibility will result in a misdemeanor charge. In addition, this law requires voters to document their U.S. citizenship when registering to vote and when voting; however, there had not been any evidence of voter fraud. A troubling consequence of this victory scored by anti-immigrant groups has emboldened similar groups around the nation. The FAIR-backed group in Arizona has launched a "Protect America Now" campaign to help proponents of similar measures around the country to organize.

3. See Dunn (1996) for a detailed account of border militarization, such as tactics, technology, and training.

4. In another paper, we describe the operations of these groups in detail (Kil and Menjívar, forthcoming).

5. At the time I conducted this research these individuals held these positions in those organizations; however, they are not permanent appointments and are likely to change.

6. Some of the founders of the Sanctuary movement are also involved in efforts to assist immigrants. However, as a volunteer of Humane Borders observed, "Some of them [founders of the Sanctuary movement] are getting older and can't do the work anymore, but they certainly are an inspiration for others to continue."

7. BorderLinks has always resisted engaging in charity work for people in Mexico, but the fortuitous acquisition of Casa de la Misericordia has led them to rethink this posture, and now they provide direct assistance through this house.

8. The nun went on, "And then I added one phrase to my part of it, which I know not all of them did, but I did. I will not transport an immigrant when I'm working directly with Humane Borders, I said, when I'm staff or when I'm on a water trip, but in my own car that is personal, then it's not part of work. Of course the Border Patrol was not happy with that."

9. At Humane Borders they even communicate with some of the vigilantes. After a television appearance by a prominent vigilante organizer in which he pointed to an area of the desert with trash left behind by crossers, the administrative coordinator wrote to him indicating that Humane Borders could clean the site. I read this email communication.

10. The Tohono O'Odham nation initially opposed the water stations on reservation land because they were concerned about the effects of migration not only on the land but also on the increased presence of the federal government in their lands. However, a prominent member of the nation, Mike Wilson, has been an active volunteer with Humane Borders.

9

Religious Reenactment on the Line

A Genealogy of Political Religious Hybridity

PIERRETTE HONDAGNEU-SOTELO, GENELLE GAUDINEZ,
AND HECTOR LARA

Faith-based activists have adopted and embraced a liturgical calendar based on Catholic and Mexican traditions in order to underscore the connection between faith and commitment to social justice along the U.S.-Mexico border. The Posada Sin Fronteras, the Via Crucis del Migrante Jesus, and Dia de los Muertos are now celebrated at multiple points along the U.S.-Mexico border by ecumenical faith-based, binational groups, and in some spots in the interior (a Posada Sin Fronteras, for example, was held in Washington, D.C.). These collective reenactments, usually conducted in situ, in strategic sites along the border fence, constitute part of an expressive culture. This culture is used to denounce government immigration and border policies that have prompted thousands of migrant deaths, to commemorate the migrants, and to renew activists' commitments to faith-based social justice work. As we see it, these events suggest the emergence of a Christian, particularly Catholic-Latino influenced culture of social activism responding to border issues.

The Posada Sin Fronteras, celebrated now for over ten years at the Tijuana–San Ysidro border, appears to be the grandmother of these hybrid events. Organizers commemorate the plight of contemporary Mexican and Central American migrants by using the biblical story of Mary and Joseph being turned away from the inns of Bethlehem. On the third Saturday of December, a few hundred people gather on both sides of the fence to sing songs, read aloud the names of those who died while crossing the border, and reenact through testimonials, symbols, and gestures the seeking of hospitality and sharing across borders. Organizers say the event allows people to see immigration and border issues through a religious lens, and that it offers people hope and faith that the border divisions and policies will change. Here's how some describe it:

> Jesus didn't find Posada. . . . that's why he was born in the stable. . . . So for
> me, I don't think there is any place in the world where the message is more

striking (than the border) because that is the place, you know, you see just the opposite of that hospitality. There is a wall that divides two nations. This is where the message is very strong. (Brother Gioacchino Campese)

It puts flesh and blood on our beliefs, it gives meaning to us to be creatures of God, creatures of the Divine community and in relation to each other, and there's tension. . . . There is a drama associated when you go to the border, and you are at the fence, and people can't cross the fence, and you can't cross the fence, and yet you are standing together. (Pastor Art Cribbs)

It's such an obvious metaphor for the whole immigration issue in terms of Joseph and Mary going from place to place seeking shelter and being turned away and the great rejoicing when the innkeeper says, "Well, I've got a stable and you can stay." . . . To hold that vision in our minds in the midst of all this xenophobia is very important, and what's so neat is that we celebrate with the people of Tijuana at the border fence. (Rosemary Johnston)

It's moved from, you know, "No room for Jesus and Mary," to a real shift in looking at policy and looking at, really, just the plight of immigrants. (Former Franciscan Brother Tom Thing)

The Posada Sin Fronteras, in its twelfth year now, is a creative, flexible event. Different gestures and symbols are used to represent hospitality: one year wristbands with the names of the dead were distributed through the small holes in the fence. Candy is regularly thrown over the fence, in both directions, to signal the sharing of sweets and hospitality, and in the 2004 Posada, people from the United States side threw across to Mexico colorful fleece scarves to symbolize the offering of warmth. In an era when crossing the border is criminalized, the biblical frame of Joseph, Mary, and Jesus seeking shelter gives legitimacy to the very act of migration.

In this essay, we draw on in-depth interviews with key organizers of the Posada Sin Fronteras in order to write a genealogy of the event. Who are the people who make the Posada Sin Fronteras happen, and what are the main strands of influence on their lives, and hence on the Posada Sin Fronteras? By addressing these questions, we seek to provide an agent-centered model that is attentive to the realm of culture and belief, following the social movement research pioneered by James Jasper, Verta Taylor, and others. Doing so allows us to highlight the important and complex role of religion in addressing contemporary immigration policies and their outcomes.

We also rely on in-depth interviews to offer a macroregional perspective on the Posada Sin Fronteras. Our main argument is this: the form and content of the Posada Sin Fronteras suggests the emergence of a borderlands faith-based culture of social activism that is richly informed by Latin American, Chicano, and

Mexican traditions. Latino immigration to the United States has many cultural and political reverberations. Social movements of the late twentieth century—and, importantly, the ideas and cultural forms associated with these movements—have shaped the Posada Sin Fronteras. The influences include Latin American Liberation Theology, with its preference for the poor; the Catholic left of the 1960s, which brought Catholic symbols and rituals to the streets for antiwar efforts; the United Farm Workers (UFW) movement, where Cesar Chavez's organizing projects for migrant workers incorporated religious leaders of various faiths, as well as pilgrimages, fasts, rituals, and symbols with decidedly Mexican-Catholic origins; and the solidarity movement's faith-based commitment to the liberation struggles and witnessing in Central America. All of these movements find contemporary resonance in the United States, we argue, because of the recent history of Mexican and Central American migration.

In the process, we find that Anglo American Protestants and Catholics are embracing, adopting, and promulgating forms of Latin American popular religiosity and notions of faith-based social activism rooted in Latino culture. These instances provide a stunning contrast to the predictions of assimilation theory and secularization theory, paradigms that anchored sociological thinking in the twentieth century. The ineffectualness of these paradigms to predict social life in the late twentieth and early twentieth centuries are well known. What is surprising here is the extent to which processes completely *counter* to orthodox assimilation and secularization characterize the activist movements for social justice at the border. These processes, we argue, are rooted in the long and complex history of Mexican and Central American immigration to the United States.

We can think of this emergent culture as forming counterhegemony to NAFTA and neoliberal forces of globalization that open doors to trade and capital, but selectively close the front door to migration from the South while keeping the back door ajar. This culture is U.S.-based, but it is also binational, bicultural, and ecumenical. It reflects the history of United States involvement in Latin America throughout the twentieth century, and the subsequent legacies of U.S.-bound migration organized around labor needs. This culture also reflects, importantly, the faith-informed social movements and mobilization efforts that have sought to bring about structural change to ameliorate human suffering caused by those socially disruptive transnational flows of capital and labor. The context in which this develops is largely the U.S.-side of the border, where religion is less hegemonic than in Mexico and hence more adaptive.

In this chapter, we examine the influence of these various movements as these are mediated through individual biographies. Religious people who were inspired by movements from other times and places, either vicariously or through hands-on involvement, bring together these traditions to create and sustain the Posada Sin Fronteras. As we will see, the influences include some of the major social movements that took place in the Americas during the late twentieth century.

Religion and Culture in Movement

The secularization thesis, the idea that society would become increasingly secular with modernization, has had nails in its U.S. coffin for at least a decade. Its replacement, the New Paradigm, emphasizes the significance of religion in modern society and it has been fueled by scholarship examining immigrant social life (Warner 1993). Religion, we now recognize, is critical and foundational in the lives of most immigrants, as studies have documented the role of religious institutions in fomenting ethnic identities, in establishing transnational ties, and in providing social services, resettlement assistance, and coping support for immigrants and refugees (Ebaugh 2003; Ebaugh and Chaftez 2000, 2002; Levitt 2002; Warner and Wittner 1998). How immigrants mesh religion and social activism has received less attention.

Yet we know that religion has long played an important role in American civil society and in mobilizing collective groups to pursue social change (Demerath 2003; Smith 1996; Williams 2002; Wood 2002). In fact, myriad social and political movements in the United States draw from the well of religion, specifically Christian religion. The Bible, it turns out, is a very flexible text, as Abolitionists and Klansmen, antiwar protestors, and "family values" conservatives have all laid moral claim to their causes by basing their movements in Christian religious teachings (Williams 2002). Additionally, we have a growing scholarship that examines the role of religion in various social justice movements (Nepstad 2004; Shupe and Misztal 1998; Warren 2001; Wood 2002). Meanwhile, a growing social movement's literature encourages a cultural turn, emphasizing the realm of belief, ritual, creativity, and emotion in formulating protest (Jasper 1997). In fact, all protest can be seen as moral protest (Taylor and Rupp 1993; Jasper 1997).

What's been relatively ignored in the studies of migrants and religion, however, are the legacies of faith-based movements for social justice that immigrants from Latin America bring with them, and the faith-based movements for immigrant social justice that these migrants and their advocates devise together in the United States. As we see it, faith-based activists are on the frontlines of a fledgling immigrant rights movement today. Coming from strong Catholic and Latin American traditions, rituals have become central to many of these organizing efforts. Rituals, James Jasper reminds us, are critical to social movements: "Collective rites remind participants of their basic moral commitments, stir up strong emotions, and reinforce a sense of solidarity with the group, a 'we-ness.' *Rituals are symbolic embodiments, at salient times and places, of the beliefs of a group. . . . .* affirmation of basic beliefs seems to connect participants with deep truths about the world, and hence with the past and the future" (Jasper 1997).

In *Convictions of the Soul*, Nepstad (2004) shows that participants in the Central American solidarity movement relied on religion to provide "cultural resources of Christianity," such as rituals, symbols, songs, biblical teachings, and narratives, to advance activist causes. We see something similar happening here, but we underscore how these changes derive from Latino immigration and the emergence of a new regional culture. Here, in the borderlands of San Diego and Los Angeles, we find that it is not just Christianity, but more specifically Latin American popular religiosity and traditions of social justice religion, that helps advance immigrant civil and human rights.

In an earlier article on the Posada Sin Fronteras, we examined the different constituencies who gather at the event, and the multiple meanings they bring to and take from it (Hondagneu-Sotelo et al. 2004). This work is intended to complement that earlier effort with a focus on the organizers and purveyors of this particular manifestation of "disruptive religion" (Smith 1996). Here we trace the factors that have shaped their innovative response to the crisis of immigration policies at the U.S.-Mexico border.

Description of Research and Interview Subjects

We conducted twenty audiotaped, open-ended structured interviews with the founders and key organizers and participants of the Posada Sin Fronteras; two of the tapes were lost, so we draw on eighteen fully transcribed interviews. The interviews were conducted in San Diego, Tijuana, Los Angeles, San Francisco, and Chicago, and lasted, on average, about ninety minutes and most of the transcripts are about twenty to thirty pages long. We asked interviewees about the details of putting together the Posada Sin Fronteras, how the event had changed over time, and we asked about their views concerning the significance, concrete outcomes, and religious and political meanings of the event. We also conducted minioral histories about the role of religion in their lives. Additionally, ethnographic observations inform this study. In groups of two to four, we have attended the Posada Sin Fronteras for four years in a row, from 2001 to 2004. At these events, we participated in the activities, but we also wrote field notes and took photos and video. During the 2002 event, we conducted mini-interviews with forty-four participants and wrote an article based on those responses (Hondagneu-Sotelo et al. 2004).

All of the people interviewed for this chapter are currently, or have been in the past, intimately involved with the Posada Sin Fronteras. These include the individuals who actually make arrangements for the event—by getting permission from California state park authorities to hold it at Borderfield State Park, by devising ideas for the themes and bringing the materials on the day of the event, setting up, contacting youth groups or singers to perform, recruiting attendees, and so on. Interviewees also include the key participants, the people who have a visible presence at the annual Posada Sin Fronteras because they read the scripture, emcee the event, or play guitars and lead the songs.

Together, they constitute a remarkable group of individuals. All of them express strong moral commitments to social justice—they express this in their talk and in their daily practice. In this regard, they act from strategic structural positions, as they held or currently hold jobs largely defined by religion and social justice work. They share biographies rich in social activism, and many of them maintain multiple commitments.

Most of these people are nonclerical religious professionals who hold midlevel administrative jobs devoted to faith-based social action. They are educated and they mostly work in offices, where access to phones, Internet connections, and fax technology facilitates their organizing and networking. They seem to know a lot of people. As Christian religious professionals, they enjoy legitimacy and respect in society—but they are also on the fringes of mainstream religion. As lay leaders and members of religious orders or faith-based groups, they have almost all received some formal training in theology, or they are currently involved in ongoing theological education; some of them spoke of their daily practice as "living theology." All of them have received some higher education, and more than a few have graduate education, such as a master's in divinity, and one was studying for his doctorate in theology. At least two of them have written books.

Many of them maintain commitments to multiple social causes, and the plaques of community service adorning the walls in the homes and offices where we interviewed them were testament to this. The combination of structural position in faith-oriented nonprofits, and their theological grounding enables these activists to organize people and events, and to access the narrative tools that go into creating the Posada Sin Fronteras. All of the interviewees hold—or held, before retirement—jobs that were explicitly defined by the connection between religion and social justice. They mostly work in the NGO (nongovernmental organizations) and nonprofit sector for organizations that are generally ecumenical or interfaith in name and design, or explicitly affiliated with a religious order. Most of these individuals are Catholic, although they do not necessarily work at Catholic organizations.

Only two of the organizers we interviewed were clergy leading a flock of congregates. These two men were both Protestant clergy with remarkable résumés of activism garnered in Latin America (Bill Radatz) and the Philippines (Art Cribbs), and they continued to spread their considerable talents and efforts to multiple social action projects in San Diego. For example, Pastor Art Cribbs, who heads up a United Church of Christ congregation in San Diego, cofounded the Council of Concerned African American Clergy and Laity in San Diego and the Interdenominational Ministry Alliance of San Diego County, and he was also active in AIDS-health awareness. Pastor Bill Radatz came to San Diego to head up a Lutheran congregation after doing mission work in Cuzco, Peru, during the time of Sendero Luminoso. In San Diego he volunteered with American Friends Service Committee, cofounded an organization called Survivors of Human Torture, which offers refugees legal assistance and counseling services in seeking asylum, and he had participated with the now-defunct AFSC-sponsored Border Peace Patrol for migrants in transit in the pre-Gatekeeper era. We are not sure why Catholic priests who lead congregations are absent from the organizers; providing sacraments in large parishes may leave them little time for extracurricular activities, or perhaps the hierarchical structure of the Catholic church precludes their involvement. The only Catholic priest who had regularly participated as an organizer is Padre Luiz Kendzierski, a Brazilian Scalabrini Order priest who serves as the director of the Tijuana-based migrant shelter, Casa del Migrante. While most of the interviewees regularly interacted with church congregations, only two were leaders of congregations. Unlike the black preachers in the civil rights movement, who would preach and perhaps command the congregation's involvement, the Posada organizers are not in the same position.

The Posada Sin Fronteras has become a fluid, annual institution. Many of the people who initiated it and who worked on it during the early years (the mid-1990s) have since moved away or are retired. We interviewed a few of these people in retirement and two of them as faraway as Chicago. The Posada organizing work is carried on by a new cohort of participants and organizers, and they don't necessarily know one another on a face-to-face basis. In this way, the Posada Sin Fronteras is like a tapestry with many threads, old and new, woven into it. Each person who works on it may only have a glimpse or dim memory of who worked on it previous to them and what symbols they used, or who has taken over the responsibilities. Yet they all leave an indelible imprint on the event.

A Regional Culture of Faith-based Social Activism

The Posada Sin Fronteras is a truly popular, collective event of the people; in fact, no one we interviewed rushed to take credit for its origins. It was created and continues to be organized by a diverse committee of people. Two individuals, however, were instrumental in formulating the first Posada Sin Fronteras, and we tell their story in some detail in order to show how their biographies of activism, achieved in different places and with different organizations, came to influence the Posada Sin Fronteras. They are Noreen Sullivan, a former nun who left the Dominican sisters after a four-year stint of working with UFW during the 1970s, and Roberto Martinez, a Chicano activist influenced by the Chicano Movement, Liberation Theology, and the American Friends Service Committee. A Lutheran pastor, Bill Radatz, also involved in the initial effort, told us that there was already by then a social justice Posada held in downtown San Diego. And Ched Myers, who worked with the AFSC in the early 1990s and also helped come up with the idea, told us that the Posada at Dolores Mission in Los Angeles "had proven to be a real galvanizing force for community organizing." So the Posada Sin Fronteras evolved as mimetic process, even if this was not necessarily conscious or deliberate on the part of the organizers.

Roberto Martinez, referred to as the "grandfather of immigrant rights" by one of our respondents, has left a lasting legacy in social activism and human rights work along the U.S.-Mexico border. He became an activist at an early age, he said, because of his own personal experience with police brutality and racism. As a teenager in San Diego, he suffered both police and Border Patrol harassment during Operation Wetback in the 1950s—even though he was fifth-generation U.S.-born and spoke no Spanish. "It's always been that way for us," he recalled. "It's always been an issue for Mexicans to be harassed by the police, sheriffs, border patrol, Texas Rangers." While organizing against police brutality is a longstanding concern in Chicano communities, Roberto Martinez, from his vantage-point on the border, and propelled by key transformations in Catholicism, expanded that organizing impulse to include migrants in transit. His personal experience with unfair arrests led him to start the U.S.-Mexico Border Program of the AFSC.

> We were always being harassed by police, followed around, couldn't go anywhere, you know, so that's what (it was like) for us in the 1950s, 1960s, 1970s. The whole immigration thing began to surface, and then by the early 1980s, we had massive groups of migrants, immigrants crossing from Mexico, Central America—because in Central America the civil wars, so police began getting involved in that. . . . I evolved from a Chicano activist, to an immigrant rights activist, to a human rights activist at the border.

How exactly did this transformation unfold? Certainly a good deal has to do with individual resolve, but this process was guided along by opportunities and positions in particular organizations. In the early 1970s, Vatican II created the space for new lay leadership positions in the Catholic church, and Roberto Martinez came forward to organize around issues of concern to the Mexican American community. He was then recruited by Bishop Chavez, a Chicano bishop, to work for the Catholic diocese, which then included San Diego and San Bernardino counties, and it was in this capacity that Martinez was exposed to the teachings of Liberation Theology, an activist religious movement rooted in the Latin American struggle for the poor. "The first thing Bishop Chavez did was send me to study at the Mexican American Cultural Center in San Antonio, Texas," he recalled, "and most of our teaching was by South American liberation theology teachers, like Gustavo Gutierrez." They urged attendees to make a lifetime commitment, to "Ver, Analizar, y Actuar" (See, Analyze, and Act) for the poor. Roberto Martinez took this message to heart. When another bishop in San Diego later told him his work had become too focused on fighting for justice, Martinez left the diocese, and after a brief stint with the Chicano Federation, where he began addressing violence at the border, he started what would become a long career with the American Friends Service Committee, the Quakers.

At that time, AFSC had a small U.S.-Mexico Border Program that provided services to migrant agricultural workers, but Martinez added a focus on protecting migrant human and civil rights and monitoring violence at the border. During the 1980s, as both illegal migration from Mexico and Central America and public sentiment against it increased, the San Diego-Tijuana border became an increasingly dangerous and violent place, with attacks on migrants from government authorities and roaming gangs of thieves. Roberto Martinez was determined to do something about it. As a Catholic going to work for a Quaker organization, he experienced a confluence, rather than conflict, of religious and political beliefs. No one tried to convert him, and AFSC granted him autonomy to do the work he saw necessary as long as he abided by the Quaker beliefs of nonviolence and simplicity. In fact, some of the Catholic institutional structure and beliefs that had weighed down his previous work with the diocese were now gone. He reported that he found a more hospitable environment with the Quakers than he had with the Catholic diocese, one that allowed him to do the kind of work he wanted to do. "Quakers are not a structured religion, they don't have a hierarchy like Catholics do. But you don't miss that," he said. "Quakers support Liberation Theology, so for me it was a perfect."

As Roberto Martinez molded the AFSC program to include a focus on border violence, he continued his longstanding interest in monitoring and stopping police and Border Patrol brutality by joining former nun Noreen Sullivan in forming a small group of religious-based volunteers of different denominations, a group he referred to as a type of "witness abuse group" at the border. The group, he said, tried "to show the Border Patrol that there was another way, rather than violence." The Border Peace Patrol was congruent with the Quaker philosophy of nonviolence, but conversant with the methods then being developed by the Central American solidarity movement. In the Witness for Peace projects of the 1980s, American lay and religious leaders traveled to Central American civil war zones to observe close-up conflicts and thereby attempt to deter gross violations of human rights. Similarly, the Border Peace Patrol group walked along the border, wearing armbands to identify themselves, in an effort to preserve peace and nonviolence. Among the volunteers in this group were Noreen Sullivan and Lutheran Pastor Bill Radatz. According to Roberto Martinez, "the group wanted to do something religious down there," and Noreen Sullivan "came up with the idea that we would have a Posada there at the border, and it began developing from there. We formed a committee, and got funding from the Quakers."

Vatican II had also opened up new spaces and new opportunities for Noreen Sullivan. The third sister of nine siblings to join the Dominican nuns, she described, without a trace of bitterness, life as a nun in the 1950s as being akin to living in medieval days—cloistered, restricted, and under deeply hierarchical rule. With Vatican II, nuns gained more options, and Noreen Sullivan found that she no longer had to obey the little white cards that gave directives on what one would do the following year. With approval from the Dominican authorities, she chose to teach drama to children, she wrote a book, and in 1974 she decided to come to California, intending to work with the UFW for one summer. Those intentions gave way to a four-year stint with the UFW, where she joined other religious volunteers in the revolutionary effort to improve living and working conditions for Mexican farm workers in California. "It was life changing for me," she recollected of her time with the UFW. "Every single day, we were making history, just by virtue of our existence."

The UFW's use of fasting during strikes and the public marches with religious symbols such as crosses and religious banners are well known. Religion permeated the UFW. Vigils and Catholic masses were held in the fields, Cesar Chavez's office featured religious pictures and statues, and the Virgen de Guadalupe was "present at nearly every single meeting, procession, or march" held by the UFW (Hammerback and Jensen 1998). The UFW theme song, "De Colores," was taken from the Catholic *cursillo* movement, and the first UFW march during the spring of 1966 broke new ground in U.S. civil rights struggles by incorporating Mexican Catholic traditions. In a short document called *"Peregrinacion, Penitencia, Revolucion,"* Cesar Chavez laid out a plan for the march that included, as commentator Alan Watt (1999) put it, "a Mexican religious pilgrimage, a Lenten penitential procession, and an act of defiance, all in one." That event alone seems to presage the Posada Sin Fronteras.

For Noreen Sullivan, the UFW pulsated with religious faith and reverence: "When the religious came into the union," she said, "we were accorded an immediate respect." Yet she felt ambivalently as the recipient of this respect. She wanted to be treated like any other person, but in the UFW, highly educated nuns, quite reasonably, were put to work doing specialized tasks, and she circulated among jobs that included writing pamphlets, directing a medical clinic, and providing paralegal assistance, first in Delano and later the Coachella Valley. In exchange, she received room and board and a stipend of five dollars a week. A major turning point in her life, one that still brought tears to her eyes almost thirty years later as she recounted it, was being arrested in the fields during a UFW strike—cloaked in nun habits that she put on for the occasion. Eventually, she left both the Dominicans and the UFW in 1978 and made her way to San Diego.

Noreen Sullivan and Roberto Martinez came from very different social points of origin, but by the 1970s both of them were deeply informed by Catholic social teaching, the Chicano Movement, and the UFW, and they were dedicating their respective lives to working for social justice. Yet both of them found that institutional Catholicism did not allow them to do the work they wanted to do or to be the people they wanted to be. Neither one of them rejected Catholicism or walked away from the church, but Martinez left employment with the diocese and Sullivan left the Dominican Order of nuns. They continued carrying out Catholic social justice teachings outside of Catholic institutions, yet they innovated the Posada Sin Fronteras by relying on popular Catholic religiosity to express a collective commitment to stopping violence against migrants at the border.

Together with Lutheran Pastor Bill Radatz, Catholic social activist Ched Myers from the AFSC office in Pasadena, and later a coterie of religious activists from both sides of the border, they creatively designed a celebratory event that focused initially not on deaths at the border but on providing the positive imagery of hospitality to migrants, one based on biblical text. Although Quakers and Catholics lie at opposite ends of the spectrum when it comes to liturgy, both religious traditions share deep commitments to social justice.

Another person who played an important role in the early years of the Posada Sin Fronteras was Ched Myers, who then worked at the regional AFSC offices in Pasadena. Raised in an affluent, white community in a nominally Christian family, he told us that he was "mentored out of the Catholic Left," and that as a young person he had been deeply moved and influenced by events in the 1960s and 1970s. He recalled particular events, such as when "Daniel and Philip Barrigan poured their own blood on the [draft] files and then took them out and burned them with homemade napalm. That sort of symbolic public action was really sort of a new thing. You know the civil rights movement had had marches and pray-ins, but *this kind of sort of high level symbolism was really clearly coming out of the Catholic symbolic stock.*" As a consequence, by the 1990s, he said, "there were literally dozens and dozens of places around the U.S. and beyond where there would be [for] Holy Week, Stations of the Cross that would be going to a weapons installation, or going to a jail, or going to a State Department office to, you know, protest something." As he put it, these events "really grew organically from the faith-based social activist community," but in the southern California landscape, these were then nurtured and propelled by Latino immigration and the faith-based social movements and traditions that accompanied it. He singled out the Sanctuary movement as bringing in "more elements of Latin American theology and liturgy" to Los Angeles, where "there were many public actions with the sanctuary movement and the Central American solidarity movement that oftentimes were pegged to a liturgical holiday of some kind." He said, "All kinds of sort of organic social movements [were] growing and then they start touching each other and then they start cross-fertilizing. . . . . You had a whole bunch of people who were becoming more and more comfortable with this notion of liturgy as public action."

For the second Posada Sin Fronteras, organizers in San Diego were joined by likeminded people from Tijuana. These included members of the Scalabrini Order working at the Casa del Migrante migrant shelter and others from human rights and faith-based nongovernmental agencies. Maria Lourdes Arias Trujillo, a Scalabrinian laity, worked closely in the hands-on organizing of the Posada Sin Fronteras from 1995 TO 2000. She came to the border from the interior of Mexico to live her faith by serving migrants as a Scalabrinian layperson. She brought tremendous creativity to the event, introducing symbolic elements of spirituality and liturgy that she was using in her Scalabrini mission work. In the 1995 Posada, doves were released from the Mexican side of the border fence and sent to fly over the border fence. Another year, to dramatize the deaths of migrants due to Operation Gatekeeper, white balloons floated over the fence, one by one, as names of the dead were read. As Maria Lourdes recalled her participation during these years, she remembered the power of images and the sharing with *gringos* on the other side:

> *Entonces cuando ibamos nombrando. . . .* So when we would call out each name of the migrants who had died that year, we'd let loose one white balloon. That's one of the deepest images I hold. To see that white balloon go up towards the border, and [*speaking slowly, for emphasis*] to cross *la frontera.* These were very strong, significant gestures and symbols. . . . And with a wall dividing us . . . and with immigration policies causing these deaths of so many of our brothers and sisters, and yet to see that people from that side who were deeply hurt by what was happening, who were in solidarity with us, and who weren't necessarily Mexican but rather gringos and American. . . . We'd say, what do we believe? That one day, this wall will disappear.

Lourdes Arias reported that she had never been involved in explicitly political actions, such as marches or demonstrations, but she stated that her work as member of the laity in the Scalabrinian mission of helping migrants shaped her own contributions to the Posada Sin Fronteras:

> *Durante estos años . . . .* During those years, I was in a mission community. We were opening shelters (for migrants), many of them, in Tijuana, Cuidad Juarez, in Central America, and doing many liturgical activities. I think that experience, of working with liturgical celebrations, in the middle of migrants, and surrounded by refugees in the refugee camps, that's what gave me the capacity to see how liturgy, that aspect of faith, religion could be used.

Although the Scalabrini Order began with the charitable outreach to Italian American immigrants by an Italian priest, as it extended to Brazil, Mexico, the Philippines, and other parts of the world, the Order added adherents in the late twentieth century of Liberation Theology. Guided by the influence of Brazilian Liberation Theology, the mission work of the Scalabrinis along the U.S.-Mexico border extended to include more social change work. Scalabrinian Brother Gioacchino Campese, who worked at the Tijuana shelter for seven years, said that he believes "service and protest are two dimensions of the same mission." While committed to offering material and spiritual service, he also said, "Then there is another dimension, which is the more you know, I would say the public dimension, the social dimension of the work of Casa del Migrante—which starts with events like Posada Sin Fronteras, Via Cruces del Migrante Jesus."

Gioacchino Campese, originally from Italy, came to Tijuana in 1995, after spending several years studying in the Philippines, and he attended his first Posada Sin Fronteras that year. "I didn't even speak Spanish!" he laughed, as he recalled his first time. "I didn't even know about the whole tradition of the Posada, so it was new. The border was new to me. I didn't even know there was this wall dividing Mexico and the U.S.A. But in the following years, I have been deepening my knowledge, my view of what is the Posada. What is the Posada? And how do we apply it to border issues?" Gioacchino Campese was a quick study, and from the Mexican side of the border he worked to deepen the theological significance of the Posada Sin Fronteras. Inspired by the Posada Sin Fronteras, he worked with Lourdes Arias and others to start, in 1997 or 1998, a Dia de los Muertos Eucharist Mass, to commemorate migrant deaths at the border, at Casa del Migrante, and in 1999 they organized during Lent, the first Via Crucis de Jesus Migrante (Way of the Cross of the Migrant Jesus). For the latter, Gioacchino Campese wrote a short book, with biblical readings, reflections, and special songs and prayers that serves as a guide for reenacting Jesus' journey in the Stations of the Cross as the migrant journey of suffering. The intention, as explained in the introduction of the book, is to celebrate faith in God and to show how "Jesus continues to walk today with the marginalized and insignificant, and the migrants who are the living symbols of this humanity on the move. . . . This Way of the Cross is intended for all those communities and people who are living the difficult experience of migration, for those who work with migrants building a better world, a world without borders" (Campese 2000).

Incorporating scripture, in fact using the Bible as a guide, has been key to Campese's approach to these public liturgies and migrant reenactments. As he reflected during our interview "There are many passages in the Bible that speak of migration. The Bible could be interpreted completely from the viewpoint of migrants. . . . the first Christian communities were formed by immigrants basically, you now, by people who were not citizens of the places of the cities where they were living. . . . You can go to Exodus, you can go to Leviticus, you can go to the book of Deuteronomy." In his eyes, the Posada Sin Fronteras brings together a positive message of spirituality together with "a protest against what was going on there at the border, people dying at the border, and the hypocrisy that is behind immigration reform or immigration laws."

While commentators may be ready to proclaim that Liberation Theology, if measured by the diminishing number *of comunidades de base*, is dead, the ideals and methods of Liberation Theology seem to live on through individuals, their activism, and institutions such as the Scalabrini Order dedicated to immigrants and social justice.

Another person who participated intimately in the organization of the Posada Sin Fronteras was Franciscan Brother Ed Dunn, who came to the San Diego area in the mid-1990s, working as a community organizer for the Interfaith

Coalition for Immigrant Rights. Among central influences in his life, he cited Martin Luther King, Archbishop Oscar Romero, Cesar Chavez, and Liberation Theology. He brought with him a rich legacy of hands-on experience with faith-inspired social justice activism working in Mexican American communities from San Jose to Las Vegas. He had worked with the UFW in California during the late 1970s as well as with Communities Organized for Public Service (COPS) and Ernie Cortez in Texas, he received Industrial Areas Foundation training in community organizing in Chicago, and he had also studied Liberation Theology in Texas. The Posada Sin Frontera, he said, reminded him of how the UFW used Catholicism to draw in Protestant support for Mexican migrant workers: "The celebrations of the Posada [was] very similar to the UFW because there was a lot of Protestant support for the UFW and the farmworker movement. And there was a huge amount of respect that Protestant leaders and grassroots leaders brought to the celebration of the mass and the celebration of religious events with the farmworkers. So I think there's the same thing with the Posadas. There was this great respect that people brought and said, 'We understand this is part of the tradition and we want to learn from it.'" In this regard, Ed Dunn saw the Posada Sin Fronteras appealing to a broader audience, particularly Protestants and non-Mexicans who lacked strong liturgical celebrations, allowing them to make "a switch from witnessing other people's expression of faith, in this case the Latino expression of faith through the Posadas, and somehow making it a challenge of spirituality for ourselves too."

Two musicians, Rosa Martha Zarate and Francisco Herrera, regularly animate the Posada Sin Fronteras with their guitars and lead participation in songs. Like Noreen Sullivan, Rosa Martha Zarate is a former nun, but not by choice, as she was expelled after suing the San Diego diocese for labor exploitation. In fact, she and Roberto Martinez had both worked together in the San Diego diocese during the 1970s. Originally from Mexico, she cited among her earliest influences the examples set by her Communist-leaning father, and her mother and grandmother, both of whom were always involved in popular religiosity and helping the poorest in the community. Rosa Martha entered the convent in Guadalajara, Mexico, in 1962, and it was there that she met Paolo Freire and became a disciple of his theory of empowering the poor, pedagogy of the oppressed. The nuns brought her to San Diego—illegally, she said, without papers but dressed in habits—and she recalled in explicit detail the blatant and brutal racism she experienced as a Mexican in the white dominated Catholic church. Yet it was here that the UFW, the Chicano movement, the Cuban Revolution, and Liberation Theology converged in life-transforming ways:

Cuando comienzo yo a involucrarme con . . . . When I began getting involved with Cesar Chavez, I got into conflict with the congregation, with the religious community, because of my insistence in getting permission to attend the strikes and demonstrations. I got to meet Dolores Huerta, and Chicano priests and nuns that were in the movement. . . . So when I'm asked why I do what I do, I say it's because of my cultural *herencia*, for having lived at this historical moment where Liberation Theology was infiltrating into this country too, where the Chicano movement was vindicating my cultural roots of origin, of our indigenousness that was very strong. . . . All of this was influenced by the Cubans too, and by the popular movements arising in Latin America.

Today, Rosa Martha Zarate is the director of a nonprofit community agency in San Bernardino and she works tirelessly for numerous causes, including the movement to regain the ex-Braceros the earnings taken by the Mexican government. She primarily identifies as a singer-songwriter, in the tradition of popular, socially committed Latin American folk music, and she has three CDs, including one with her musical collaborator, Francisco Herrera, called "Posadas Sin Fronteras." The title song, coauthored by both of them while they were driving on the freeway to the Posada one year, features special lyrics focused on migrants and the border.

Today, the Posada Sin Fronteras is largely in the hands of three women, Leticia Jimenez of the AFSC, Linda Arreola of the Catholic diocese, and Rosemary Johnston, who, among many other activities, is executive director of the Interfaith Shelter Network in San Diego and is a board member of the Interfaith Coalition for Immigrant Rights. Rosemary Johnston identified herself this way: "I'm a Roman Catholic and I've long had a great admiration and respect for social justice teachings." After raising four children, she began working at the Catholic diocese in the social ministries office, and as she has pursued theological training she has become a key faith-based activist in San Diego. Raised in an Irish-Catholic family and educated in Catholic schools and colleges, she now organizes the Annual Homeless Death Vigil on All Souls Day in front of the steps of San Diego City Hall; she is active in the local Ecumenical council, through which she promoted an interfaith Christian-Muslim dialogues after September 11, 2001; and she has worked to organize a Stations of the Cross organized around social justice issues in downtown San Diego. Although she had not been active in the Central American solidarity movement of the 1980s, nor any sort of socialist or workers' justice movement, she cited among her sources of inspiration Archbishop Oscar Romero and Catholic Worker founder Dorothy Day. In fact, she keeps handy in her busy office inspirational quotes written by both of those figures. She had never practiced or attended Posadas while growing up in Southern California. Now, though, Posadas and other Mexican-Catholic rituals enacted as public piety have become natural to her. "I think these rituals are full of meaning—what's the point if they're not?," she said. "But it's a meaning that transcends the walls of the church, and that's what we need to, we need to have that vision if we're going to make a difference in the world."

A Final Note on Religion and Politics, Biography and History

The iconoclastic sociologist C. W. Mills long ago wrote that the promise of sociology is to understand the interaction of biography and history. People and their actions shape history, and, in turn, historical processes—including social movements—are created by individuals and groups. The synopses of biographies presented in this chapter show how the lives of a unique group of faith-based activists dedicated to social justice at the U.S.-Mexico border have been shaped by Latino immigration and, more directly, by the religious and political traditions of Latino culture. The legacies of the UFW, Liberation Theology, the solidarity movement, and popular Latin American religiosity now constitute part of the cultural landscape informing faith-based progressive activists in the United States, at least in the border region. Part of this legacy is an emphasis on the expressive culture of antiborderism.

At the same time, many of these activists are situated in an American context, and they remain deeply influenced by American political and cultural traditions. One aspect of this is the relative devalorization of politics. In the current era, many Americans shy away from embracing overtly political identities and actions. Politics, the thinking goes, is perceived as dirty, self-serving, and corrupt. The hybridity of American and Latino culture is not without tension, and one of the points of tension involves the blending of religion and politics.

Is the Posada Sin Fronteras a political or a religious event? The organizers from the U.S. side expressed some reluctance to embracing the notion that it is an explicitly political event. Among interviewees from the Mexican side, or those who were from Mexico, this was not the case. But Brother Dunn insisted that it was a religious ceremony, not a political protest, and Pastor Art Cribbs added that "it is not a protest as such and it is done cooperatively." Roberto Martinez first said that the Posada was a religious event, but when pressed for clarification, he reflected and said that the Bible is political, musing, "Well, the flight from Egypt, you can say that it was political too because of why they were being driven out of Egypt." Rosemary Johnston clarified that she only participated in social actions that were "prayerful," in part because she did not want to be "co-opted by other groups with different agendas," and in part because as a religious person she did not want to "demonize the other." As she explained: "If I organized an event, it's going to be prayerful. I think that makes it more inclusive, that you're for something rather than against something. You know, we're for a more inclusive society, we're for recognition of the dignity of all people regardless of their immigration status and that they have certain rights like to medical care and housing and education because they're human, not because they're citizens. You know, we avoid ad hominem attacks against Bush or Ashcroft or anyone else, or against the Border Patrol."

Certainly, these are understandable perspectives. Yet this delineation of the Posada Sin Fronteras was puzzling to us as the event brings religion to the public square to make a seemingly political statement: participants denounce government immigration and border enforcement policies that kill, and they use religious text, ritual, and narratives to imagine a different future, one of hospitality and unity. Moreover, the forerunners—in the UFW, the Central American solidarity movement, the Catholic left, and Liberation Theology—had all meshed Christian religion and the politics of social action.

Yet many participants in this new regional culture of religious-based social activism and protest remain reticent about embracing terms such as "political" and "protest." Why this hesitance? We are not sure. One possibility is that this regional culture of faith-based social justice activism, as binational as it is, is mostly operating in a particular place, the United States, where politics and religion have come to signal the power of the Christian right. Another reason may have to do with their structural location as employees in mostly nonprofit, tax-exempt, nongovernmental agencies that must advocate no partisan political allegiances; perhaps purely practical real-politik reasons explain their choices. Finally, another possibility is that we sociologist observers may be imposing our own meanings and definitions of the situation here, seeing it as a religious-political event, while many of the organizers identify with the former and not the latter.

We celebrate the tenacity, creativity, and courage of the organizers of the Posada Sin Fronteras. We see them collectively weaving together a living regional culture of religious protest, one that serves as a faith-based counterforce to the militarization of the border, neoliberalization policies, and the new racialized nationalism and xenophobia in the United States. The threads holding this all together come from diverse skeins, but they can all be seen as rooted in responses to the crisis of immigration that rely on what Nepstad (2003, viii) calls "the cultural resources of Christianity." In this instance, the response is based on Latin American popular religiosity, as well as radical religious traditions associated with Latin American and Chicano movements. There are diverse viewpoints within the tapestry, but perhaps a good voice to choose for closing the chapter is Noreen Sullivan's. Before we met for our interview, she typed up two pages of notes on her detailed recollections of the Posada Sin Fronteras, and she included views on combining politics and religion. Here is what she wrote: "We had many discussions in the beginning about not getting too 'political,' partly for fear of getting shut down by the BP [Border Patrol] and partly because 'political' was seen as antithetical to 'spiritual.' Our thinking gradually evolved and we realized that everything is political, that there is no spirituality without the political, that the border/immigration situation is completely political and that we must speak out and act in order to change things. And that speaking/acting is the highest form of a true spirituality rooted in justice."

PART IV

Faith-Based Nongovernmental Organizations

10

Welcoming the Stranger

Constructing an Interfaith Ethic of Refuge

STEPHANIE J. NAWYN

The majority of organizations that resettle refugees in the United States are faith based. The religious affiliation of these organizations varies, from the large Jewish organizations that have been active in assisting refugees since the nineteenth century to the Protestant organizations who have come into resettlement within the past few decades. Although these organizations are grounded in different religious traditions, their staff describe the organizations' missions in strikingly similar ways: showing hospitality to the stranger, providing refuge to the cast-out, and honoring the rights of human beings regardless of national boundaries.

Using interviews, printed materials, and field observations from thirty-six refugee resettlement and assistance organizations in four cities, I explore the language used to describe organizational missions and individual motivations of staff working at refugee resettlement and assistance organizations, both faith based and secular. In my analysis, I demonstrate how faith-based resettlement organizations have constructed an interfaith ethic of refuge that connects to similarities of major world religions. Faith-based staff use interfaith language that is necessarily generic in order to appeal broadly across religious traditions, emphasizing openness and acceptance of the mostly non-Christian and non-Jewish refugees they serve. The ethic of refuge is also a tool by which resettlement NGOs mobilize their organizational networks to access material and human resources, and create space for alliances with faith-based organizations from different religious traditions.

Religious Persecution and Faith-based Mobilization

Religion has conflicted with nationalism and national interests in at least two ways: state actors have perceived religion as a threat to the nation, and faith-based movements have acted against the state to protect human lives across borders. The earliest refugee migrations in the twentieth century were brought on by religious conflict and persecution. Groups who practiced religions other than the dominant religion in a society were often deemed disloyal to the nation and thus a potential threat to national survival. This was the case with the Armenian genocide and refugee migration that occurred roughly from 1894 to 1919. Armenia came under the control of the Ottoman Empire in the fourteenth century, and because the Armenians were not Muslims the Turks considered them outsiders. As nationalism and nation-state consolidation within the Ottoman Empire progressed in the nineteenth century, the Turks' treatment of Armenians and other minority groups worsened (Kushner and Knox 1999). The outright massacres and forced relocations to the desert resulted in the deaths of 1.5 million Armenians by the early 1920s (Marrus 2002).

Nationalism mixed with scapegoating of religious outsiders was also a factor in the Holocaust. The otherness of Jews made them not only easy targets for genocidal nationalism but also less sympathetic to states that could have offered them asylum (Kushner and Knox 1999). But shared Jewish identity also provided grounds on which to build a movement against religious persecution and nationalist exclusion of Jewish refugees. Between 1908 to 1925 over one million Jews immigrated to the United States (Marrus 2002). The Jewish population in the United States formed numerous organizations that lobbied unsuccessfully to increase refugee admissions for German and Eastern European Jews before World War II, but their efforts increased the strength and influence of their organizations. Following the Allied victory in Europe they were influential in convincing President Roosevelt to raise the ceiling on refugee admissions (Nichols 1988). More than a dozen Jewish organizations were operating on an international level at this time, the most important being the American Jewish Joint Distribution Committee, which funneled financial assistance from the United States and helped 300,000 homeless Jews in Eastern Europe to resettle or repatriate (Marrus 2002). Later, Catholic and then Protestant refugee assistance organizations emerged, modeling themselves after the earlier Jewish organizations (Nichols 1988).

The refugee assistance efforts of religious organizations have resulted in the U.S. government expanding their protection of other refugee groups, such as Central Americans (Coutin 1993, 1998). During conflicts in El Salvador and Guatemala in the late 1970s and 1980s, civilian Salvadorans and Guatemalans were not often targeted explicitly because of their religion, but the governments were concerned about Catholic church members' involvement in liberation theology and empowerment movements among the poor, which were considered revolutionary. On March 24, 1980, Archbishop Oscar Romero was assassinated while leading mass, and on December 2 of that same year four U.S. nuns were assassinated by government forces (Smith 1991; Hamilton and Chinchilla 2001).

The U.S. government did suspend economic relations with El Salvador for a short time but were reluctant to criticize a government to which it was providing military aid to fight communist insurgents. Liberation theologists in the United States joined forces with churches in El Salvador and Guatemala to form the Sanctuary movement, which provided safe havens for Central Americans entering the United States illegally and lobbied the U.S. government (with limited success) to recognize Central Americans as refugees (Coutin 1993; Golden and McConnell 1986). The American Baptist Church spearheaded the lawsuit against the Immigration and Naturalization Service, which pressured the federal government to extend Temporary Protected Status to many Salvadorans (Coutin 1998, 2000). Clergy, church congregations, and other religious organizations continue to serve and advocate for migrants crossing the U.S.-Mexico border in the Sonora Desert to this day (Greenberg 2005; Martinez 2005; Rotstein 2004).

How Religion Operates in Resettlement Nongovernmental Organizations

Religion involves more than the religious affiliation of resettlement nongovernmental organizations (NGOs); it encompasses organizational practices, rhetoric and doctrinal mandates, and networks. Resettlement NGOs can observe religious holidays, use religious doctrines to guide the mission of their activities, and network with other organizations and individuals sharing their religious affiliation. In the past, Christian congregations sponsoring refugees have made conversion a requisite for receiving resettlement assistance (Hoskins, this volume; Ong 2003). But current federal regulations prohibit resettlement NGOs receiving federal money from spending that money on religious activities. However, faith-based resettlement NGOs reflect their religiosity in their rhetoric and organizational networks (Nawyn, 2006). Religious rhetoric, as I conceive it in this study, includes any organizational mission statement or published literature that mentions religion, as well as the religious talk of organizational staff and volunteers. While religious rhetoric can take many forms within faith-based NGOs, religious rhetoric in resettlement NGOs supports refugee assistance and resettlement by connecting religiosity to human rights.

Religious Roots of Human Rights Language

Although the major world religions contain vast differences and contradictions between them, scholars have identified some shared elements that have given birth to the current concept of human rights. Lauren (1998, 5) cites the "universal interest in addressing the integrity, worth, and dignity of all persons and, consequently, the duty toward other people who suffer without distinction." He identifies this universal interest in the Torah's shared fatherhood of God to all people, the Buddhist valuing of all people regardless of their social position, the place of charity as a pillar of belief in Islam, and Christian parables told by Jesus, including the story of the good Samaritan. Reformations within Hindu thought also support equality and the inherent divinity (and thus worth) of all people (Mitra 1982). Scholars have even found roots of human rights in Confucianism (Lauren 1998; Slingerland 2004). While not all these religious traditions conceptualize human rights in the same way or in a way consistent with more secular conceptions (such as in the United Nations 1948 Declaration of Human Rights), these scholars argue that across major world religions there is room for a consistent language of human rights.

Summary of the Refugee Resettlement System

Federal agencies set limits on new refugee admissions, and they approve which individuals are given refugee status. They also define the array of services that legally constitute resettlement. These services include, for the first thirty days, transitional cash assistance, food, housing, clothing, health screening, and referrals for other social and medical services. Other assistance includes welfare benefits (amounts varying by eligibility), employment assistance, and language instruction. The federal government subcontracts these resettlement services to NGOs. The government allocates all new refugee arrivals to a national voluntary agency (also called a Volag), which in turn subcontracts with a local NGO to resettle each refugee. The national Volag subcontracts with either one of their local offices or a mutual assistance association. Mutual assistance associations are secular ethnic organizations serving a particular immigrant group. A group of immigrants that has become more settled forms an association in order to assist others from that group to adapt to life in the United States (thus providing mutual assistance to their compatriots).

Volags can be faith-based (such as Church World Service or Catholic Charities) or secular (such as International Rescue Committee or Ethiopian Community Development Council). All local Volags serve only refugees, providing the government-mandated resettlement services and occasionally other services intended to assist refugees to adapt and become economically self-sufficient. Not all mutual assistance associations serve refugees, and not all do resettlement. The ones that do resettlement tend to provide a broader range of services (especially cultural services), and may also provide services to nonrefugee clients, depending upon the requirements of their funding. In general, Volags focus on refugee resettlement, whereas mutual assistance associations focus on assisting a particular ethnic immigrant group (which may be composed largely of refugees).

There are other organizations that provide assistance to refugees but are not contracted to provide resettlement services. I call these organizations support agencies. This includes faith-based NGOs, secular NGOs, and government agencies that provide any type of assistance to refugees (or broadly to people in need, at least some of whom are refugees). Some support agencies provide cultural programming, including interceding between refugees and American institutions such as schools or the police. Some support agencies recruit volunteers who collect items to furnish a refugee family's apartment or provide refugees transportation to job interviews and other necessary appointments.

Human rights principles sustain the practice of all resettlement NGOs, but no one has studied the rhetorical strategies by which these principles are expressed. The ethical principles contained in resettlement NGO literature and the way resettlement staff talk about their work reveals a great deal about why resettlement staff believe their work is important and how they convince others (specifically government agents, potential donors, and/or volunteers) of its importance. In this chapter I examine the rhetorical strategies of faith-based and secular resettlement NGO staff. Specifically, I address three questions: (1) How is religion used in the rhetoric of faith-based NGOs? (2) What are the similarities and differences between religious and secular rhetoric? (3) How is rhetoric used strategically to mobilize resources?

Methods

I use qualitative data collected from fifty-eight interviews with staff and volunteers at thirty-six refugee resettlement and assistance organizations in four metropolitan areas; Los Angeles, Chicago, Sacramento, and Minneapolis/Saint Paul. The thirty-six resettlement and assistance organizations consisted of twenty Volags, ten mutual assistance associations, five support agencies, and one county government resettlement office. Eighteen of the NGOs in my sample were faith based. The four cities were chosen because they represent both traditional gateways (cities that have a long history of receiving refugees, such as Los Angeles and Chicago) and emerging gateways (cities that have recently received refugees at a faster rate than the national average, such as Minneapolis/Saint Paul and Sacramento).

Interviews cover the services NGOs provide, how they fundraise, what the needs are of refugees they serve and how they try to meet those needs, how the NGOs mission and religious affiliation (in the case of faith-based NGOs) shapes the work the organization does, and what vision they have for successful resettlement. Thirty-seven interviews were with the directors of resettlement NGOs or lead coordinators of resettlement programs within a larger umbrella agency. The remainder of the interviews were with other staff, volunteers, and board members.

Results

While faith-based resettlement NGOs may not be any more religious than secular NGOs in their practices (Nawyn, forthcoming), they do express their religiosity through organizational rhetoric and networks. Faith-based NGO staff are acutely aware of government limitations on their religious activities, but they still view their work within a framework of religious faith. Deborah from World Relief in Sacramento told me, "I think it's a faith, you know, it's connected to your faith. You know, as a government contracted organization, you know, we can't go out and do religious activities per se. So we don't make any effort to proselytize, but I think it impacts our attitude." Roger at Catholic Charities expressed it this way: "we serve refugees not because they are Catholic, but because we are." In this chapter, I describe in more detail the religious rhetoric used by faith-based resettlement NGOs and how it is mobilized in the service of refugees. Also, I show how the religious rhetoric of faith-based resettlement NGOs intermingles with the secular rhetoric of international human rights discourse to form a cohesive ethic of refuge that NGO staff use to justify their work. This ethic of refuge comprises the ethical and moral language used to justify the admittance of and social welfare assistance extended to refugees, what Ruben Rumbaut (1989) called the structure of refuge. Finally, I explore the ways in which refugee resettlement and assistance NGOs use this ethic of refuge to serve and advocate for refugees.

Religious Doctrine and Judeo-Christian Values

All of the faith-based resettlement NGOs in the United States are affiliated with Judaism or Christianity. Thus, there are many common doctrinal elements to the religious rhetoric of faith-based NGOs. The basic themes within the ethic of refuge are (1) extending hospitality, (2) the Divine's concern for refugees, (3) themes of refugeehood in religious history, (4) service to those in need, and (5) the sanctity of human life (regardless of nationality or other social position). The religious rhetoric of Jewish and Christian resettlement NGOs reflect these basic themes. For example, Regina at Exodus World Service, a faith-based support agency in Chicago, stated, "we felt that there was a faith-based mandate that we had, as Christians, to walk with the stranger, and that that was something that the Christian community wasn't doing to the degree that we wanted to see it engaged in that type of service." She felt there was a mandate for Christians to show hospitality, or "walk with the stranger," and in order to provide that opportunity to Christians she cofounded World Exodus. Regina gave the title "New Neighbor Program" to their one-on-one mentoring program in order to reflect the ethic of loving one's neighbor that she felt was an important part of Christianity.

Shane at Interfaith Refugee and Immigration Ministries spoke of a "biblical imperative to feed the hungry or to help a stranger." He stated that "Christ was a refugee. He was a refugee as an early child fleeing from the Middle East to Africa," so therefore it was an important part of the Christian faith to welcome refugees. Beth at Hebrew Immigrant Aid Society connected hospitality to the Jewish faith, saying, "the Jewish dimension [to our services] is helping people realize that America is a place that welcomes all." Judith at Jewish Children and Family Services also felt that the Jewish faith including a mandate to help others, saying it is "the Jewish way of life to help, to help people and helping those who are helping captives . . . a lot of Jewish religion speaks about helping people who need help."

Some faith-based staff also emphasized equality when discussing the importance of helping refugees. Caroline at Opening Doors (which was affiliated with several Protestant Volags and local churches) quoted scripture in her explanation of her personal convictions about assisting refugees. She said, "Well, in terms of me, personally, in the first chapter of Genesis, God said, 'Let us make man in his image.' He didn't put any 'let us make white, upper middle class, man in his image.' You know, he didn't fit any qualifications on that . . . and I take that very seriously." Resettlement staff use equality rhetoric not only to support their work but also to educate the public about refugees, specifically using equality as a synonym for similarity. In their educational programs and written materials, resettlement staff promote the notion that refugees are "just like you," thus minimizing the sense that native-born Americans might have that refugees are an Other. By arguing that refugees are the same as everyone else, resettlement staff attempt to increase empathy for refugees and make it more difficult to deny refugees assistance.

Connecting Judeo-Christian Values to Other World Religions

Although all the faith-based resettlement NGOs in my study were either Jewish or Christian,[1] the staff at these NGOs sometimes spoke of religious values in terms of all world religions or attempted to connect the Judeo-Christian religious values of their organization with non-Christian or Jewish faiths. Caroline at Opening Doors in Sacramento stated, "We have on staff two people who are more or less Buddhist, one very explicitly so, and in Buddhism they talk about Buddha nature, that everything, every sentient being, has Buddha nature, you know. And so again you recognize the Buddha nature [when you help refugees]." Beth at Hebrew Immigrant Aid Society stated that "one of the most moving things that we've ever done is at Ramadan, providing food baskets for the celebration for Ramadan," and she related this service to Muslim refugees to her responsibility as a Jewish person not to "shut her eyes to the world" when terrible things happen to other people. Shane at Interfaith Refugee and Immigration Ministries gave an explanation of his NGO's name change from "Interchurch" to "Interfaith" that illustrates the point of rhetoric that spans different religious orientations: "The first things that I realized was that while our links are to the mainline protestants . . . many of the supporters and other houses of faith that work with us to help refugees resettle may not be strictly Christian. We have people of the Jewish persuasion or Buddhist persuasion that might work with us. Certainly the people with whom we work, those whom we are privileged to serve, by and large are not Christian. They are Buddhists, most certainly Muslim, and a hand full of others." Shane expressed an interfaith ethic of refuge, saying, "I think any of the good faiths of the world; all of the world's faiths preach the idea of helping our neighbor. The so-called golden rule is to treat your neighbor as you wish to be treated yourself."

It is not just Interfaith's networks of resources that span religions; Shane's rhetoric about refugee assistance bridges different religions as well. Resettlement staff who used interfaith language to talk about their work did so to create a sense of inclusiveness with their refugee clients. From 2000 to 2003, six of the ten largest nationality groups came from predominantly Muslim countries (Afghanistan, Bosnia-Herzegovina, Iran, Liberia, Somalia, and Sudan). During those same years, over ten thousand refugees arrived from predominantly Buddhist Vietnam, and the arrival of Hmong refugees during 2004–5 brought in even more non-Christian and non-Jewish refugees. When I asked staff at Jewish and Christian resettlement NGOs about how their organization's religious affiliation effected their work, they frequently cited preponderance of non-Christian, non-Jewish refugees they resettled. Maintaining an interfaith ethic of refuge enabled resettlement staff to use Judeo-Christian ethics without excluding their refugee clients. Also, interfaith language created room for building relationships with potential supporters from non-Christian and non-Jewish organizations. Shared ethical concerns provide points of similarities that facilitate organizational collaborations.

Secular Human Rights Rhetoric

Both secular and faith-based staff frequently used secular human rights discourse when explaining the ethics of their work. While this discourse has roots in various religious traditions, the absence of explicit religious reference reflects the influence of the international human rights discourse that emerged particularly post–World War II during the formation of the United Nations (Dacyl 1996; Redman and Whalen 1998). Secular resettlement NGO staff most frequently expressed the ethic of refuge in terms of increasing the number of new refugees admitted to the U.S. Refugee admissions and human rights have been intertwined from the beginning. The Universal Declaration of Human Rights, created in 1948, responded directly to the nonadmission policy directed at German Jews, Roma, and other refugee groups fleeing Nazi persecution in the 1930s (Kjærum 2002). Thus, an interest in human rights and a desire for increased refugee admissions go hand in hand. Katya at International Rescue Committee in Los Angeles, referring to the total number of new refugee arrivals, told me that "what you see here for the entire county is what our agency alone used to resettle." Senada at Catholic Charities was also concerned about refugees trying to enter the United States, saying, "there are about 15 million refugees all over the world. And you know, they are waiting to enter third country." Beth at Hebrew Immigrant Aid Society in Chicago used this illustration to express her frustrations about the sharp decrease in refugee admissions following September 2001: "Now you have to think about Wrigley Field . . . think about the fact that Wrigley Field holds more people than all the refugees that were allowed into the United States. There are 13 million refugees in the world and sorrowfully we let in 22,000."

Like many other resettlement staff, Joshua at the International Institute in Los Angeles felt that increasing new refugee admissions was the most important thing to change about the current resettlement system in the United States: "The thing I would change the most is getting people out of harm's way, getting more people who we've authorized to come here . . . that's most urgent because people are sitting there. Just yesterday I got a press release from our national office describing what has happened to refugees in Africa. They were [stuck in refugee] camps and some 150 of them were killed." Every resettlement NGO director I spoke with thought that the current number of admissions was too low, and many considered low admissions as the top problem in the resettlement system. Increasing the number of refugees brought safely to the United States was the clearest example of human rights rhetoric in the ethic of refuge.

Secular resettlement NGO staff also expressed the ethic of refuge in terms of giving voice to disenfranchised refugees. Hoa from the Vietnamese Association of Illinois described her organization's advocacy program that trained native-born volunteers "to use their voices to speak up on behalf of refugees because refugees are impacted by policies over which they have no control." Jasmine at the Bosnian and Herzegovinian American Community Center concurred that an important task for her organization was to "speak for people who cannot speak."

The rhetoric of faith-based NGO staff is often similar to the rhetoric of secular NGO staff. Understandably, people working in refugee resettlement tend to value the rights of refugees over state sovereignty, whether they are working in a faith-based or secular setting. Staff at secular NGOs differ from staff at faith-based NGOs in that they draw upon the secular rhetoric of human rights rather than religious doctrine or scripture. But the words and ideas they use are similar to those invoked by faith-based staff. Secular NGO staff frequently talked about the humanity of refugees, placing the importance of human life above the interests of government. Lan at Center for Asian and Pacific Islanders stated, "the government is suppose to be helping people. They have a basic obligation [to help people] regardless of their [immigration] status." Kelly, who volunteered with refugees at Heartland Alliance, felt that her personal experience with refugees made them seem like real humans rather than "a bunch of statistics, or numbers," and that once you realize that refugees are real humans with needs, "you can't ignore them." And Shane at Interfaith Refugee and Immigration Ministries expressed the importance of hospitality in more secular terms: "It is our job to ensure that if nothing else as concerned citizens of the United States that we do ensure that our country continue to welcome the hungry, the down trodden, that we do still stand as the shining beacon of hope for these people wherever they may be because, believe me, one of the few things that they ever have left of them is hope."

Both faith-based and secular resettlement staff feel extreme frustration with the small number of refugees admitted to the United States, relative to the number of people currently in refugee camps. As Joshua noted, many of these camps have poor security and minimal health resources, making the camps themselves almost or just as dangerous as the situations from which people fled. People working on resettlement want more refugees to enter the United States and are less concerned about state sovereignty than saving the lives of refugees. Therefore, human rights rhetoric, drawing upon either religious or secular principles, comprises a central component to the ethic of refuge.

Advancing the rights of human beings over the rights of states became much more important for resettlement NGOs after September 11, 2001. In the months immediately following the attacks on the World Trade Center and Pentagon, refugee admissions were halted. Refugees who had already been approved for admission were denied access, and their cases were reevaluated under the new security restrictions overseen by the Department of Homeland Security. Even after the U.S. government began admitting refugees again, they entered a political climate that was more hostile. Many resettlement NGOs that had not conducted advocacy activities before September 11 started public education campaigns and outreach efforts to schools, churches, and businesses to advocate for refugee rights. The International Rescue Committee in Los Angeles started a speaker's bureau to educate people in the local community about refugees, because, as their director Katya explained, "some people mix refugees with illegals." Katya could more easily justify the right of refugees to be in the United States, whereas it is more difficult to argue that the state does not have the right to control undocumented immigration. Resettlement NGO staff also need to rhetorically separate refugees from terrorists, as Shirley at Lutheran Social Services described: "I mean, I think part of it was just making sure people understood that refugees were not terrorists and you had to go out and say that quite a few times; that these are people who have been waiting to come here, they are victims of terrorism themselves."

Because resettlement NGOs administer federal welfare programs, they serve as agents of the state. However, when it comes to the rights of people to cross national borders in order to achieve safety, resettlement staff are deeply invested in the ethics of human rights.

Melding the Sacred with the Profane

The ethical rhetoric of secular and faith-based resettlement NGOs intertwine to form a cohesive ethic of refuge. NGOs use the ethic of refuge as a bridge between secular and faith-based organizations, creating a common language, common set of interests, and common agenda between them. This allows faith-based NGOs to collaborate with secular NGOs in ways that may not occur outside of refugee resettlement. As Demeke from the Ethiopian Community Association of Chicago put it, "if our needs coincide with their interests, we work with them." Peter at the U.S. Bahá'í Refugee Office stated that "basically at one time or another, if there is a human rights organization or an organization which works for the same type of principles that the Bahá'ís have, which are the elimination of prejudice, the equality of men and women . . . if there's an organization that holds those principles, at one time or another our organization . . . probably worked with that organization." The U.S. Bahá'í Refugee Office used the common ground of human rights to collaborate on a project with Amnesty International, a secular human rights organization, in which the two organizations worked on the United Nations' Convention to End Discrimination Against Women (CEDAW).

The similarities between religious and secular rhetoric are what make it possible to understand the two as part of a cohesive ethic of refuge. But it is the interaction between faith-based and secular NGOs that creates a unified ethic. The ethic of refuge provides a universal language with which different types of NGOs can communicate with each other, forming collaborative relationships around their shared principles and goals. It is how Bach-Viet, a secular mutual assistance association, can collaborate on a Healthy Marriages program for refugees with a Christian Church and a Buddhist Temple in Sacramento. It is how Opening Doors and Lutheran Social Services, both faith-based Volags, can collaborate on projects with secular mutual-assistance associations. Their shared goals, expressed in either religious or secular rhetoric, allow faith-based and secular resettlement NGOs to form overlapping organizational networks. As Harold of Sacramento Employment and Training Agency put it, in regards to collaborations "there is nothing mandated. It is more of a 'we'll all benefit from doing this together.'" Every city in my sample had a coalition organization of refugee service providers that met at least once a month, with the shared discussions providing more basis for a similarity in rhetorical strategy. And by working together on refugee resettlement, the rhetorical strategies of faith-based and secular NGOs continued to develop in overlapping language, further reifying the ethic of refuge.

Using Religious Rhetoric to Mobilize Religious Networks

Faith-based and secular resettlement staff invoke similar language when describing the ethic of refuge, but differences likely exist in how powerfully each discourse mobilizes resources. Faith-based staff use their religious ethic of refuge to motivate members of the Christian or Jewish communities to help refugees, whereas it is unclear how useful a secular ethic of refuge is for mobilizing individuals outside a faith community. Faith-based and secular NGOs in my sample used volunteers about equally. The real divergence may be in how easy or difficult it is to recruit both volunteers and material resources.[2] For faith-based NGOs, common religious values between an NGO and a faith community facilitate recruitment of volunteer labor and in-kind donations. Beth at Hebrew Immigrant Aid Society used her networks with synagogues in Chicago to mobilize a wealth of resources for refugees: "Synagogues have been involved in giving space to us to run citizenship classes, they have been involved in celebrations of new citizens, they have been involved in welcoming new refugees to communities . . . when refugees from Kosovo came, synagogues were very active in actually going to airports and meeting Kosovo refugees and bringing them baskets and donating food and shelter and support and friendship."

Sveta at Jewish Family Services also sought assistance from synagogues in Sacramento. When organizing a Jewish cultural event, she said, "I ask them for community hall . . . [and] they gave me this big room and it was very nice. Just because they are affiliated with us." One of Jason's primary responsibilities at World Relief is to lead outreach and recruitment at churches in the Minneapolis area, and he used a religious ethic of refuge to speak with church members. He rarely had the opportunity to address an entire congregation but found that speaking to smaller groups within the church, like a youth group, proved successful: "We had a youth group this last winter that helped a family from Sudan. What they did is they went back to their parents and said, 'Here are these people that need furniture and household goods,' and they collected it." Stella at Saint Anselm's Cross Cultural employs the ethic of refuge to gain assistance from local churches sharing Saint Anselm's affiliation with the national Volags Church World Service, Lutheran Immigration and Refugee Services, and Episcopal Migration Ministries. Stella provides reports about the work they do to these national Volags, who in turn send updates to their affiliate churches. The churches in turn contact Stella about donating to Saint Anselm's.

It was common among faith-based resettlement NGOs to use the ecclesiastical structure of denominations and the faith-based national Volags to tap resource networks. These ecclesiastical structures are not available to secular NGOs. Joshua at the International Institute explains that "we [resettlement NGO directors] just kind of have agreed that the Jewish community will seek support from Jewish or from temples and the Catholics will seek support from the Catholic churches, etc. So we don't recruit faith-based groups, to avoid stepping on toes of other organizations." It was more common for secular Volags to have collaborative relationships with faith-based NGOs rather than religious institutions like churches, mosques, or synagogues. Faith-based NGOs, on the other hand, had access to networks with both secular NGOs and houses of worship, which gave them expanded capabilities of mobilizing resources compared to secular NGOs.

Faith-based NGOs employ scriptures supporting a divine mandate to assist refugees. The World Relief national office in Baltimore, Maryland, makes scriptural mandates explicit in their organizational literature. Their Web site states that "God makes it clear that He takes extraordinary interest in refugees and He expects His people to do the same." Specific biblical scriptures are cited as proof that God loves refugees (Prov. 31:8–9 and Deut. 10:16–19), that God will bless those that help refugees (Heb. 6:10, Prov. 28:27, and Deut. 24:19–21) and refuse to answer the prayers of people who turn their backs on refugees (Prov. 21:13).[3] Exodus World Service, the faith-based support agency in Chicago, focuses entirely on recruiting volunteers and in-kind donations from area churches. Exodus World Service also cites scripture as part of their volunteer mobilization. The manual for their New Neighbor Program (connecting church members to refugees for one-on-one mentoring and relationship building) cites Deuteronomy 10:19 (*"Love the sojourner therefore: for you were sojourners in the land of Egypt"*) and Matthew 25:34–35 (*"Then the King will say to those at his right hand, 'Come, O blessed of my Father, inherit the kingdom prepared for you from the foundation of the world . . . for I was a stranger and you welcomed me"*), among others. Cited scriptures focus on showing hospitality to strangers, and in several places the manual identifies Jesus as a refugee. Such invocations of religious teachings (and especially to a religious teacher as a refugee) undoubtedly provides faith-based NGOs with a powerful tool to mobilize resources.

The religious rhetoric and accompanying networks of faith-based Volags give them an audience and potential pool of resources to which secular Volags and MAAs do not have access. Michael at International Institute of Minnesota believed that recruiting volunteers was easier for faith-based NGOs than for secular agencies like his, saying, "the churches have the whole ecclesiastical structure that they appeal to, we don't use that method." Secular NGOs tended to recruit volunteers and donations from area universities, and some operated joint programs with local colleges and universities, like the Bosnian and Herzegovinian American Community Center in Chicago did with Loyola University. But faith-based NGOs could also take advantage of these networks. Additionally, it is also possible that the secular rhetoric of human rights is not as powerful a motivating tool as religious rhetoric. When I asked secular NGO staff how they obtained private donations, most admitted they received very few donations, and those NGOs that successfully acquired donations usually enlisted refugee ethnic communities. But former refugees who have only recently resettled themselves cannot provide many resources for newly arrived refugees, so these networks do not provide the amount of resources to secular NGOs as religious networks provide to faith-based NGOs.[4]

Faith-based and secular resource networks shared one striking similarity: most resource mobilization (as well as advocacy on behalf of refugees) occurred through national institutional networks. When Caroline at Opening Doors needed material donations, she did not go directly to local congregations; rather, she worked through the denominational structure of member churches associated with her national Volag affiliates, Church World Service and Lutheran Refugee and Immigration Services. Similarly, Katya at International Rescue Committee in Los Angeles leaves private fundraising to the national IRC office, rather than taking on that task within her local organization. While there is some grassroots organizing of volunteers and collecting donations from congregations, much of the contact between local faith-based resettlement NGOs and individual congregations initiates through regional or national offices. This is analogous to findings by Kurtz and Fulton (2002) and Olson (2002) that mainline Protestant activism frequently occurs with national offices. This also affirms, at least in part, Skocpol's (2003) thesis that professionalized NGOs commonly engage in political activity, shifting responsibility for civic engagement from local communities to national offices. However, faith-based networks differ from secular networks in that local congregations still provide a readily available grassroots audience for public education and resource mobilization. Faith-based refugee organizations clearly address these audiences with their religious rhetoric, and, based on my interviews with faith-based NGO staff, those audiences are responding.

Conclusions

Although faith-based resettlement NGOs are prohibited from spending federal dollars on religious activities, they still operate as religious organizations through their rhetoric and networks. In the literature that they publish and the language their staff uses, faith-based resettlement NGOs explicitly express their religiosity. Whether Jewish, Catholic, or Protestant, faith-based resettlement NGO staff draw upon the (not exclusively) Judeo-Christian values of showing hospitality to a stranger, assisting those in need, and valuing human life over states' rights to justify the importance of their work. The literature that faith-based NGOs publish describes God's calling for people to provide aid and comfort to refugees. And faith-based NGOs invoke images of Jewish suffering or Jesus' status as a refugee to encourage Jews and Christians to assist in the resettlement effort. Faith-based NGO staff sometimes attempt to describe the ethical principles underlying resettlement in interfaith language, connecting to ethics in other world religions. Interfaith language may be expressed in generic terms that lose their specific religious quality; faith-based NGO staff use interfaith language to construct a sense of inclusiveness to all refugees and to other refugee organizations, regardless of religious affiliation. Finally, all resettlement NGO staff use human rights rhetoric to argue for increased refugee admissions and assistance.

There are many similarities between religious and secular rhetoric in refugee resettlement. Both rhetorical strategies connect to the concept of international human rights, which values the rights of people above the rights of states. My study only looks at a cross-section in time of these two types of rhetoric, so I cannot determine with certainty how they each developed over time within resettlement work. However, my data clearly show that resettlement staff use the similarities between religious and secular rhetoric to build organizational networks across religious or secular affiliations. My data demonstrated that resettlement NGOs, like other service providing agencies, do compete for scarce resources. However, resettlement staff described more collaboration than competition, using the similarity in the ethical principles and goals underlying their work to building relationships with other resettlement agencies regardless of religious or secular affiliation.

I anticipated that religious rhetoric would serve as a more powerful tool in accessing human and material resources, and I did find some support for that. However, the fact that faith-based resettlement NGOs were able to access more resources through their organizational networks was confounded by their affiliation with a particular religion. In other words, it might not be the power of religious rhetoric to mobilize resources, but rather the mere access to those resources through a religious affiliation. I suspect that affiliation and rhetoric go hand in hand. While a Jewish resettlement NGO may have access to synagogues that can provide meeting space and furniture donations, the NGO must first mobilize the members of the synagogue to provide those resources, and that mobilization occurs through a rhetoric that entices the synagogue members to act.

Organizational affiliations also make it difficult to know the usefulness of an interfaith ethic of refuge. Faith-based NGOs avoid crossing religious boundaries to access resources, as they do not want to encroach on another organization's funding stream. Secular NGOs also generally avoid accessing resources from religious institutions for the same reason. Therefore, while an interfaith ethic of refuge may make it possible for faith-based NGOs from different religions to communicate, or for faith-based NGOs to collaborate with secular NGOs, it is impossible to know how effective an interfaith ethic of refuge is for mobilizing resources from a broad donor audience.

Perhaps the real power of an interfaith ethic of refuge lies in its capacity to educate the public about the situation of refugees and to advocate for increased admissions, more services, and to elicit more compassion for refugees. While the secular rhetoric of human rights has long been a part of refugee assistance and resettlement, religious rhetoric contains the emphasis on human rights but adds doctrinal mandates of compassion and caring for refugees and a divine calling to serve refugees. Yet faith-based resettlement staff use religious language that is not exclusive to Christianity or Judaism; rather, it has a generic quality that weaves together similarities across different faiths. The similarities in religious rhetoric across different religious traditions make an interfaith ethic of refuge appealing to people from diverse religious backgrounds, and many faith-based resettlement NGOs in my study used an interfaith ethic of refuge in their advocacy efforts. Unfortunately, I do not have data on how effective those advocacy efforts were. I expect, however, that such language could be an effective tool in a political climate in which politicians frequently interweave vaguely Judeo-Christian language with patriotic imagery.[5] One could speculate that in a time of increased religious language and references to the divine, using an interfaith ethic of refuge to advocate for refugees would be a more effective strategy than trying to appeal to the public in secular terms alone.

NOTES

1. One support agency, the U.S. Bahá'í Refugee Office, was affiliated with the Bahá'í religion. This was the only non-Jewish or Christian faith-based NGO in my study.

2. Religious or secular affiliation is not the only factor in volunteer recruitment. NGOs' use of volunteers is also affected by the need for volunteers. NGOs with very small numbers of new refugee arrivals, particularly those resettling predominantly family reunification cases, have less need for volunteers.

3. The Web address for this page as of this writing is http://www.wr.org/gettinginvolved/volunteer/usministries/godlovesrefugees.asp.

4. Resettlement NGOs with access to a long-settled refugee community or relatively affluent refugees (generally Eastern European) were able to raise significant funds from this community. The Bosnian and Herzegovinian American Community Center and Catholic Charities in Los Angeles (with strong ties to the Vietnamese community in Los Angeles and Orange counties) held fund-raising events within their respective refugee communities. However, local NGOs rarely organized fund-raising events among refugees.

5. For a timely example of this language, read President George W. Bush's March 1, 2005, address to the Compassion in Action Leadership Conference (available at http://www.whitehouse.gov/news/releases/2005/03/20050301-4.html).

11

The Catholic Church's Institutional Responses to Immigration

From Supranational to Local Engagement

MARGARITA MOONEY

In the last twenty years the United States has had its highest levels of immigration since the early twentieth century, with about one million new immigrants entering annually (U.S. Immigration and Naturalization Service 1999). Given these trends, immigration policy and immigrant adaptation have risen to the forefront of public debate in recent years, but little is known about how different religious organizations, many of whom do substantial grassroots work with immigrants, have attempted to influence public debates. This chapter addresses one particular religious tradition in the United States—Catholicism—whose public role in American civil society has been profoundly shaped by immigration. I emphasize two new ways of understanding the Catholic church and immigration: (1) its attempts to influence the public sphere and (2) how the church's vertical and horizontal networks allow for the transfer of financial and political resources to disadvantaged immigrants. Specifically, I explore how the U.S. Conference of Catholic Bishops engages immigration in the public sphere. I then use this theoretical lens to explore how national-level Catholic institutions have an impact on the adaptation of one particular immigrant group—Haitians in Miami.

To capture this role of the church in the adaptation of Haitians in Miami, I develop the concept of the church as a *mediating structure* between individuals and the state. Although previous theorists have argued that religious groups generate a parallel set of institutions that allow immigrants to achieve upward mobility (Gordon 1964; Herberg 1983; Hirschman 2004), I argue that the *interaction* between religious institutions, civil society, and the state facilitates successful immigrant adaptation by helping newcomers to overcome unfair government policies and hostile societal attitudes toward them.

The question of social justice for immigrants takes on particular relevance for the case of Haitians in Miami, as Haitians arguably have been one of the most discriminated immigrant groups to the United States of the last three decades. Although much has been written about the Catholic church's social doctrine (Novak 1989; Weigel and Royal 1991), I use a sociological lens to explore how particular institutions and actors apply Catholic teachings on social justice. I identify two ways the Catholic church has promoted social justice for Haitians: (1) by advocating for more fair immigration policies and (2) by providing social services to help adaptation.

Research Design

The data for this chapter form part of a larger project I carried out for my doctoral dissertation in sociology from 2001 to 2003 (Mooney 2005). In my thesis, I compare the role of the Catholic church in the adaptation of Haitian immigrants in Miami, Montreal, and Paris. This present work addresses only the Catholic church in the United States, but the comparative angle of my larger project alerted me to the importance of not only studying the Catholic church's social teachings—which are the same for all countries—but also examining how particular institutions and actors implement these teachings, which varies across time and space.

In order to examine how national Catholic structures may influence the adaptation of a particular immigrant group, I conducted interviews with Catholic leaders at three levels: national, diocesan (city), and local (parish). Because I wanted to see the church as part of civil society, I also interviewed leaders of secular Haitian associations in Miami about their interactions with religious organizations. In total, I conducted thirty-five interviews with Catholic and secular leaders in the United States. In addition to these formal interviews, I carried out seven months of participant observation in Notre Dame d'Haiti Catholic Church in Miami's Little Haiti.

Immigration and the Public Sphere

Most historical and contemporary scholars who have studied the Catholic church and immigrants have written about how the church contributes cultural and economic resources for immigrants in their local communities (Herberg 1983; Hirschman 2004; Menjívar 2003; Thomas and Znaniecki 1927; Zhou and Bankston 1998). However, many of today's immigrant groups such as Haitians may see their adaptation hampered by unfavorable immigration policies and racial discrimination. We know little about how disadvantaged immigrant groups confront challenges to their adaptation that are ultimately questions of social justice—such as protecting basic legal rights, even for noncitizens or undocumented immigrants—and accessing basic health care and education.

Studying how religious institutions contribute to social justice for immigrants broadens our understanding of civil society, as scholars often overlook the important role of religious ideas and institutions in shaping public opinion and policy (Berger and Neuhaus 2000). Rather than just focusing on how internal solidarity with a church community may support immigrants' adaptation, I view the church as an actor in the public sphere, understood as that space in civil society where various actors—governmental and nongovernmental—exchange information and ideas that shape public policy (Cohen 1999). Rather than just noting that the church helps immigrants form many voluntary organizations, we should ask whether the church's public role in supporting immigrants has an impact on our concept of civil society.

Studying the Catholic church's vertical and horizontal networks can also shed light on current debates about civil society and democracy. As Skocpol and Fiorina (1999) argue, much of the scholarship on voluntary associations emphasizes the importance of local-level connections and overlooks that majority of local associations, such as the Rotary Club, belong to federal structures. Given the hierarchical structure of the Catholic church, we can explore whether the church's national and even supranational institutions influence the actions of local-level Catholic leaders.

The Catholic Church and Immigrants: Local, Federal, Binational, and Supranational Structures

At the time of the first U.S. census in 1790, Catholics comprised only 1 percent of the U.S. population (Gordon 1964). Although all Protestant groups together had more members than the Catholic church, by 2000 Catholics had grown to 22 percent of the U.S. population, making Catholicism the single largest religious denomination in the United States (Jones 2002). The massive immigration of Irish, Polish, German, and other European Catholics in the nineteenth and twentieth centuries shaped the church in the United States as largely an immigrant church. What does this mean? First, it means that many of today's members of the Catholic church and its hierarchy are comprised of immigrants and their descendants. A second, and perhaps less commonly understood, meaning of "immigrant church" is that the church's social institutions, including its schools, orphanages, and hospitals have been formed in order to support immigrant adaptation (Oates 1995). In other words, studying the network of Catholic institutions that support immigrant adaptation is a strategic research site to explore how social justice is promoted in specific circumstances.

Although I focus here mostly on the network links between national Catholic institutions and the Haitian community of Miami, it is important to recall that the Catholic church is a supranational institution. Only the pope can define Catholic teachings, but each bishop bears the responsibility of applying church teachings within his jurisdiction. In other words, the central authority of the church in Rome defines *what* the church teaches, and bishops decide *how* to implement those teachings.

The Vatican, and in particular the pope, also may choose to emphasize particular aspects of Catholic teachings at a given point in time. Because of the global importance of migration, and because migration touches the Catholic church in both sending and receiving countries, Pope John Paul II (1978–2005) highlighted migration as one central social question where all members of the church are called to contribute to social justice. For example, during each of the last ten years of his papacy, Pope John Paul II organized a World Migration Day. Each year on this day, he issued a statement reminding Catholics of a particular aspect of the church's teachings that bear on immigrants. These letters, and the other papal documents to which they refer, serve as guides for national and local Catholic leaders about where to focus their efforts to promote social justice.

Because many aspects of national politics influence how the church carries out its mission, for centuries Catholic bishops in the United States, Europe, and elsewhere have been meeting to discuss common challenges, with regards both to public policy and to internal church affairs. In particular, since World War II the U.S. Conference of Catholic Bishops has assumed a greater public role, both calling on the government to serve the needs of the poor and expanding its own outreach to the most vulnerable members of society, including immigrants (Dolan 2005). Despite the fact that in the last fifty years social justice for immigrants has been a central focus of the Bishops Conference, little is known about how this national institution has influenced immigrant adaptation. In this chapter I argue that (1) local Catholic institutions should also be analyzed as being *embedded within a set of horizontal and vertical networks* and (2) Catholic social institutions should be understood *in their relationship to the state rather than as replacing the state.*

One piece of evidence to support this perspective comes from the fact that the structure of the Bishops Conference has evolved along with changes in the U.S. government. The federated organizational structure of the Bishops Conference and its emphasis on social justice began to take shape after World War II when the Catholic church began to partner with the government in resettling the large flows of refugees from Europe. Although many local Catholic institutions had been working on immigrant adaptation and refugee resettlement for years, the bishops decided that their efforts could be better served by creating a central structure to support these local organizations.

Although some might argue that a strong civil society reduces the need for a strong state, other scholars have argued that voluntary organizations may actually grow in tandem with state expansion (Kaufman 1999). A view of civil society that emphasizes the complementarity of rather than competition between civil society and the state more accurately describes the growth of the Bishops Conference. In the 1960s, when the U.S. federal government greatly expanded its role in providing social services, the Bishops Conference also expanded its social outreach programs, in part by bringing what previously had been a separate organization run by Catholic laypeople—the U.S. Catholic Welfare Conference—under its wing.

The choice of Washington, D.C., as the home of the permanent offices of the Bishops Conference further demonstrates this organization's political role. In the eighteenth and nineteenth centuries, cities such as Baltimore in the East, Saint Louis in the Midwest, and Portland, Oregon, in the West had some of the largest Catholic populations and often hosted the meetings of Catholic bishops in the United States. However, the choice of Washington, D.C., as the home to the permanent offices of the Bishops Conference in the twentieth century resulted in the church's desire to strengthen its public role vis-à-vis the expanding federal government (Dolan 2005). The Bishops Conference has not given up its ties to cities that are the heartbeat of Catholicism in the United States today, but it seeks to balance its presence in cities with large numbers of faithful Catholics and with physical proximity to powerbrokers in the District of Columbia. For example, the Bishops Conference holds two annual meetings: the first is generally held in a large archdiocese such as Denver or Saint Paul/Minneapolis and the second is always held in Washington, D.C. Whereas cities such as Philadelphia or New Orleans may claim to have a much stronger Catholic history and culture, there is no doubt that the center of gravity of the Catholic church's political work is located in Washington, D.C. The physical presence of the Bishops Conference in Washington gives the church a voice in federal politics, where lawmakers decide much of immigration policy.

Let us now consider one more evolving aspect of the structure of the Bishops Conference that influences its work on immigration. In 2003, the Bishops Conferences of the United States and Mexico issued a joint pastoral letter about migration between the two nations entitled "Strangers No Longer: Together on the Journey of Hope." Although the content of this binational bishops statement largely reiterates earlier church statements calling for greater social justice for immigrants, the decision to publish a joint statement further demonstrates how the church's structures evolve to mirror the government. As the United States and Mexico move forward in trade and migration agreements, the bishops follow suit by joining their voices to speak to both national governments. Just as the national offices of the Bishops Conference fortify rather than replace local church organizations, binational public statements do not substitute for the church's public work in each nation-state, but this greater cross-border collaboration reinforces the church's mission as a mediator for the poor and disadvantaged.

The U.S. Conference of Bishops and Immigration

Now that we have seen how the Catholic church's structures have evolved as national and international politics have changed, let us turn to the specific content of the church's statements on immigration. The conference's work on migration is coordinated through the office of Migration and Refugee Services, which in turn has three divisions: (1) migration policy, (2) refugee resettlement, and (3) pastoral (spiritual) care. Ten lay Catholics staff these three offices and advise the bishops on their public advocacy. According to its mission statement, Migration and Refugee Services is a central coordinating body for "a network of national pastoral centers, pastoral consultants and diocesan personnel who minister with various ethnic groups" (U.S. Conference of Catholic Bishops 1997). Information flows from different points in the church's local-level agencies up to national-level offices where the lay staff of Migration and Refugee Services work with the bishops who attempt to influence policy through statements and lobbying. In other words, the Catholic church's local-level engagement with immigrants guides the work of the bishops and laypeople at the Bishops Conference.

The specific content of the bishops' statements are shaped as responses to issues that emerge from the many Catholic parishes, refugee resettlement programs, and social service centers such as Catholic Charities. For example, Migration and Refugee Services has offices in dioceses throughout the country carry out the daily work of advising new immigrants, such as helping them apply for legal status or social benefits. In the case of refugees, local offices of Migration and Refugee Services administer government funds to find housing and support the refugees for the first few months. Thus, the church is both a partner of the government and a lobbyist; in fact, the church's history of promoting social justice for the poor and immigrants strengthens its lobbying voice in Washington.

The Bishops Conference is not the only organization in Washington that makes policy suggestions on immigration. What is unique is that the Bishops Conference's statements combine ideas of human rights and religious ideas to justify its call for social justice for immigrants. For example, one Bishops Conference statement that addresses undocumented migration states that "without condoning undocumented migration, the church supports the human rights of all people and offers them pastoral care, education, and social services, no matter what their circumstances of entry into this country, and it works for the respect of the human dignity of all—especially those who find themselves in desperate circumstances" (U.S. Conference of Catholic Bishops 1988). The language in this statement, such as "human rights" and "human dignity," does not refer to any particular biblical passage. However, as the statement continues, it makes more explicit reference to ideas that are rooted in Christian tradition, such as that "all human persons, created as they are in the image of God, possess a fundamental dignity that gives rise to a more compelling claim to the conditions worthy of human life" (U.S. Conference of Catholic Bishops 1988). Whereas the first formulation of human rights does not necessarily require one to ascribe to any particular religious beliefs, the second formulation links concepts of fundamental human dignity to the idea of a single creator. This is significant because, in the public sphere of discourse on immigration, the church frequently refers to ideas that *do not emanate from the political state* (such legal status or citizenship) but from one's human condition, a topic in which the church claims an authority higher than the state.

Other Bishops Conference statements on immigration are intended for internal use in dioceses and parishes. These internal documents more frequently use religious language, such as specific passages from the Old and New Testament, the church's social teachings, and writings of Pope John Paul II. One of the most common biblical passages quoted is Matthew 25:35 "For I was hungry and you gave me food, I was thirsty and you gave me drink, a stranger and you welcomed me." This passage is used to legitimize Migration and Refugee Services' work on behalf of immigrants and refugees as being rooted in "the Gospel mandate that every person is to be welcomed by the disciple as if he or she were Christ himself" (U.S. Conference of Catholic Bishops 1997). These documents serve to remind Catholic faithful that they are responsible to a higher authority than the political authority: their duties as Christians may often go beyond their duties as citizens. Even if a person is undocumented, and thus does not have some political rights, Christians are supposed to welcome that person as if he or she were Christ.

This example further illustrates how the church influences public discourse—by framing public behavior as answering to God's authority, not only the state's authority. When the church makes statements about migration, it calls on sources outside of the political system itself—religious revelation, the gospel, and concepts of human rights. Although the church does not directly determine policy, it reserves the right to critique state action based on principles outside of the state. The church's statements can influence public discourse and public policy either directly by influencing government officials and policies or indirectly by influencing the actions of Catholic faithful. Thus, whereas most lobbyists may be perceived as promoting their self-interest, the church argues for particular policy recommendations based on what it perceives to be universal rights.

Now that it has been shown how the church's national, binational and supranational structures attempt to influence public discourse on immigration, one should ask whether these teachings on social justice have had an impact on the experience of specific immigrant groups. In order to explore this question, I examine the case of Haitians in Miami. Haitians in Miami are a good case to study the Catholic church and immigration because Haiti is a majority Catholic country (Alemán and Ortega 2001) and because many Haitian immigrants in Miami begin their adaptation with little education and urban work skills.

Although the Catholic church is an important cultural force in Haiti and different Haitian communities of the diaspora, I focus on how the structure of the Catholic church influences its public role in the Haitian community, in particular in shaping public opinion and policy regarding immigration. I develop the concept of the church as a mediating structure in the Haitian community that promoted social justice through providing political advocacy and social services to this needy population. The macrosociological lens I developed in the previous section shows how the Catholic church forged its central role as an advocate and social service provider to Haitians in Miami.

The Local Setting and Contexts of Reception of Haitians in Miami

Since the 1960s, when migration to the United States began to include large numbers of Latin Americans, Miami has become one of the top gateway cities for immigrants to the United States. According to the 2000 U.S. Census, by 2000 more than half of Miami's population was foreign born, and of the foreign born nearly all were from Latin America (including the Caribbean).

Miami is distinct from other major U.S. immigrant gateway cities, such as New York or Los Angeles, because it was a relatively small city before the 1960s. The arrival of millions of Latin Americans to Miami in the last few decades has created what scholars have called "the most dramatic ethnic transformation of any major American city this century" (Grenier and Stepick 1992). The influx of immigrants to Miami, which started with the Cuban refugees in the early 1960s, transformed Miami from a sleepy resort town to a booming regional economic hub for Latin America and an international tourist destination (Portes and Stepick 1993). Although white (also called Anglo) Americans maintain an important business presence in Miami, one can safely say that Miami's cultural and political environment is a melting pot of American and Latino cultures. One result of this Latino-Anglo melting pot is that Catholicism, the largest religion in Latin America, has a strong institutional presence and cultural influence among immigrants to Miami. As with previous waves of Italian and Polish immigrants to cities of the Northeast in the early twentieth century, in Miami the Catholic church has flourished as an immigrant church, supporting immigrant adaptation in the cultural, economic, and political realms.

Despite the fact that one might expect Haitians to be welcomed in a majority immigrant city, Haitians who migrate to Miami found a more negative context of reception than in other cities of the Haitian diaspora in North America such as New York, Montreal, or Boston. As Haitians began to arrive in Miami in the 1970s, many of them by boat, the U.S. government created specific policies to prevent Haitian boat people from entering the United States and to make it difficult for them to obtain asylum if they managed to enter undetected (Stotzky 2004). In Miami, Haitians were quickly placed at the bottom of the so-called ethnic queue. In addition, specific stereotypes were formed that harmed the image of Haitians. For example, the Centers for Disease Control (CDC) classified Haitians as one of the main carriers of a new disease in the early 1980s—AIDS.

There was a hysterical scare that tuberculosis was endemic among Haitians and could spread to the entire population of south Florida. Although these fears were later disproved and the CDC eventually removed the classifications, many Haitians reported losing their jobs due to fear of their infection (Stepick 1992).

Despite this negative host society and government reception, the Haitian community of Miami grew to become one of the city's most visible immigrant groups, centered in a residential and business area known as Little Haiti. But how did an immigrant group with low levels of human capital and many undocumented members establish institutions and spokespersons to promote social justice in their community? In the following sections, I describe how the vertical and horizontal networks of the Catholic church and its position as a public advocate generated mediating structures that addressed Haitians' social justice needs.

Mediating Structures

Given the negative publicity surrounding Haitians' arrival in Miami, the lobbying efforts of church leaders in Miami and in Washington were crucial to opening up paths for the legalization of Haitians and to attaining greater government funding to support their settlement and initial insertion into American society. Because the Catholic church has an important political and cultural role in Haiti (Nérestant 1994), Catholic parishes in Miami became a central place to organize volunteer work and leadership among this highly discriminated immigrant group. Different Catholic parishes, in particular an all-Haitian ethnic parish that was founded in Little Haiti, Notre Dame d'Haiti, are embedded within church organizations that have both national and local offices, such as Catholic Charities and Migration and Refugee Services, that provide services for immigrants and the poor. By combining the leadership and experience of Haitian social service workers with money and buildings donated by the Catholic church in Miami, the leader of Notre Dame, Father Thomas G. Wenski, founded a social service center—the Pierre Toussaint Center—on the same property as Notre Dame. This service center, which is faith-based but open to all regardless of religious observance, was started with Haitian volunteers and church funds and since 1981 has grown to be the largest social service center for Haitians in Miami.

Political Advocacy

To understand how the Toussaint Center and Notre Dame came to be central institutions in the Little Haiti, one must also understand the church's public advocacy work on behalf of Haitians. Church leaders drew on the ideas contained in the bishops' statements on immigration, and individual bishops and priests, such as Archbishop McCarthy or Father Wenski (who was later named a bishop) publicly critiqued government treatment of Haitians. Whereas the church was certainly not the only group protesting the treatment of Haitians, the church was unique as a public advocate because it had a grassroots presence in the community and because its leaders had also established themselves as political advocates in Miami and Washington.

The church's national structures supported the social justice work of local church leaders in Miami. For example, Edward J. McCarthy, the archbishop of Miami from 1977 to 1994, relied on the church's national structures to lobby President Jimmy Carter on behalf of Haitians. The director of Catholic Charities in Miami in the 1980s, Monsignor Brian Walsh, influenced one of the judges in Miami who made several favorable decisions for Haitians that opened the door to greater consideration of Haitians' asylum claims (Miller 1984). Statements published by individual bishops or the Bishops Conference made the political climate more welcoming toward Haitians (Laguerre 1984, 1999). Catholic priests in Miami attempted to sway public opinion by visiting the Haitians being held in Immigration and Naturalization Service detention and informing journalists about their conditions. Another way the church helped sway public opinion in favor of Haitians was by informing the press about the political causes of Haitian migration, strengthening sympathy for Haitians' claims to asylum (Miller 1984).

The church's ability to influence the public sphere with regard to policy and attitudes towards Haitians was fortified by its national structures. When Haitian immigrants and refugees began arriving in Miami en masse in the early 1970s, the church already had national structures in place that helped local Catholic leaders—such as Archbishop McCarthy, Monsignor Walsh, and Father Wenski—gain an audience among government officials in Washington. The relationships between the bishops and lay staff members of the Bishops Conference provided local Catholic leaders in Miami with a way to lobby the federal government on behalf of Haitians. In addition, several preexisting church-run programs were expanded to include Haitians, such as the local Migration and Refugee Services office that organized the resettlement of Haitian refugees.

Notre Dame and the Toussaint Center

Although I have thus far emphasized the political advocacy aspect of the church's social justice work on behalf of Haitians, the Catholic church in Miami became an important political actor in the Haitian community in part because of its successful efforts to incorporate Haitians in local church structures. Despite the fact that the Catholic church in Haiti has a large public and social role, this should not obscure the fact that Haitians in Miami had to be "churched"—or incorporated into local church structures in the United States (Finke and Stark 1992). As has historically been the case with the Catholic church and immigrants (Finke and Stark 1992; Hirschman 2004), local church leaders in Miami created new parishes, ministries, and programs to keep Haitians in the church in Miami.

Although many Catholic schools and social programs have helped Haitians' adaptation, the church's efforts to support the Haitian community have centered around a pair of institutions located on the same property: Notre Dame d'Haiti Catholic Mission and the Toussaint Center. These institutions' success in supporting Haitians' adaptation resulted from their connections to vertical and horizontal networks that provided access to resources outside the ethnic community itself.

In the nineteenth and early twentieth centuries, the Catholic church often created national parishes, organized on linguistic lines, to incorporate new immigrants. Although today the Catholic church in the United States prefers to create ethnic ministries for immigrants within an existing parish rather than creating a national parish, church leaders in Miami decided to replicate the national parish model precisely to counteract the strong discrimination against Haitians. The creation of Notre Dame d'Haiti Catholic Mission for Haitians provided Haitian leaders a central organizing place for the Haitian community. At the request of Father Wenski, who led Notre Dame for fifteen years before being nominated as a bishop in 1996, Archbishop McCarthy donated ten acres of property in the center of Little Haiti to build Notre Dame and the Toussaint Center. This support from the archdiocese gave leaders in the Haitian Catholic community a valuable and centrally located piece of property upon which to build an ethnic parish and a social service center for Haitians.

In a context where Haitians were ostracized because of their race, language, and legal status, the church provided them a bridge to participate in civil society by creating an environment that was culturally familiar. In the early 1980s, when virtually no government programs were serving Haitians, the Toussaint Center brought together Haitian volunteers experienced in teaching and social services to launch social programs for the steady flow of Haitian immigrants. This skilled volunteer work—teaching English, teaching Creole literacy, administering emergency financial provisions from church funds—was strengthened by the availability of physical space and startup funds donated by church organizations. In some cases, volunteers from Catholic agencies outside the Haitian community also helped start social programs. Bringing these resources together—Haitians' volunteer work, a physical space (buildings), and the financial resources of the Catholic church—allowed this poor immigrant group to provide a welcoming structure to support Haitians' initial settlement and adaptation. Many of the Haitian volunteers already had experience working in social justice programs in Haiti. By linking up with local offices of Catholic Charities and the leadership of Father Wenski, Haitians were able to transfer those civic skills into a new environment.

Although the church was crucial to attracting volunteer workers and providing startup resources, the programs at the Toussaint Center grew because they attracted outside funding from other Catholic organizations, private foundations, and the government. For example, as Randy McGrorty, the director of the Legal Services Project at the Toussaint Center recounted, he began the Legal Services Project in 1993 with three volunteers, funds from the Jesuit Refugee Service, a shared desk, and a single telephone. By 2002, Legal Services had grown to have thirty-five staff members and had expanded its offices to two other locations in Miami-Dade County. Although Catholic Charities provides some funds for buildings and maintenance for this program, more than half of Legal Services' funding comes from federal funds for refugees, and the rest comes from fund-raising with foundations. The Job Placement Service was a second high-growth program started at the Toussaint Center. What began as a volunteer project in one room of the Toussaint Center has expanded to its own building, a staff of fifteen, and funding from the state government.

Another example is the day care center, which benefited directly from horizontal network ties to other church programs and links to the government. For example, the Archdiocese of Miami transferred an already-existing day care center into the first floor of the Toussaint Center. As enrollment at the day care increased, and as the center received positive evaluations, the director of the day care center, Marie-Laure Fils-Aimé, described how the center began to receive funds from Head Start and United Way; meanwhile, the archdiocese has invested more than half a million dollars to renovate the building. By 2002, the day care center had expanded to have ten classrooms with twenty children in each classroom. Similarly, English and Creole literacy programs were begun with volunteer work and church funding for the building and materials, but now these two programs are funded by Miami-Dade Public Schools. According to the director of the Toussaint Center, by 2002 around 80 percent of the programs offered at the Toussaint Center received government funds administered by Catholic Charities of the Archdiocese of Miami. At its height, around 1996–97, more than one thousand people came to the Toussaint Center daily. By 2002, the flow had decreased to six hundred people a day because legal services and job training now have their own buildings a few blocks away.

The church's mediation for Haitians in Miami is observable not only at the level of public discourse, but also in the daily lives of thousands of Haitians in Miami. With 600–1,000 people coming daily to the Toussaint Center for social services and another 2,500 coming to Notre Dame every week for religious services, the corner of 69th Street and 2nd Avenue is one of the busiest intersections in Miami's Little Haiti. The central location of Notre Dame and the Toussaint make it easy for people to take public transportation, either a bus or a van. The property's familiar cultural symbols make it a welcoming place for Haitians in an unwelcoming environment. As Emile Viard, the director of the Toussaint Center, recounted, at one point there was a proposal to close Toussaint Center's English school and merge it with the one in the neighboring African American area, but leaders of the Toussaint Center protested and claimed people would not go there because *"nou pa gen moun"* (we do not have people there); in other words, Haitians do not feel at home there. The church's cultural and geographical proximity to Haitians, combined with its vertical and horizontal networks that provide access to social programs Haitians need for their settlement and adaptation, has made the church a central institution in Little Haiti.

One should not overlook, however, that Miami may be unique even among other cities where Haitians have settled. In Miami, a city whose population is mostly foreign born, government officials recognize that community organizations, such as churches and religious nonprofits, can help them reach new immigrant groups, whose members are often among the most vulnerable residents. Although many government programs in Miami at first excluded Haitians, with time, local and state government accepted that many Haitians would remain no matter how negative immigration policy was, and some officials began to reach out to the Haitian population. Because the relationship between Haitians and the state was very tenuous, the church's social service agencies, such as the Toussaint Center, provided a needed link between Haitians and the state. When state agencies began to look for an organization to carry out programs in the Haitian community, the Toussaint Center was already in place and had a recognized service record. Thus, the Toussaint Center has grown to be a partner with the state even while maintaining its autonomy and ability to critique government policies.

The church's ability to provide this mediation also rests on the fact that many government officials in Miami themselves are first-generation immigrants accustomed to collaboration with religious organizations in social affairs. For example, Dr. Lumane Claude, a Haitian immigrant who directs a city government office that aims to increase contact between residents and the government, exemplifies the extensive cooperation between church leaders and government officials in Miami. Because the Haitian state is very weak and often oppressive, Dr. Claude recognizes that few Haitians will go directly to the government when they have a problem. Haitians are more likely to trust the church than the government, both because of political repression in Haiti and their negative reception in Miami. Dr. Claude explained that "the church is the only place people can really trust. . . . You see the priest if you don't have food. Hey, you're not going to the government, you're not going to the social services. It's a shame to go to those places, but it's okay to tell the church that you have a problem. They're [Haitians] not thinking of social services, they're thinking of the church." The trust Haitians have in the church leads them to perceive the church as a mediating structure that helps them access resources for their adaptation. State resources are more efficiently distributed because they are channeled through an organization that has a broad grassroots network.

In addition to a favorable local context for church-state partnerships in social programs, the national context also facilitates the church's mediating role in civil society. For example, the Toussaint Center has expanded its programs because it has attained government funding. Although organizations such as Catholic Charities already received government funding before the 1996 Charitable Choice Act (Campbell 2002), the passage of this act and George W. Bush's Office of Faith-Based and Community Initiatives have created certain conditions that strengthened the church's mediating role with the state.

Although local and national politics may create conditions that enable churches to engage public discourse and social services, not all religious organizations take advantage of these opportunities. In fact, many studies have found that some religious groups have a stronger orientation than others toward direct engagement with civil society by founding nonprofit organizations or directly engaging community politics (Ebaugh and Chaftez 2000; Guest 2003; McRoberts 2003; Wuthnow 2004). In Little Haiti, despite the existence of perhaps one hundred Christian churches in Little Haiti, Notre Dame is the only one whose leadership founded a successful community-oriented social service center, the Toussaint Center. A combination of factors—Haitians' trust in the church, skilled volunteers and leaders from Haiti, the archdiocese's donations of land and money, and Catholic church leader's national and local political advocacy that created a more favorable climate and greater funding for social programs for Haitians—coalesced to alter Haitians' context of reception in Miami and create more favorable conditions for their adaptation to American society. Although other religious groups or family networks are also important to Haitians' adaptation, only the Catholic church is positioned as a mediator between Haitians and the state. As a group of immigrants with many undocumented and low levels of human capital, this mediating role between Haitians and the host society is crucial to creating more favorable conditions for Haitians' settlement and adaptation.

Conclusions

Whereas concerns about religion and immigration have often focused on the local level, understanding the national and even international structures of religious institutions furthers an understanding of how local-level religious institutions may promote social justice for immigrants. For the case of Haitian immigrants in Miami, national-level Catholic institutions provide a set of resources—both material resources and political advocacy—that facilitate their adaptation. The church was an effective mediator for Haitians in Miami because it organizes volunteer resources, provides information to the state about the needs of the community, and provides a structure through which the state can channel its resources to Haitians. In some circumstances, religious institutions can become much more than just a place where immigrants re-create their culture or generate social ties that support their employment or education: for the case of Haitians in Miami, the church provides an institutional buffer against discrimination and has become a mediating structure that promotes social justice for disadvantaged immigrants.

As a large institution with a history of philanthropy in the United States, the church can generate valuable resources to support immigrant adaptation through its network of nonprofit organizations and its leaders' mediation on behalf of particular immigrant groups. However, the church would not be an important mediator if Haitians themselves—even those who are not personally religious or are not Catholic—did not look to the church as a place of organizing collective action. Many Haitians who arrived in Miami had participated in the Catholic church's political and social activities in Haiti. They carry this cultural schema with them and seek to organize collective action around the church in Miami. Although the Catholic church in Miami provided important resources such as meeting space and initial seed money to start social programs, Haitians contributed their own resources: leadership experience and volunteer work. It was this combination of preexisting resources in the Catholic church of Miami and Haitians' own resources that allowed Haitians to build an institution—the Toussaint Center—that would serve tens of thousands of Haitian immigrants annually over the past two decades. The Catholic church in Miami provides important resources to help Haitians' adaptation not just because many Haitians have strong religious beliefs, but also because the church draws on its national structures such as the Bishops Conference, and horizontal networks such as Catholic Charities, in order to mediate with the state.

Despite increasingly restrictive policies on immigrant entry and regularization of undocumented immigrants, immigrant flows to the United States do not appear to be slowing down. In this scenario, important elements of immigrant incorporation that were untheorized—such as how immigrants become actors in civil society—take on increasing importance. Until recently, questions about religion and immigration have not been looked at from the angle of civil society and the public sphere. In the United States, although scholars may be aware of the Catholic church's long philanthropic tradition, they have paid relatively little attention to how the church's social justice work influences American politics and civil society. Religious organizations' political work on behalf of immigrants has also largely escaped theories of immigration adaptation, such as the melting pot or segmented assimilation. Although previous theories of religion and immigration often painted a picture where religious institutions provided parallel structures that afforded immigrants a chance for upward mobility, taking a historical and macrosociological approach has shown that religious institutions may be most effective at promoting immigrant adaptation when they serve as a bridge, or mediator, with the government and other civil society institutions.

PART V

Theology, Redemption, and Justice

12

Beyond Ethnic and National Imagination

Toward a Catholic Theology of U.S. Immigration

GIOACCHINO CAMPESE

Christian churches in the United States have ministered to immigrants for about a couple of centuries now,[1] and yet their pastoral effort has not been matched by the elaboration of a substantial and systematic theology of immigration. A Christian "theology of migration" is still at a germinal stage both in terms of its methodology and contents. Christian churches in the United States, both Protestant and Roman Catholic denominations, have abundantly reflected about the ethical, ministerial, and practical implications of the massive presence of immigrants within society and the church (U.S. Conference of Catholic Bishops 1986, 1998, 2000, 2001; U.S. Conference of Catholic Bishops and Conferencia del Episcopado Mexicano 2003; Wilbanks 1996), but it is only quite recently that theologians have begun to grasp the crucial importance of the phenomenon of migration itself as a *locus theologicus*, meaning both a context and a source, for Christian theology in today's world (Campese and Rigoni 2003; Castillo 2004; Espín 2000; Phan 2003, 2004; Schreiter 2003). The relevance of such systematic theological reflection was unambiguously expressed by the participants to the two recent international conferences on migration and theology that took place in Tijuana, Mexico, in 2002 and at the University of Notre Dame, Indiana, in 2004. This audience, made up mostly by Christian lay and clerical ministers—some of them immigrants—voiced the urgent need not only to discern together the import of immigration for Christian life today in the United States, but also to affirm the responsibility of Christian theology to provide the foundations for sacramental, social justice, and advocacy ministry among the immigrants. This essay continues this ongoing conversation by suggesting a number of essential elements for a theology from the experience of immigration in the United States.

A number of important clarifications are in order before I go into the main body of this chapter. First of all, my proposal draws especially from the Roman Catholic tradition. One of the principal developments of the Roman Catholic church has been the birth and proliferation of a great variety of religious groups or orders, which, inspired by their charismatic founders, have developed specific gifts and ministries at the service of the mission of the church. Some of the prominent religious orders in Roman Catholic history are the Franciscans, the Dominicans, and the Jesuits, founded respectively by Saint Francis of Assisi, Saint Dominic, and Saint Ignatius of Loyola. The Missionaries of Saint Charles (or Scalabrinians), the religious institute I belong to, were founded in 1887 by the Bishop of Piacenza (Italy) Giovanni Battista Scalabrini to minister among Italian people immigrating to and settling down in the Americas, particularly the United States and Brazil. In the course of the years the original mission of this religious group has been expanded to include migrants and refugees of all nationalities in twenty-nine different countries around the globe. Today the Scalabrinians are involved in multiple activities within the world of human mobility, such as centers for the study of migration, parish ministry, ethnic missions, border ministry (Casas del Migrante), centers for displaced people, and refugee ministry. Among other things, the Scalabrinians have cosponsored, with the University of San Diego and the University of Notre Dame, the two conferences on migration and theology.

Second, the interpretation of the term "Catholic" that I will employ here points to the original, and more pertinent, meaning of this word. In fact, the term "Catholic" did not emerge as the proper designation of any particular Christian denomination—even though nowadays it is commonly used to refer to the Roman Catholic church—but as an essential dimension of the Christian faith with profound ecumenical, intercultural, and interreligious implications. As it will be explained in the last part of this chapter, the term "Catholic" refers to the fundamental inclusiveness of Christianity.

Third, as an exercise of theological reflection, this chapter follows the traditional definition of theology as *fides quaerens intellectum*, or "faith seeking understanding," originally coined by Anselm of Canterbury (1033–1109). This means that theology begins with a faith commitment in a gracious and loving God in whom we believe and tries to explicate this primary commitment in categories that make sense in a particular time, history, and cultural context. This definition of what theology must be has been influenced by the relatively recent traditions of Christian contextual, liberation, and political thought (Bevans 2005). Consequently, theology is not, and cannot be, simply an intellectual discourse that responds to abstract and conceptual concerns about God. In the words of Kevin Burke (2005, 42): "Theology not only 'thinks' about God, but commits to God's way and acts on God's word. It integrates conceptualization, commitment, and praxis." Liberation theologians observe that "praxis" does not mean simply "practice," but must be rather understood as "intelligent action"—action, analysis, and reflection working together—that liberates and transforms the world. In this way they modify the classic definition of theology into "faith seeking intelligent action" and affirm that theology cannot be authentic if it does not lead to a "praxis" of liberation, social justice, and solidarity (Bevans 2005).

Fourth, in my reading there are two major factors that contribute to the development of a theology of migration today. The first is the constant concern of the church for migrants, which has been expressed in numerous documents issued by the Vatican, such as *Exsul Familia* (1952), *De Pastorali Migratorum Cura* (1969), *Church and People on the Move* (1978), *Refugees: A Challenge to Solidarity* (1992), and *Erga Migrantes Caritas Christi* (2004).[2] These documents constitute the official teaching of the Roman Catholic church on migrants and refugees. At the local level, the U.S. Conference of Catholic Bishops has dedicated major documents to the issue of migration, such as *Together a New People* (1986), *One Family Under God* (1998), *Welcoming the Stranger among Us* (2000), *Asian and Pacific Presence* (2001), *Strangers No Longer: Together in the Journey of Faith* (2003), and has recently launched "Justice for Immigrants," a nationwide campaign for immigration reform in the United States.[3] All these represent important resources for the construction of a theology of migration. The second factor is the emergence of new discourses in the theological scene highlighting the experience of particular groups of disenfranchised people, like the economically poor, women, indigenous people, and "racial others," who were normally excluded from the process of theological reflection. This new development began in the 1960s and 1970s with the birth of Latin American liberation theologies, followed by black liberation theologies, feminist theologies, Asian and African liberation theologies, Latino/a and Asian American theologies in the United States, etc. The objective of these new theological discourses has been the liberation of their oppressed constituencies by affirming and placing their particular experience and concerns at the center of Christian theology. The different proposals for a theology of migration that have emerged, particularly at the two conferences on migration and theology, are deeply influenced by both the official teaching of the church on migration and the new theological developments that underline the liberating potential of Christian faith.

Finally, a theology of migration has to be considered as an interdisciplinary effort that draws upon the social sciences for describing the material realities of migrants, particularly the most vulnerable among them, and interprets them from the perspective of Christian biblical and theological traditions. This interpretation, in turn, forms and inspires Christians to go beyond cultural and national boundaries in order to promote and practice attitudes of compassion, social justice, solidarity, and finally harmonious *convivencia* among and with the migrants.

Migration As a "Sign of the Times"

In the document *Gaudium et Spes* (1965), the Second Vatican Council makes it unmistakably clear that the church has the responsibility of "reading the signs of the times and interpreting them in the light of the Gospel."[4] What does this council mean by "signs of the times"? Theologian Jon Sobrino interprets this concept in two interrelated ways (Sobrino 1995, 2003): in a historical-pastoral sense, as the characteristic marks of a particular period in history, and in a historical-theological sense, as a way in which God reveals Godself and manifests God's presence to humanity and the whole creation.[5] In the framework of this theology of the signs of the times, historical reality is understood both as a material reality that must be thoroughly analyzed and as a theological reality that helps one understand how God is communicating with human beings today (Burke 2005; Sobrino 1995).

Migration fits perfectly this bidimensional profile of the signs of the times. In fact, human mobility, in a historical-pastoral sense, is a major characteristic of the globalized world and contributes significantly to its ongoing globalization. Migrations are not a recent event in world history. People have been migrating from time immemorial, and the Bible offers some of the most important ancient written testimonies of the migration of peoples, tribes, and individuals.[6] What is different today is the quantity, intensity, and global reach of the movements of people. And even though migrants and refugees represent a very small percentage of the world's population, their social and political significance has increased considerably, especially in Western nations. Indeed, this is partly the reason why the current historical period has been defined as the "the age of migration" (Castles and Miller 2003). Migration is also a sign of the times in a historical-theological sense. God's mysterious and elusive divine presence is revealed today in the journey of millions of people who leave their homeland with the hope of a promised land, and who, despite the obstacles and problems they face, witness in faith to a God who becomes fellow Pilgrim in this journey. This contemporary manifestation of God confirms the image of God in the Bible as a "God of the Tent," the God who journeys with God's people (Campese and Rigoni 2003).[7] Migrations can also be read from a theological perspective as one of God's unlikely instruments to bring about unity and solidarity within humankind, a unity often hindered by the rebuilding of walls, the very walls that were torn down by Jesus Christ's ministry, death, and resurrection.[8] Even in the suffering and death of thousands of immigrants at the U.S.-Mexico border, one can detect the incomprehensible presence of a God that is revealed also in the tragic historical reality of the cross (Burke 2005; Sobrino 1995).[9]

It is with the reality of the suffering of the immigrants in mind that I proceed to the next element of my proposal, where I argue that theology is also a truth-telling discourse that starts from a serious reading of the signs of the times in order to confront the reality of immigration in the United States (Copeland 2002).

A Theology from the Reality of Immigration

Theology is a discourse that deals with reality in its entirety—that is, in its historical-material and transcendent dimensions. This understanding of theology and its accompanying methodology were originally proposed by Ignacio Ellacuría (2000) and later reinterpreted by his close friend and colleague Sobrino (1995, 2003).[10] In a foundational essay written in 1975, which has already become a classic text of theological methodology (Isasi-Díaz 2004; Sobrino 1995), Ellacuría starts by drawing a comparison between European and Latin American theology that leads him to the following conclusion: while the former discourse is more interested in the meaning and the understanding of meaning, the latter's objective is the transformation of reality, and of humankind within reality. It is critical to understand the reason for this emphasis on transformation, or liberation, of reality: Latin American liberation theology was born in the context of a Christian continent ravaged by massive oppression, exploitation, poverty, and repressive violence.

According to Ellacuría, theology confronts reality following three steps: (1) *hacerse cargo de la realidad* (realizing the weight of reality), which means that the theologian must get to know reality and become aware of it by being in the midst of reality, and not by just reflecting on the idea of reality; (2) *cargar con la realidad* (shouldering the weight of reality), which is about taking responsibility for reality and realizing the ethical demands that reality makes on one, demands that cannot be evaded; (3) *encargarse de la realidad* (taking charge of the weight of reality), that is, to understand that the fulfillment of the process of knowing and comprehending reality is to become involved in the process of its transformation. To these original three steps Sobrino adds: (4) *dejarse cargar por la realidad* (letting oneself be carried by reality). With this fourth step Sobrino asserts that reality is not just negativity: yes, there is sin and evil within reality, but also grace—that is, the seeds of hope—and the promise of a new heaven and a new earth even in the midst of misery. Mysteriously and surprisingly, it is the victims of sin and negativity—namely, the poor and disenfranchised—that manifest and communicate that hope and promise, which ultimately come from a God who is in solidarity with the victims of history. The play on the term *cargar* in the exposition of this methodology is compelling. Ellacuría and Sobrino envision reality in its totality containing both negative and positive dimensions. Theology has to carry—*cargar*—and confront the negative in order to transform it (*hacerse cargo de, cargar con, encargarse de*), and let itself be carried by the positive (*dejarse cargar por*) with its hope and promise of the Reign of God, the ultimate fulfillment of God's covenant with humankind (Sobrino 1988, 1995).

Ellacuría and Sobrino's methodological proposal is critical because it shows us first of all that a meaningful theology of migration must get to know the reality of migration as it is, in its complex and multifaceted totality. One of the main problems to be faced here is the relentless misrepresentation of immigration by pundits, politicians, and media in the United States. Yen Le Espiritu (2003, 24–25) observes how the U.S. public debate on migration focuses on undocumented immigrants, yet makes invisible another important group of border crossers: "U.S. colonizers, the military, and corporations that invade and forcefully deplete the economic and cultural resources of less-powerful countries." Anti-immigrant discourse takes the attention of the public opinion away from the essential role that economic and foreign U.S. policies have in promoting the movement of peoples from the so-called Third World to the United States. A theology of migration must denounce this cover-up. Here a close conversation and collaboration with social sciences research on the causes and dynamics of international migration is necessary (Castles 2002; Castles and Miller 2003; Massey 2002; Massey et al. 1993).[11] At the same time, in order to know the reality of migration it is essential to be in the midst of it, which means that one must have direct contact with the experience and humanity of the immigrants themselves. This experiential knowledge helps one to remember a fundamental, and often ignored, truth: immigrants are human beings, and not illegal aliens, as they are often portrayed in the mass media.

Secondly, a theology of migration must also assume the responsibility for the ethical demands that emerge from the reality of migration, which are demands for social justice, acceptance, inclusiveness, and human dignity. Thus, this theology takes responsibility for the elaboration of a critical discourse that grounds these concerns and demands within the Christian tradition. In other words, it is not enough to repeat the popular affirmations that the United States is a nation of immigrants, or that the Roman Catholic church is a church of immigrants. These statements must be followed up by a serious and sustained reflection on the implications of these claims for our lives as human beings and Christian believers.

Thirdly, a theology of migration commits itself to the liberation of the reality of migration from whatever threatens the human dignity and rights of the immigrants, and to its transformation into a truly human reality. Saint Irenaeus used to say: *Gloria Dei, vivens homo*, the glory of God is the living human being (Sobrino 2003).[12] A theology from the reality of migration in the United States must claim as its final objective the glory of God in the living immigrant, the immigrant who can enjoy fully and with dignity her or his life in this land.

Finally, this theology recognizes that the reality of migration in the United States is not only a story of suffering and marginalization. In the midst of negativity and seemingly insurmountable problems, the hope, faith, and courage of the immigrants have left their imprint showing the incredible resilience and strength of the human spirit, thus revealing the incomprehensible and mysterious presence of God within this complex reality.

Interestingly enough, the ministerial trajectory of Bishop Giovanni Scalabrini—founder of the Scalabrinians—bears some resemblance with the dynamics of this methodology. Bishop Scalabrini was more a pastor and a minister than a theologian, and yet in his writings on migration (Tomasi 2000) one can discover traces of Ellacuría and Sobrino's method. The term "traces" is used on purpose, since Scalabrini's writings must be read within the potentialities and limitations of his historical, geographical, ideological, and theological context. Still, here there is a person of deep Christian faith who decided to confront directly and honestly the reality of Italian emigration; a man who got to know the reality of migration not just as an idea, but from within, thanks to his constant contacts with the migrants, which in turn led him to become a student of this phenomenon; a pastor who allowed himself to be challenged by the ethical demands emerging from the reality of migration; a church leader who asked the question "What can I do?" in terms of transforming the reality of migration; and a Christian who was able to see in this complex reality the providential hand of God.

A Theology from the Option for Undocumented Immigrants

Latina theologian María Pilar Aquino (1999, 29) rightly observes that the option for the poor "is the identifying mark of all theologies that belong to the wider family of liberation theology." The option for the poor is not just the decision to help the poor, but it is primarily an epistemological and hermeneutical option: theology realizes that in order to know God it has to opt for the poor (Aquino 1999), because God's voice can be heard, and God's presence in history is mysteriously revealed, where the poor are. It is from the poor that reality can be interpreted more honestly. The poor represent more than insignificant and helpless people: they are a fundamental *lugar teológico (locus theologicus)*, a context and source, for doing theology (Ellacuría 2000).

Following this argument, I contend that the most vulnerable immigrants are a crucial *locus theologicus* for a theology from the reality of immigration in the United States. Who are the most vulnerable immigrants in the United States? Here I prefer to avoid the term "poor" because it could be interpreted only from the perspective of economic deprivation, and generally the migrants are not the economically poorest people, both in their countries of origin and destination. Therefore, I adopt the category of "vulnerability," by which in the context of migration I mean legal apartheid, social and political invisibility, cultural debasement, family separation, gender discrimination, physical risk, etc. In other words, the most vulnerable migrants are those who risk the most—even their very lives—and are often powerless vis-à-vis the prejudice of U.S. society and harsh immigration laws: undocumented immigrants, among them particularly women and minors. It is from their epistemologically privileged perspective that theology must read the reality of migration and uncover the presence of God within that reality (Campese and Rigoni 2003).

Despite their situation of powerlessness, undocumented immigrants are not just helpless victims. It has been observed that the contemporary paradigms of immigrants *as* risk and immigrants *at* risk, while valid, do not describe the reality of immigrants in its entirety (Ruiz 2003). Immigrants are not simply to be considered as a threat to society or as victims of society's greed and hypocrisy. They are also people who *take* risks, meaning human beings who, armed with faith, hope, and courage, become aware of their human worth and precious contribution to the civil and religious community, and take the risk to assert them against great odds. This became obvious during the Immigrant Workers Freedom Ride 2003 in the United States (Campese 2004). But it is not only in these public events that undocumented immigrants are becoming active subjects of their own history; it is also in *lo cotidiano*—that is, in their daily lives (Isasi-Díaz 2004): *la lucha*—the struggle—of immigrant women to survive the journey toward *el Norte*, the crossing of the border, and the detention and abuses by *la Migra*; the effort to keep the family united and support it with great sacrifices, overcoming fear of deportation and, often, domestic violence; the responsibility to educate and raise their children who are growing up in a different world, etc. These are some of the daily stories that make up the "real" reality of migration and that unfortunately are often neglected by academic analyses and discourses. A theology of migration emphasizes the perspective of the most vulnerable, invisible, and excluded immigrants. Their story has to be included to create a comprehensive and relevant picture of the reality of immigration in the United States, and to hear God's voice within this reality.

A Critical Theology of Migration

It is not possible to do theology today anywhere in the world without seriously engaging the critique of the role of religion and God in ideologies and societies. When the name of God is used to justify wars against so-called evildoers, and when so-called believers are willing to become human bombs in order to indiscriminately cause death and fear in the heart of a community, it means that it is time for theology to deal with what Nobel laureate Jose Saramago has called the "God factor." Saramago says that the God factor has opened the door to the worst acts of intolerance in human history. In God's name everything has been permitted and justified, the worst, the most cruel, and horrendous actions (Saramago 2001). When Christianity is employed to support a hegemonic, militaristic, and neocapitalistic agenda like the one implemented after the tragic events of 9/11 by the U.S. government—thanks to the committed and influential

support of the Christian right—then we have enough reason to define this supposedly Christian ideology as a theology of empire (Wallis 2003).

Journalist Bill Moyers (2005) puts it well: Jesus, the prophet of Nazareth
who preached the Good News to the poor, who had compassion for the vulnerable and the marginalized, who proclaimed forgiveness and love of enemy as a
way of life, has been hijacked by the Christian right in the United States. He, the
champion of the poor and oppressed, has been transformed into a guardian of
privilege. In the meantime, prophetic Christianity appears to be overwhelmed
by the powerful Christian right and seems to have lost its voice. This development hinders the elaboration of a liberating theology of migration. While, as
Pierrette Hondagneu-Sotelo has rightly observed in the introduction to this volume, the Christian right has not been directly involved in the immigration debate
in the United States, its kind of theology certainly does not promote the cause of
vulnerable immigrants, but, in the context of the war on terror, encourages
people to view them rather as potential enemies. A theology that loses sight of the
prophetic Jesus of Nazareth loses sight also of the disenfranchised and excluded
people he championed and loved until death. And if one loses sight of the marginalized, such as the undocumented immigrants and asylum seekers, then one
will miss the main features of a theology from the reality of migration: liberation, social justice, compassion, and solidarity for and with the more vulnerable
members of society. At the same time, by disregarding the marginalized immigrants, one disregards crucial sources to know reality and God properly. In other
words, to have a theology of migration, it is imperative, as Moyers says, to "get
Jesus back" from those who are using him to bless inhumane, and ultimately
un-Christian, economic and political agendas.

A Political Theology of Migration

A theology of migration must necessarily be a political theology, not only because,
like any authentic theology, it is geared toward the transformation of the *polis*—
the society—but also because it deals with one of the most controversial political
issues of the times. Here are some of the challenges that, in my reading, a political theology of migration must face. This theology must denounce and unmask
the structures of inequality and the myths about international and U.S. immigration, which serve the purpose of maintaining the privilege of the few while
allowing the exclusion and exploitation of the many. Stephen Castles (2004,
223) has remarked that "migration control is really about regulating North-
South relationships and maintaining inequality." To support the option of migration control, "one of the great fictions of our age" has been fed to the public
opinion: "that the 'new economy' does not need '3-D workers' [dirty, demand-
ing, and dangerous] anymore." (Castles 2002, 1152). This kind of hypocrisy has
led to the implementation of U.S. border control policies that are costing the

lives of thousands of immigrants in the U.S.-Mexico border region, and billions of dollars to U.S. taxpayers. The truth is that behind these policies there are hidden political agendas: the government has to give the impression that it is protecting the sovereignty of the nation and securing it from terrorists and unwanted foreigners, when in reality it cannot stop immigration "because this meets important economic or labour market objectives" (Castles 2004, 214). The ideal would be to deal with the root causes of migration, but this is not as politically and economically viable as enforcing restriction measures to supposedly stop migration (Castles 2004). The cost that immigrants, native laborers, and the taxpayers have to shoulder is not the issue. The real issue is what the market economy and the American way of life need to keep on going.

The reality of immigration calls for the transformation of the internal politics of U.S. Christianity itself. This is certainly true for Roman Catholics faced with a critical political challenge that Brian Hehir has described by questioning the usual description of the Roman Catholic church as just an immigrant church:

> We are both a "post-immigrant Church and a "newly-immigrant" Church. . . . Catholics, whose ancestors came here from the mid-nineteenth to the mid-twentieth century, now sit in every major profession and institution in this country. Catholics are now at the center of American life. That means post-immigrant. But that is no longer the whole story; we are a newly immigrant Church. The immigrants today do not come from northern Europe or southern and eastern Europe so much; they come from Asia, Latin America, Central America, and more recently the Balkans and Africa. And we, therefore, are now a Church that is both at the center of American life and back out at the edge again. We are a "center-edged" Church. . . . This is not just an interesting fact; it is a fact with potential. People at the center of society often do not know people at the edge; people at the edge have few contacts with the center. A Church that is a "center edged" Church cannot be two Churches. (Hehir 2003, 21)

How are we going to realize the potential Hehir is pointing at if the post-immigrant does not communicate with the newly immigrant and vice versa? Can immigration, the plight of undocumented immigrants, become an issue around which the post-immigrant and the newly immigrant churches unite and struggle for a better and more inclusive society and Christian community? The stakes are high, and the post-immigrant church is not quite ready to share power and give up some of its beliefs and customs to build up a different church. Yes, a different church, because the new immigrants come from everywhere except Europe, and as Stephen Warner (2004, 20) has observed, they "represent not the de-Christianization of American society, but the de-Europeanization of American Christianity." Is U.S. Christianity, and the U.S. Roman Catholic church, ready and willing to be "de-Europeanized"?

This is also the challenge that the whole U.S. society, and not just U.S. Christianity, must confront, a challenge that has led academics such as Samuel Huntington (2004) to write the apology of the supposedly Anglo cultural identity and integrity of the United States. If U.S. society, church, and theology want to honestly engage with the new immigrants and their different cultures, then they will have to deal with what German theologian Johann Baptist Metz calls the "dangerous memories," which are not the memories of the "good old days," but memories "that make demands on us" (Burke 2005, 35). They are the old and recent immigration memories of discrimination, suffering, and death. They are the memories of the anti-Catholic and antiforeign powerful nativist movement that developed before the Civil War in response to the massive influx of Irish and German Catholic immigrants (Dolan 2002), a story of persecution and prejudice that has been conveniently forgotten today in the face of Catholics and other immigrants coming from Third World countries. They are the memories of immigrants' most recent struggles for dignity and rights (Campese 2004). They are memories that question one's responsibility vis-à-vis the injustices that new immigrants suffer. These memories challenge the two traditional modes of incorporation in the society of destination: assimilation, which means to basically renounce to one's culture of origin and adopt fully the local social and cultural practices in order to become a citizen; and differential exclusion through which immigrants are accepted just as workers with no right to family reunification and permanent stay, and are excluded from social and political participation. Castles (2002, 1155–1156) notes that "both assimilation and differential exclusion share an important common principle: that immigration should not bring about significant change in the receiving society." A political theology of migration in the United States cannot side with "a cheap recognition of cultural diversity," which will repeat the same story of the good old days when immigrants were really assimilating to U.S. culture—meaning Anglo dominant culture. This ideology will include diversity superficially, as an embellishment just to give color to public rituals, but not to share power and certainly not to bring about significant change. A political theology of migration must, on the contrary, foster a costly recognition of cultural diversity that will allow one to know the dark or dangerous side of the story of U.S. assimilation and differential exclusion, and eventually can lead to conversion, significant changes, and real inclusion of the diversity of the immigrants (Burke 2005).

A political theology of migration must also become aware of the global responsibility that the immigrants themselves acquire by simply residing in the United States. Peter Phan (2004, 738) reminds us: "New immigrants in America, willy-nilly, are part of this system of racial, gender, economic, and political exploitation and domination. None of them now have clean hands, even though they may have come to the United States from poor and oppressed countries." In other words, immigrants do not have to forget that they now live in the only

remaining superpower in the world, a superpower that with its policies has
shown its desire and will to dominate, exploit, and oppress. In this context
immigrants can either turn a blind eye to imperialistic U.S. policies or can opt
to become a prophetic voice that denounces international abuses of power and
promotes global compassion and solidarity (Min 1999; Phan 2004).

A Catholic Theology from the Reality of Migration

The irruption of liberation theologies in the theological scene in the 1960s has
also represented a renewed emphasis on the relevance of context in Christian
theology. Theology has become once again a conscious contextual discourse that
takes ethnicity quite seriously, as shown by the proliferation of local theologies
such as African American, indigenous, Latino/a, and Asian American theologies.
Yet, from some of the same theologians who have been among the protagonists
of this contextual and ethnic development comes now an important call: it is
time to go beyond a theology of identity and particularity; it is time to elaborate
a theological discourse that builds on solidarity, communication among different constituencies and cultures—an intercultural theology—and common eman-
cipatory projects (Aquino 1999; Min 2004; Phan 2003; Valentín 2004).

A truly Christian theology has to balance its attention between local and
global concerns (Schreiter 1997). A truly Christian theology cannot be bogged
down with sheer particularism. Anselm Min (2004, 138) elucidates this point
well: "A God in whom only a particular group can find itself to the exclusion of
other groups, even when that group is an oppressed group, is only a tribal God,
not the Christian God; a discourse about such a God may be tribal lore but not
Christian theology." In other words, we need a truly catholic theology. It is necessary to emphasize that "catholic" is not used here as the proper name of the
Roman Catholic church. The original meaning of this term needs to be urgently
recovered, and to do that we have to go beyond its confessional or denominational use (Bosh 2001). "Catholic," in its root sense, means "according to the whole,
or to all." For example, the witness about Jesus from the Gospels was considered
catholic because it included all perspectives, the four different Gospels. The
church was catholic because it was the church according to the witness of all the
apostles, and not just one of them. In other words, "catholic" is not so much, as
it has been traditionally taught, about universality, being everywhere, but about
inclusiveness (González and Pérez 2002). It is the inclusion of all, concern for
the whole (Marzheuser 1995) and commitment to dialogue (Bosh 2001) that
makes the church and theology catholic. Orlando Espín explains it beautifully:

> The Church is "catholic" because its doors are open to every human being,
> and to every human group, without distinction and without barriers. The
> Church is "catholic" because it refuses to assume that one human culture

is superior to others, or that one human culture or nation is better suited as witness and bearer of the Christian gospel. Indeed, it is part of the very definition of catholicity that national, cultural, racial, political, gender, and economic barriers must come down as a direct consequence of God's revelation in Christ. (Espín 2000, 55)

To be Catholic is not just a quality and a gift, but a vital challenge for Christian churches and theology. I believe that this challenge can be realistically faced by relying more on the power of imagination. Sandra Schneiders explains the crucial importance of imagination in a world in which individuals have been taught mainly to function as rational beings. She says that imagination is "our constructive capacity to integrate our experience into dynamic and effective wholes which then function as the interpretive grids of further experience" (1986, 16). Anthony Gittins (2002, 48) adds: "If we are to be led by the Holy Spirit or if we are to look creatively to find where the Holy Spirit might actually be working, then we need imagination. Without it we will be imprisoned in the indicative way of thinking; with it we will be able to ask *What if?* and *Why not?*"

Yet, it is not enough to assert that imagination is needed to nourish the catholic quality of theology and Christian life. Perhaps the problem here is not lack of imagination, but that our imagination is sick and needs healing. Schneiders maintains that "a healthy spirituality requires a healing of imagination which will allow us not only to think differently about God but to experience God differently" (1986, 19). In other words, to have a healthy theology from the reality of migration we need to heal U.S. imagination so that we will not only start thinking about God and immigrants differently, but also experience and relate to both differently.

What is the problem with U.S. imagination? The problem is, in my opinion, the absolutization of limited goods, such as nationalism and sovereignty, over against truly absolute goods, such as the interdependence and solidarity of the human family (Hehir 2003). The problem is that "we have allowed our imaginations to be so bounded so that we are left with a nation full of borders, borders that too easily become fault lines" (Chang 1997, 251). Linda Bosniak (1996) in her analysis of the debate surrounding the opposition to Proposition 187 in California shows how even the progressive critics of this proposition were bounded by a national imagination that did not allow them to radically question this proposal, and to include the lives of undocumented immigrants in the discussion simply because they are beyond the borders of the national political community.

Taking her clue from Bosniak, Cuban American theologian Daisy Machado (2002) detects this national imagination at work even in U.S. progressive Christian theologies. She recognizes that the suffering and struggle of undocumented women are not being included in the Christian theological discourse in the United States because "women, feminists and womanists, still speak from a culturally and historically shaped social location that in very real ways limits their perspective" (Machado 2002, 173).[13] The point is that if theology remains within the boundaries of a national imagination, the reality of migration, the experience of immigrants, the plight of undocumented immigrants will all be left out. And as Stephen Kim has observed, with the exclusion of immigrants, the concept of U.S. community is truncated and falsified (González 1992). In the same way, the concept of U.S. Christian theology will be truncated and falsified if we do not include the immigrants. This is why theology needs an imagination that stretches beyond the borders of the U.S. national reality. It needs, in other words, a catholic imagination, meaning an open and inclusive imagination, which allows us to discover God's presence in other cultures, religions, and indeed in the whole cosmos. What is at stake here is our very Christian identity, and the relevance and significance of our faith. We either believe in the catholic God of all nations, the God who created all things, or we believe in a tribal God, who, as Min warned us, is not the Christian God, and whose theology is not Christian theology.

How do we acquire and promote a Catholic imagination? There is no definitive answer, but I am quite sure that we will not get there by simply professing every Sunday that we are a Catholic church.[14] I do not believe we are making that case very well yet, and certainly many, perhaps too many, of us Christians, and Roman Catholics, did not get it. As a matter of fact, it is not uncommon to hear Christian churchgoers and leaders making demeaning and un-Christian comments about immigrants. Jürgen Moltmann reminds us that to be Catholic is a movement, a mission, and a hope. In other words, it is an endless journey. Perhaps a good way to start is precisely by confronting honestly the reality of immigration in the United States, by relating to immigrants, especially undocumented immigrants, and by looking at reality from their perspective. After all, it is migrants who are today the most credible prophets of catholicity (Tassello 2001), the people who with their sheer presence challenge us to be Catholic, to be open and inclusive, and to worship and give glory to a God that mysteriously and surprisingly reveals Godself within the diversity, movement, and vulnerability that characterizes the experience of immigrants and the reality of immigration in the United States.

Conclusion

The goal of this chapter has been to elaborate a tentative framework for a theology from the reality of immigration in the United States. I have proposed this framework in terms of six essential, and interrelated, elements, which do not, and cannot, encompass the complexity and variety that characterizes the phenomenon of migration. Much more reflection, interdisciplinary research, and experience from within are needed in this relatively new field of theological reflection. The hope is that the present proposal can at least provide an idea of the importance and complexity of this task, and at the same time stimulate more discussion and interest in the theology of migration.

In conclusion, I can say that this must be a theology done with memory and imagination (Phan 1999). It has to thoughtfully remember and reflect on the dangerous memories of the old and recent past, from those of our migrant ancestors in the faith—Abraham, Sarah, Moses, Ruth, and Jesus himself, the Incarnate God who adopted a border crossing and border stretching attitude and vision as a way of life—to the struggles of the new immigrants to be recognized within U.S. society. And it requires a Catholic imagination that makes people aware of and inspires them to take on the intercultural, interreligious, and liberation challenges that the multifaceted reality of migration presents today in the United States (Phan 2004). It is by accepting these challenges that Christians will start realizing the *Gloria Dei*, "the immigrant fully alive," and imagine and work on a different U.S. society, a society that is more compassionate, humane, inclusive, and just.

NOTES

1. For more information regarding the ministry of Christian denominations among immigrants in the United States, see, for instance, the Web sites of the Lutheran Immigration and Refugee Service at http://www.lirs.org, the Presbyterian church at http://www.pcusa.org/immigrant, and the Migration and Refugee Services of the United States Conference of Catholic Bishops at http://www.usccb.org/mrs.

2. Some of these documents are available at http://www.vatican.va.

3. Some of these documents are available at http://www.usccb.org/mrs. The "Justice for Immigrants" campaign has a bilingual (English and Spanish) Web site at http://www.justiceforimmigrants.org.

4. In the Roman Catholic tradition, an ecumenical council is a meeting of the leadership of the whole church. The Second Vatican Council (or Vatican II) represents a watershed in the recent history of the Roman Catholic church, whose consequences and implications are still felt today. During this council, bishops and lay observers from around the world met in Rome in different sessions between 1962 and 1965 to discuss the state and mission of the church. One of the outcomes of this event was a series of documents covering different aspects of the life of the church (Flannery 1975).

5. The historical-pastoral and the historical-theological readings of the signs of the times are supported respectively by paragraphs 4 and 11 of the document *Gaudium et Spes* (Flannery 1975, 905, 912).

6. See Gen. 12:1; Exod. 1: 8–14; the Book of Rut; Ps. 137: 1–4; Matt. 2: 13–15; I Peter 1:1.

7. See Exod. 33: 7–11; 2 Sam. 7: 1–7; John 1:14.

8. Ephesians 2:14–16 reads: "For he [Jesus] is our peace; in his flesh he has made both groups into one and has broken down the dividing wall, that is, the hostility between us. He has abolished the law with its commandments and ordinances, that he might create in himself one new humanity in place of the two, thus making peace, and might reconcile both groups to God in one body through the cross, thus putting to death that hostility through it."

9. An essay on this topic entitled "¿Cuantos Más? The Crucified Peoples at the U.S.-Mexico Border" was published in the proceedings of the International Conference on Migration and Theology, University of Notre Dame, September 19–22, 2004.

10. Ignacio Ellacuría and Jon Sobrino are two Basque Jesuits who lived and worked in El Salvador beginning in the late 1940s, except from some years of further studies and forced exile in Europe. They are considered among the most outstanding voices of Latin American liberation theology. Ellacuría was killed together with other five Jesuits, an employee, Julia Elba, and her teenager daughter, Celina, on November 16, 1989, by special units of the Salvadoran army. At the time of his assassination, Ellacuría was the rector of the UCA (Universidad Centro Americana "José Simeón Cañas") in San Salvador, El Salvador.

11. Also in this area I follow the lead of Latin American liberation theology. For centuries theology's closest conversation partner has been philosophy, traditionally defined as *ancilla theologiae*, the servant of theology, but liberation theology, with its focus on the transformation and liberation of reality, has emphasized the primary importance of social sciences to obtain a better knowledge of the causes and dynamics of its social, economic, political, and cultural context. This development in no way diminishes the significance of philosophy in the elaboration of liberationist theological discourse.

12. Irenaeus was bishop of Lyon (southern France) during the second century C.E.

13. Womanist theology is a current within black women's liberation theology in the United States that addresses the racism of white feminist and white male theologians, and the sexism of black and white male theologians.

14. The Nicene-Constantinopolitan Creed, or profession of faith, that is proclaimed every Sunday or during the major liturgical celebrations of the main Christian denominations professes that the church is "one, holy, Catholic, and apostolic."

13

Caodai Exile and Redemption

A New Vietnamese Religion's Struggle for Identity

JANET HOSKINS

Caodaism is a new religious movement that was born in French Indochina in 1926 with a vision of religious unity and interracial harmony, formulated in contrast to colonial dislocations and repressions. From its inception, Caodaism has been preoccupied with seeking justice in this world and healing the wounds of colonialism, as well as combining the Asian spiritual traditions of Buddhism, Confucianism, and Taoism in a new and dynamic religious organization that borrows from Catholicism and the French and American constitutions. Its scriptures, or sutras, come from spirit messages revealed to mediums, so its practice offers the possibility of a more personal conversation with God. The most famous Caodaist of the twentieth century, Pham Cong Tac, often erroneously called the "pope" of Caodaism, was in fact a spirit medium with the title "Defender of the Faith" (*Ho Phap*), whose college of mediums (Hiep Thien Dai, or Palace to Unite with Heaven) presented the doctrines and laws of the new religion.[1] He taught that justice could only be achieved when the people of the world realized that all religions came from the same origin, and accepted to live peacefully with others of different cultures and races.

Caodaism grew rapidly in early twentieth-century Indochina and had about four million disciples by the 1940s and 1950s. Although persecuted by both the French colonial government and the U.S.-sponsored Diem regime, it encountered its greatest hardships after the fall of Saigon in 1975, when the Communist victory virtually closed the religion down for many years. In the 1980s and 1990s, Vietnamese refugees began rebuilding their religion in exile, and by the turn of the twenty-first century there was a well-established transnational organization. The largest congregations of overseas Caodai disciples are found in California, and it is here that diasporic politics are also most accentuated, in both the "little Saigon" of Orange County and the "littler Saigon" of Silicon Valley.

This chapter examines how efforts to reconstitute Caodaism as a religion in California have been linked to struggles for social justice on four fronts. First, Caodaist exile is pictured as an exodus from the homeland in search of religious freedom, with a divine mission to spread this new faith of tolerance and unity around the world. This retrospective vision provides a meaning and a theodicy for the many years of war and suffering that Vietnamese refugees experienced, and it explains why the hardships of persecution, concentration camps, and dangerous escapes have only reinforced their faith. The trauma of flight is reinterpreted as a triumph of God's plan to globalize his message.

Second, diasporic politics focusing on the homeland have led to political activism in the field of human rights, religious freedom, and interfaith relations. There is a division between those activists most concerned with rebuilding the religion in Vietnam and those most concerned with expanding it to reach a wider audience in the United States. I refer to these two positions as the "religion in exile" vs. the "global religion of unity."

Third, Caodaism was founded as a more worldly version of Asian spirituality, and so its American disciples have also focused on various forms of social work, community activism, and resettlement efforts. These have included networks to help refugees find lost family members, reunite separated siblings and/or parents and children, and train for professional jobs. There are those who argue that during the early period, from 1975 to 1990, virtually all activities were directed primarily to social goals, but since 1990 it has been possible to pay more attention to theological and philosophical questions, as many refugee families are now established in new homes and professions in California.

Fourth, the help extended to Vietnamese refugees by Christian churches was not in fact disinterested charity, but part of a carefully calibrated campaign to gain converts from vulnerable refugee populations. Caodaists argue that since their faith is a modern one, an updated version of Asian traditions, it has been able to resist some of these pressures better than Buddhism, which has been described as hiding its face in California immigrant enclaves, where many other refugees have been pressured to convert to Protestant Christianity or Mormonism (Ong 2003).

I will begin with ways in which Caodai religious visions have always been preoccupied with issues of social justice, and the intersection between prophecy and history that has created the Caodai overseas mission. Then I will look more closely at the social and political issues that engage Caodaists in California today and their oscillation between a diasporic perspective and one more focused on global evangelization.

Caodaist Visions of Social Justice: Origins in Anticolonial Struggle

Caodaism was born in French Indochina at the same time as the nationalist movement for independence, and its political history is closely tied to the spiritual needs of a new generation of intellectuals, trained in the finest French language schools but unable to assume positions of any real responsibility in the colonial bureaucracy. They worked as civil servants for a regime that educated them in democratic ideals but refused to follow these ideals in practice. In 1925–26, as student strikes shook the capital with protests, a group of younger office workers, hoping to find poetic inspiration by contacting the great literary minds of the past, began to practice spiritism, inspired both by Alain Kardec and by many centuries of Taoist automatic writing. They received a series of messages preaching that a unified religion was needed to make the brotherhood of man a reality, in which Jesus joined voices with the Jade Emperor, the Chinese poet Li Tai Pe, and the female Bodhisattva Quan Am in arguing for a truly multiracial pantheon combining elements of Eastern and Western traditions.

On Christmas Eve 1925, the Supreme Being, using the name Caodai ("roofless tower") announced to his disciples that this new faith was born to address the new needs of people in a global age of communication: "Formerly people lacked transportation and therefore did not know each other. I then founded at different epochs and in different areas, five branches of the Tao: Humanism, Shintoism, The Way of the Saints, The Way of Immortals and The Way of the Buddhas, each based on the customs of the respective race. In present days, transportation has been improved and people have come to know each other better but do not live in harmony because of the very multiplicity of their religions. That is why I have deigned to unite all of the religions back into one, to return them to the primordial unity" (Bui and Beck 2000, 14–15). The new religion emerged as a response to the crisis of modernity and particularly literacy—the Supreme Being made his first appearance as the first three letters of the Romanized Vietnamese alphabet (a á ae). It was born, as it has been argued nationalism was also born, in the context of the new possibilities opened up by print capitalism (Anderson 1983), and it is expanding now through an online network where the divergent branches and orthodoxies are best identified by their Web sites.

Caodaists worship a pantheon of nine deities, beginning with the Left Eye of God, whose radiant light shines out from the top of every one of its temples and cathedrals. Below that stands Buddha, flanked by Lao Tse on his right and Confucius on his left, then Li Tai Pe (a Tang Dynasty poet of nature), flanked by Quan Am (sometimes called "the Chinese goddess of mercy") and the terrifying red-faced warrior Quan Cong. Jesus Christ stands on the third level, showing his bleeding heart, and Khuong Thai Cong on the fourth level, representing East Asian traditions of venerating heroes, spirits, and ancestors.

The saints of Caodaism—who famously include figures like Sun Yat-Sen, Joan of Arc, Shakespeare, Descartes, La Fontaine, Lenin, and Louis Pasteur—are not the products of a bureaucratic canonization process, as in the Catholic church, but are instead the spirits of great men and women who chose to reveal themselves to Caodai spirit mediums and engage in a conversation with sages of all ages about the proper direction that the new religion should take. The main scriptures of Caodaism—its sutras or sacred texts—are derived from 170 spirit messages received by Tay Ninh mediums from Christmas Eve 1925 until 1935, and these spirit messages instructed the original twelve disciples on how to build their churches and cathedrals, which prayers and offerings to make, and how to lead a religious movement that should eventually establish peace and harmony between all peoples, races, and religions. The conversations made possible by séances with European literary and historical figures created a space for a moral critique of colonialism, within the context of the early twentieth century, when the religion itself made an argument that Asians and Europeans were part of the same moral community and should obey the same ethical principles.

Caodaism was envisioned in the 1920s and 1930s as an autonomous community that had many of the characteristics of a Catholic mission station— schools, hospitals, weaving, and craft centers, even a fledgling university, with a governmental structure of its own. French colonial policies—which shifted from persecution to accommodation and alliance in the mid 1940s and 1950s—turned this into a state within a state in the overwhelmingly Caodaist province of Tay Ninh. During its heyday of political influence, Caodaists had their own police and armed forces, collected their own taxes, and lived out a Gandhiesque vision of a separate peace (Thompson 1937). Western journalists described the Holy See in Tay Ninh as a medieval walled city ruled by a Pope with a private army, but it is perhaps more accurate to see it as a hierarchical religious community similar to Buddhist theocracies in Tibet (Fall 1995; Greene 1955; Jensen 2000; Lewis 1951). During many long years of war, the Holy See served as a sanctuary for many people fleeing violence, although it was itself twice invaded—first by the French, who exiled its religious leaders from 1941 to 1946 for allegedly prophesying a Japanese victory, and second by the U.S.-supported Diem government, which wanted to crush its political and military influence. The American war was fought bitterly in Tay Ninh province, near the border with Cambodia, but since Caodaists were seen as overwhelmingly anti-Communist, their religious sanctuaries were generally respected.[2] One of the iconic images of the Vietnam war—the naked girl running in pain from napalm burns—is Kim Phuc, a ten-year-old Caodaist in Trang Bang, on the road to the Great Temple in Ta Ninh, who came to represent the suffering of Vietnamese children and civilians to the world (Chong 2000).

American and Russian writers (Blagov 1999; Buttinger 1967; Fall 1955; Werner 1981) have treated Caodaism as primarily a peasant political movement and have documented the ways in which Caodaists were caught in the cold war battles of 1950–75. But although this emphasis is understandable in the light of efforts on both sides of this conflict to win the hearts and minds of the Vietnamese people, it is resented by Caodaists today. They argue that Caodaism was founded and led by Vietnamese intellectuals, and that despite its mass following it should be seen as an expression of cosmopolitan spirituality. More serious studies of it as a religion (Smith 1968, 1970; Oliver 1976) acknowledge its Chinese literary heritage and the blending of influences from Theravada Buddhism, Taoist occultism, Western spiritists, and theosophists.

Exodus from Vietnam and Refugee Resettlement

Many present Caodai leaders were part of the first wave of Vietnamese refugees who were airlifted out after Saigon fell in 1975. The sudden military collapse of South Vietnam took almost everyone by surprise, and few of the people who left at that time saw themselves as immigrants. "We were just trying to get to a safer place," many told me, fully expecting that the country was not lost but simply under siege. They believed that after a big battle, the South Vietnamese would be aided by American forces and the country would be theirs. The evacuation itself was chaotic and disorganized, so many authorized people never got out, while others—particularly students—seized an opportunity and managed to escape, planning an interval of study abroad and then a return after just a few years. Ultimately, 130,000 of the Vietnamese rushed into planes and boats while the city fell were brought to the United States for resettlement—most of the relatively young, educated, urban, and professional. The country lost half of its medical doctors and many engineers, pharmacists, and professors. While there were few high-ranking Caodai dignitaries among the refugees, there were many of their sons and daughters. Because they were willing to work hard at jobs well below their previous positions, and to get themselves retrained in English, this first wave of immigrants proved quite successful: Just ten years after entering the country as state-supported refugees, most of them were earning above the national median income (Freeman 1999).

High levels of employment and educational achievement, however, tell only part of the story of families shattered and separated in wartime conditions, with many members never found and many others bearing burdens of survivor's guilt and traumatic memories. For the boat people who escaped illegally from 1975 to 1983, conditions were even worse, since they often suffered starvation, rape, and abandonment for several years in refugee camps on the way. A total of 700,000 Vietnamese came to the United States as refugees, and since 1980 another 200,000 have come as immigrants, under the Orderly Departure Program (established by the UN High Commission for Refugees to end the dangerous illegal departures) or the Humanitarian Operation established in 1987 for prisoners who served more than three years in reeducation camps (Freeman 1997). There are now about two million Vietnamese-Americans, and perhaps 20,000 of them are practicing Caodaists, although the number of former Caodaists who have yet to make contact with their coreligionists is probably as great as those who have.

The most traumatic policy of refugee resettlement was the breaking apart of extended families into nuclear families so that they could be dispersed and resettled with different sponsors (Freeman 1997; Kelly 1977). The scattering of Vietnamese refugees all over the country also worked against the formation of a sense of religious community and seemed likely to prove fatal to a minority religion like Caodaism. It is therefore nothing short of amazing that, after a decade of struggling for survival and many secondary migrations to reunite families, leaders of the religion have managed to reestablish a national and even international organization. They have done so because they have merged their religious commitment with a new diasporic consciousness, developed in the Vietnamese enclaves in California, Texas, and the Washington, D.C., area. Using modern technologies like the Internet and desktop publishing, they have come to make the overseas Caodai community into a new and influential force in both California and Vietnam.

The Diasporic Perspective

Citizenship and working for national and international harmony are important themes in Caodaist theology, but today they are been contested and reinterpreted within a diasporic framework. I use a narrow definition of diaspora developed by Hans von Amesfoot (2004, 153) in a discussion of Moluccans in the Netherlands: "A diaspora is a settled community that considers itself to be 'from elsewhere' and whose concern and most important goal is the realization of a political ideal in what is seen as the homeland." The idea of the diaspora developed from Zionism but is also found among Cuban exiles in Miami and among many refugee groups who migrated in circumstances of persecution or civil war.

Under this definition, the two most important diasporic communities of Vietnamese Americans are without doubt the "little Saigon" in Orange County and the "littler Saigon" of the Bay Area around San Jose. Half of America's 2 million Vietnamese live in California. In Orange County, some members of the 135,000 Vietnamese American community have supported special anti-Communist zone ordinances in the cities of Westminster and Garden Grove that require prior notice for Vietnamese government delegations to visit and discourage official contacts with Vietnam. They also protested for months in 1999 when a video store displayed a photo of Ho Chi Minh or raised the Vietnamese flag. In January 2004 a State Department sponsored visit by Hanoi officials to Little Saigon was canceled when Westminster officials refused to ensure their safety.

In the Bay Area, by contrast, San Francisco has had a sister city relationship with Ho Chi Minh City since 1994 and a Vietnam government consulate since 1997. The Bay Area is home to about 100,000 Vietnamese Americans, and in December 2004 it also established the first direct air service between the United States and Vietnam in nearly thirty years (Moore and Tran 2004). For many years a number of Vietnamese American leaders discouraged contact with Vietnam, including doing business there or even traveling to visit family members, since they saw all contact as offering implicit support to the Communist government. In 1993, when the United States normalized diplomatic relations with Vietnam, the number of Vietnamese Americans who returned to visit their homeland increased significantly, and in the first nine months of 2004 about 10,000 people flew to Vietnam from the United States to visit friends and family, according to the U.S. Department of Commerce (Moore and Tran 2004). Vietnamese Americans make up about 10 percent of all foreign tourists to Vietnam, in a rapidly expanding industry that recently topped the million mark.

Among those returning for visits were Caodai religious officers, bringing funds to rebuild the Caodai Sacerdotal Center (Hoi Thanh) in Binh Dinh that was destroyed during the American war. Others have returned to arrange for the shipment of Caodai altars, gongs, and religious icons to California, to give courses at the Caodai Teaching Center in Saigon (CQPTGL) and to consult with religious leaders in the homeland. The diasporic perspective is strongest among refugee groups who migrated in circumstances of persecution or civil war, and for these very reasons many Vietnamese who came to the United States after years in reeducation camps share some of the political conviction of Holocaust survivors and Cuban exiles. While some, particularly older, members of the Caodai community are most concerned with defending freedom of religion in the homeland, others, many of them now American born, are trying instead to build a larger understanding of the religion in the wider American public.

Problems in the "Land of Religious Freedom"

While the United States is seen as a land of religious freedom, and there are few direct efforts at suppression as in Vietnam, there are many more subtle problems that Caodaists have encountered as refugees and as new American citizens. The first and perhaps still most important is the ignorance of the American public about Vietnamese culture, despite almost two decades of military involvement. Since 1930 Caodai has been the third religion of Vietnam, and in 1975, the year of the fall of Saigon, it claimed 15–25 percent of the population of South Vietnam, but it was not even listed as a possible religious affiliation for incoming refugees, who had to choose from Buddhism, Catholicism, Confucianism, Hinduism, or Islam. For this reason, there are no statistics on how many Caodaist refugees actually came to the United States at entry points such as Camp Pendleton. When I asked committed Caodaists what they put under the category of religion, most said Caodai, but this may have been recorded as "form of Buddhism," or perhaps "Confucianism," since there was no category for "other." It is remarkable that despite the fact that several thousands of Caodaists undoubtedly did enter the United States at Camp Pendleton and other refugee camps in Arkansas, Virginia, and elsewhere, they did so without leaving any official trace.[3]

In addition, church sponsorship of refugees was generous and offered great practical assistance, but it almost always came along with heavy pressures to convert. Nine voluntary agencies assumed the task of finding sponsors for Vietnamese refugees, and over 80 percent of the refugees were placed by faith-based groups, including the United States Catholic Conference (the largest sponsor, which resettled almost 50 percent of all Vietnamese refugees), the Lutheran Immigration and Refugee Service, and the Church World Service. Early reports about refugees' religious affiliation stressed the surprising fact (to Americans) that nearly half of all the refugees were Catholic (Montero 1979) and many had been educated in French. Since many Caodaists were among the French-educated elite, they may have been counted as Catholics, especially given the rushed conditions of arrival at refugee camps and the fact that both names employ the same initial letter.

Church sponsorship scattered Vietnamese refugees all over the country, where Christians would provide housing, clothing, and assistance with job training, usually with the expectation of regular church attendance and the hope of conversion. The Caodaist refugees I interviewed were all assigned to Protestant churches, and many were initially sent to rural areas of the South or the Midwest, the Bible Belt of Christian fundamentalism. Grateful for the assistance that they received, they reciprocated by attending church faithfully during the period that they were sponsored, hiding ancestral altars when ministers visited and agreeing to paper conversions as a ritualized farewell before choosing to relocate to another region.[4] (See Andrew Pham's *Catfish and Mandala* for a vivid fictionalized account of this in one family.) Committed Caodaists who did not convert were told in several instances that all the other refugee families were now Seventh-Day Adventists, Baptists, etc. There was a clear perception that baptism of the whole family was expected as a gesture of gratitude, and some Caodaists, in fact, rationalized these baptism ceremonies with the argument that since Jesus was a part of the Caodai pantheon, giving themselves to Jesus did not contradict a commitment to Caodai doctrine.

In California, the land of the New Age, many younger Vietnamese found the opportunity to experiment with a number of religious affiliations, usually starting with the church that sponsored their initial settlement and then moving on to dabble in Transcendental Meditation, Tibetan Buddhism, and Bahá'í. Three people now in their fifties who I interviewed had traveled through three or four faiths in the first two decades that they were in the United States, only to return to Caodai once they made contact with Caodai churches in the late 1990s. Others, such as the Web master for the Thien Ly Buu Toa temple near San Jose, had begun this experimentation in Vietnam, by frequenting the Syncretist Taoist Minh Ly temple in Saigon ("enlightened reason," a "pre-Caodaist" group founded in 1924 to unite the three traditions of Vietnam). He then became very active in Caodaism once he moved with family members to the Silicon Valley and came in contact with an exiled Caodai spirit medium and her disciples. For these reasons, many overseas Caodaist churches are much more open, tolerant, and less strictly hierarchical than the religious organizations in Vietnam, although this incorporation of new elements is also controversial and part of intergenerational dialogues within the faith.

California Caodaists and Religious Centers in Vietnam

Caodaism today is divided into about a dozen different denominations, each with its own set of spirit messages or scriptures. In Caodai oral tradition, the twelve original disciples were eventually scattered among twelve separate churches, although the historical evidence suggests a more fitful sequence of defections and returns, with ten specific branches, or *Phái*, now officially recognized by the government. Tay Ninh, the "mother church" has 500 out of 1,300 temples and retains about half of all those Vietnamese citizens who identify themselves on census forms as Caodaists (about 2.5 million).[5] It is often referred to as the Vatican of Caodaism, or its Rome, in contrast to the esoteric branch of its founder, Minh Chieu, which is sometimes called the Bethlehem of the religion, or the center of early prophecies and apocalyptic traditions, Tiên Thiên, which considers itself the Jerusalem. The new ecumenical teaching organization in Saigon, Co Quan Pho Thong Giao Ly Dai Dao (CQPTGL), draws its membership mainly from urban elites and has been described as the Jesuit branch of the religion and its intellectual center.

When asked to explain these divisions, most contemporary Caodaists blame the divisions on colonial policy. Paradoxically, I have heard *both* that Caodai was forced to split up as a strategy to escape the persecution of the French authorities (who did imprison, exile, and prosecute many religious leaders) *and* that the French themselves tried to divide the religion by rewarding dissidents with special favors (Oliver 1976). Overseas Caodaists, for the most part, are not particularly concerned with sectarian divisions and see the large number of different branches of the religion as a sign of its vitality and diversity. Many overseas temples recruit their members from all Caodaist churches and operate in a more inclusive and nonhierarchical fashion than the formal Caodaist organizations in Vietnam.

In Orange County, I collected many stories of how the religion was constrained and paralyzed under Communist control, and indeed most of the Caodai dignitaries who immigrated to the United States in the 1980s did so only after they were released from several years doing forced labor in reeducation camps. But their narrative of purity in exile—while true to the present situation of Tay Ninh—elided the fact that Caodai denominations in the heavily pro-Communist Mekong delta contained people who worked undercover for the Viet Cong. And while the temples of the Tay Ninh group remained resolutely anti-Communist, and seem to have suffered for their resistance, all of those that we visited in 2003 in the Mekong Delta displayed large portraits and busts of Ho Chi Minh, and some proudly showed pictures of the "heroes of the liberation" who had fought for the communist cause.[6]

Since 1964, a nondenominational teaching organization (Co Quan Pho Thong Giao Ly Dai Dao) in Saigon has tried to bring the different denominations together and unify the religion around a shared body of teachings. It former director, once the vice president of the National Assembly of the Republic of South Vietnam, now says he is grateful for the fact that the religion was as divided as much of the rest of the country by Vietnam's civil war. "The Caodaists who supported the communists have given us some room to move in relation to a regime which opposes all religious organizations. They have helped to create a place for us to place our feet in the new Vietnam, and since 1990 we have been able to not only survive in the shadows but even come out again on the national stage."

After the reunification of Vietnam in 1975, Communist troops seized forty out of the forty-six buildings at the Tay Ninh Holy See, arrested 1,291 Caodai religious leaders, killed 39 of them in clashes, and sentenced 9 to death. More than 1,000 Caodai dignitaries were sent to reeducation camps, and 3,000 were reeducated in the province (Blagov 2001). When young people fled in large numbers in 1975, their families were subject to surveillance and investigated for espionage.

The Great Temple at Tay Ninh, with the imposing exterior of a Gothic cathedral, and an interior filled with Asiatic images of pastel dragons coiled around pillars and pulpits and a seven-headed snake surrounding the spirit medium's throne, was closed. From every stained glass window, the left eye of God looked out at North Vietnamese soldiers trying (unsuccessfully) to fly their new flag from its parapets. The government allowed services to begin again in 1980 but forbade people from rotating prayer groups at their homes on a twelve-day cycle. Spirit séances were forbidden, and no new bishops or cardinals have been appointed since 1975. Inspired by Western visitors who described the "Disneyfied fantasy décor" of the Great Temple, the government opened up a fun fair on the grounds of the Holy See, with carnival rides near the pope's house and a stand selling beef and liquor next to the residence of the vegetarian religious youth. In spite of these measures, attendance remained strong at Caodai festivals and ceremonies held on the new and full moon, with over a thousand people regularly kneeling at the midnight mass. In 1997, a ceremony was held to celebrate the government's recognition of Caodaism as Vietnam's third largest religion, but this recognition came at a price: Instead of following their own religious constitution, Caodaists had to accept being ruled by a Communist-appointed steering committee.

It will be many years before Caodaists in Vietnam can have the same public and even political profile that they had in the 1940s and 1950s, but the resurgence of interest in religion in the post-Reformation period—combined with the fact that Tay Ninh is now the second largest tourist destination in South Vietnam (after the War Remnants Museum, usually visited along with the Chu Chi Tunnels)—have helped Caodaists to renovate their churches, refresh the paint on their brightly colored facades, and gain new adepts among the new generation. For those young Vietnamese trying to lead a religious life in a socialist republic, citizenship requires them to look to Ho Chi Minh as a moral example, and it has even been suggested that "Uncle Ho" could be incorporated into the Caodai pantheon as an archangel (*tiên*, immortal).

Religious Activism and the Internet

The most important Catholic influence on early Caodai leaders was the religious and social activism of the Catholic Mission. Unlike Buddhist monks, Caodai dignitaries do not retreat from the world, live in monasteries, or take vows of celibacy as young men. They live in society and are often professionally accomplished (doctors, engineers, pharmacists, legislators, and professors of mathematics were the most common careers I found). The mother church in Tay Ninh has also built hospitals, schools, craft production centers, and even a university. Before the formation of its millenarian sibling Hoa Hao, and long before the "engaged Buddhism" of the 1960s that opposed Diem's regime, Caodaism showed a model of how to modernize an ancient faith and make it relevant for those who want to take part in a global world.

Religious activism does not necessarily mean the same thing as political activism. Caodaists in Vietnam know enough to stay away from direct discussions of human rights issues or religious freedom; while remaining pragmatic, circumspect, and obedient to state notions of citizenship, they are also running free traditional medicine clinics for poor people in the inner city of Saigon, building a dormitory for university students who follow a vegetarian regime, and moving into the business of tourism in order to reach the many Euro-American visitors who visit their Holy See. Since 1997, Caodaism has been allowed to have a somewhat higher public profile, and its five million followers, concentrated mainly in the former South Vietnam, claim about one out of every seven people there.

Caodaists have now also forged alliances with the Catholic church, which was once resentful of its stealing converts from them. In the explosive period of Caodaism's first charismatic expansion, the new religion attracted more converts in one decade than the Catholic church had in three hundred years of proselytization (Werner 1981). They now collaborate with the United Church of Buddhism, whose self-immolating monks seared their way onto the front pages of newspapers in the Vietnam War era. And they have a relationship of spiritual fellowship and visiting with Oomoto, a Japanese religion founded in 1892, by an illiterate woman inspired to write out spirit messages by a deity now recognized as the Chinese spirit Li Po of the Tang dynasty, also the Spiritual Pope of Caodai.

Internet activism has played a particularly important role in the globalization of Caodai, especially since this globalization is to some extent based in the Silicon Valley of California, which is also a center for information technology.[7] Until recently, people in Vietnam were able to post information about religion on international Web sites. An English teacher and writer I met in Saigon had posted a series of interesting articles about the history of Caodaism and had corresponded with international scholars in English and French. A number of Web sites appeared in the United States, Australia, and Europe that detailed Caodaist beliefs and included the texts of spirit messages. The potential expansion of virtual religious communities in cyberspace was evidently seen as too dangerous by the Vietnamese government. A new State Ordinance on Beliefs and Religions issued in July 2004 and set to become law on November 15, however, "clarified" what it called the "socialist understanding of religious freedom" by forbidding any discussion of religion on the Internet, forbidding postings from anyone in Vietnam and requiring all religious officials to get government permission before speaking publicly in person, in print, or on the World Wide Web. Religious leaders in Vietnam are prevented from attending international conferences or meetings by being denied visas. In July 2004 several Caodai and Minh Ly religious leaders were invited to participate in the Parliament of World Religions in Barcelona, and none of those based in Vietnam were allowed to attend.

In spite of these regulations, Caodaists in Vietnam can still visit Web sites established overseas, even if they cannot post to them. Large and complicated Web sites in Vietnamese, English, and French are established by the Caodai Overseas Mission (http://www.caodai.net), the Tay Ninh international Caodai Mission (http://www.caodai.org), and important scholars and temples, including the Sydney Centre for Studies in Caodaism (http://www.personal.usyd.edu.au/~cdao), the Thien Ly Buu Toa Temple in San Martin, California (http://www.thienlybuutoa.org), and the French Caodaist Church (http://www.caodisme.fr). There are also dozens of personal Web sites that post documents about Caodai history and teachings, including bulletins on group activities and ceremonies, as well as archives of earlier scholarly studies. The Vietnamese government systematically blocks Internet sites that contain either pornography or religious content (two rather strange bedfellows) with firewall, but it is usually unable to cut off access entirely (cf. Amnesty International report on Internet regulations), so the internet remains an important form of communication even under heavy government restrictions.

Transnational Caodaism Takes Shape

The syncretistic beginnings of this religious movement brought together what had previously been considered Asian philosophical traditions with a new activist and engaged perspective on worldly activities. Its Confucian elements celebrated the literary achievements of an elite; its Taoist occult practices focused more on the relation of man to nature rather than to society; and its esoteric tradition was based on the Buddhist ideal of the world renouncer. What was novel about Caodaism, however, was that in contrast to all three of Vietnam's great teachings, it fostered a more personal and direct contact with God. While Confucianism can be described as an ethical system, Taoism as a metaphysical one, and Buddhism as a philosophy of self-realization, what Caodaism added to the mix was a more immediate technology of spirit communication. Caodai spirit mediums could have direct conversations with God and the various saints, and the goal of Caodai meditation exercises was to study directly from the spiritual entities themselves. Caodai, as the Supreme Being, spoke directly to his disciples and encouraged them also to communicate with the other great spiritual leaders of history. In this way, the personal relationship with Jesus that is advocated by some Christian sects was expanded to include a much wider Asian pantheon of spirits, and a more cosmopolitan spirituality was born.

This more personal, direct, and activist form of religious communication also influenced the new religion's orientation to the world. Caodai prophecies contain millenarian elements that challenge the powers that exist today, at the same time that they show respect for many forms of occult knowledge that go back for centuries. In 1926, a spirit message predicted that after reunification Vietnamese would travel all over the world—and this is often interpreted as prophesying the exodus of 1975.

Because the Socialist Republic of Vietnam has not allowed spirit séances to ordain new religious officers in Tay Ninh, the leadership of Caodaism's largest denomination is decapitated—an aging group of dignitaries forced to administer their religion not according to its own constitution but according to the rules of a Communist-appointed management committee. Membership in many of the other denominations has been feminized, with many more women attending ceremonies than men, perhaps because they are less likely to suffer the social censure that being religious may bring to professionals and civil servants in Vietnam today. This reverses certain hierarchical relationships between the Holy Sees in Vietnam and the diasporic communities in the United States and elsewhere, and it creates a series of new problems of religious inspiration and invention.

For the first generation of Caodai religious activists, the syncretic teachings of Caodaism were used to inspire a national movement and create the possibility of establishing this blended faith as a true national religion. Opposition to colonial rule coalesced around Pham Cong Tac and his conversations with spirits like Victor Hugo and Joan of Arc, who defended spiritism and the cause of Vietnamese independence as consistent with French ideals of spirituality, humanism, and democracy. For the generation that came of age during the American War, the Holy See was a sanctuary from combat, and living in the religious dormitories was a way to avoid obligatory military service. The united religious community of Tay Ninh was said to be the one region that Communists were never able to infiltrate, but after the fall of Saigon the leaders of the religion paid for their ideological purity with their lives: Tran Quang Vinh, once the commander of the Caodai Armed Forces and the defense minister of Vietnam under the Bao Dai government, was arrested and died in a reeducation camp. The head spirit medium Ho Tan Khoa advised all Caodai disciples to respond to the banning of public rituals by turning to esoteric practices of meditation and self-cultivation (*vo vi*), but he was still arrested himself in 1983 for practicing spiritism and receiving millenarian messages associated with Halley's comet (Blagov 2001). Khoa lived out the rest of his days under house arrest, and his son Ho Thai Bach was executed for participating in a subversive organization. Eight thousand Caodaists were forced to take courses reviewing the state penal code in 1984.

Virtually all of the Caodai leaders I interviewed who came to the United States after 1980 did so when they were released from reeducation camps, spending an average of five years doing hard labor and being instructed in Marxist-Leninism. Just as scholars like Peter Zinoman (2001) have argued that the colonial Bastille served as a school for revolutionaries in French Indochina, so, too, the Communist reeducation camp deserves recognition as the central fulcrum of Vietnam's new revival of religious activity, even under conditions of extreme governmental constraints. In the early 1980s, after the deaths of many thousand boat people, the new rules of humanitarian transfer allowed once imprisoned political and religious refugees to leave Vietnam to make new lives elsewhere.

There is now a new generation, born in the overseas communities of California or in the newly reunified nation of Vietnam. For those Vietnamese Americans who are growing up in the shadow of Disneyland, worshipping the left eye of God may suggest Indiana Jones and the Temple of Doom rather than solar energy, lunar calendars, and Oriental morality. Do Vang Ly, the most senior Caodai leader in the United States, is the former Vietnamese ambassador to the United States, as well as the founder of Vietnam's diplomatic offices in India and Indonesia. His daughter, Merdeka (the Indonesian word for freedom or national independence), is an Oxford scholar who has written about Caodaism, and he sees the future of the religion as lying with Vietnamese educated overseas. "We are the two peoples in the world to worship under the sign of the eye. We Vietnamese worship the left eye of God, you Americans worship the right. There is an Arab proverb that says: 'The two eyes are very close but they cannot see each other.' This shows how wrong the Arab world can be. My lifelong goal of liberating my people will be achieved when the American educated Vietnamese return to their country to bring them Western democracy with an Eastern ethical orientation."

He articulates the diasporic perspective, which sees Caodaism as a religion in exile whose members are all striving for religious freedom in their homeland so that they can return. It contrasts with another view—perhaps more common among younger members and those who are American born—of a global religion reinventing itself in the new world—in which ties to non-Vietnamese converts become more important, and the religion can receive new revelations on American soil.

Dr. Hum Dac Bui, a California physician who coauthored *Caodai: Faith of Unity* (2000), describes his perspective in this way: "Now, Americans are beginning to discover the value of the original esoteric form of CaoDai, with its practices of meditation, vegetarianism and emptying the mind to open the way for conversations with God. In much the same way as Tibetan Buddhism has attracted many Western disciples, Caodaism has begun the process of disseminating its valuable and closely held esoteric information to the West. . . . Its leaders have the desire to relate their teachings in English to Americans (both Vietnamese and non-Vietnamese) so that the first and main message received from the Supreme Being, that we are all One and must reunite under The One Nameless Divinity, can be delivered and that a path of esoteric practice toward that end (reunification of the self with the Supreme Being) may begin" (Bui and Beck 2000, 312).

In September 2005, a group of Tay Ninh Caodaists in Garden Grove ("Little Saigon") received a building permit to start construction of their own temple—a replica of the Holy See in a smaller format—and a groundbreaking ceremony was held on November 27, 2005. Projected to be finished in 2007, this Caodai Church of California *(thanh that Cali)* may become the first intentionally built temple in the New World, and the first place for Americans to see the colorful and eclectic hybrid architecture of this new religion.

Alternative Strategies: Encompassing American Religions within Caodaism

Efforts to spread the religion to non-Vietnamese Americans go hand in hand with public relations campaigns to make the teachings of this new faith better known and understood in the media and academic circles. Publishing books in English, translating Caodai scriptures and prayers, and participating in academic conferences are part of this agenda. There is an effort to gently address and perhaps even redress the patronizing attitude that many Western writers have taken toward religious innovations in Asia, and also the subtle prejudices of refugee workers and resettlement organizations. Aihwa Ong describes Mormon outreach organizations working with Cambodians in ways that resonate strongly with what I heard from Vietnamese refugees: "The recruitment and conversion of displaced populations . . . operate within a system of compassionate domination in which social support is accompanied by racial disdain, kindness is blended with cultural superiority, and acceptance is ordered by racial and gender configurations. Even as the church teaches the recruits the initiative and self-discipline for negotiating the market economy and attaining the good life, this is done within a structure of white power that is more sharply inscribed than in the wider society, though continuous with it" (Ong 2003, 227). Gifts of used clothing, furniture, food and occasionally even money to pay rent and utility bills were appreciated by refugees, but the expectation of conversion was not. Ong suggests that many young Cambodians saw Buddhism as "something intangible, and perhaps irrelevant to the lives they wanted to lead in America" (Ong 2003, 214), and complained that it was taught only by example, not through books. Caodaism emerged in the early twentieth century because of a similar unease experienced by young people in French Indochina, so it has already developed certain modern elements that might make it better able to survive in exile: It is syncretistic, flexible, has an activist tradition and preaches a personal relationship with God. Its written scriptures (translated into French as "sutras," but into English as "Bibles") are in literary Vietnamese, and often in complex verse, so they are not easy to translate, but they can be taught in Sunday school format.

Compared to Cambodian refugees, many Vietnamese were better educated and (after twenty years of contact with the U.S. military) more able to do business in American terms. The elderly woman who is now the highest ranking Caodaist in California, Archbishop Tuyet, for example, bought a Chinese herbal shop just two weeks after her arrival in the United States and has built a flourishing business in San Jose. She received a spirit message that ordered her to build a temple, and since 1977 she has worked with the female spirit medium Bach Dien Hoa to run Thien Ly Buu Toa (Court of Heavenly Reason), the only Caodai prayer hall to continue to conduct spirit séances and post the results on the Internet.

The séances in San Jose present a new mandate from heaven for the religion in exile. In the "first Bible" of spirit messages received at the TLBT temple (*Dai Giác Thánh Giáo Pháp*), there are fifty-four messages, including fourteen from Caodai (Ngoc Hoang Thuong De, the Supreme Being, also called the Jade Emperor), six from Jesus Christ, two from Buddha (Thich Ca Mau Ni Phat), two from Quan Cong (Quan Thanh De Quan), one from the Virgin Mary (Duc Me Maria), four from the founder of Caodai Ngo Minh Chieu, two from Li Thai Bach (the Spiritual Pope), one from the Mother Goddess (Dieu Tri Kim Mau), one from Noah of the Old Testament, and one American spirit—Joseph Smith, the founder of Mormonism.

Joseph Smith is appropriated by American Caodaists because his revelations from the Angel Moroni are seen as part of a tradition of spiritism that includes Caodai, and Smith's own background as a Free Mason caused him to include many Caodai symbols (like the all-seeing eye, the moon and stars, etc.) on the outside of Mormon temples. It is perhaps significant that several non-Vietnamese Caodaists, like Stephen Stratford and Ngasha Beck,[8] came from Mormon backgrounds but renounced Mormonism as racist and patriarchal, and have come to find Caodaism a more welcoming spiritual home.[9]

On November 9, 2003, a spirit medium in San Jose received a message stating that, since after 1975 the sacred centers in Vietnam (Hoi Thanh) could not communicate with Caodaists overseas, they should now listen to the direct spiritual guidance of Li Po (also called Ly Thai Bach, the Spiritual Pope), and seven of its most important twentieth-century leaders (including Pham Cong Tac and the first disciple Ngo Van Chieu): "We immortals are happy to see you going overseas and carrying the Caodai messages to new people. God created the religion to save the Vietnamese and also all of humanity. His blessings will go to the good and penalties will go to those who oppose God's will. Look at the example of the past and learn from it in order to spread the teachings in the future. When we immortals were alive, we were sometimes separated by divisions, so you should not follow that example but learn to work together more effectively. . . . You need to unify to become the lighthouse of the western world (*sáng chói o Tây Phuong dê*) so that people can find peace, salvation and happiness."[10]

This call for unity is an effort to transcend the tensions between hierarchy and egalitarianism, between a respect for the authority of religious leaders in the homeland now paralyzed by government restrictions and the leaders of refugee communities who need new messages of spiritual guidance for the new world. It speaks both to the glorification of ancient traditions and the innovations forced by the present moment.

Caodaism is now a transnational religious movement, although there are deep and significant differences between the way it is perceived and lived in the Socialist Republic of Vietnam and the New Age–influenced communities of California. But it is precisely because of these differences that a study of efforts to revitalize this faith of unity is especially important and significant today. Eighty years ago, Caodaism came into being to provide Vietnamese intellectuals in a modernizing world with a form of spiritual and religious activism, using the principles of Buddhism and Taoism in a much more this-worldly organization. Today, it is being reconceptualized as a way to heal not so much the lingering wounds of colonialism but the continuing inequities of a globalized society. This new vision of bringing the Left Eye of God to the Western world brings an Eastern perspective on universal religion to the land illuminated by the right eye on the dollar bill.

NOTES

1. The Caodaist religious hierarchy, detailed in its *La constitution religieuse du Caodaisme*, published by Pham Cong Tac in both Vietnamese and French, includes the grades of priest, bishop, cardinal, censor cardinal, and pope (using terms similar but not identical to Vietnamese Catholic grades), and its sacred city in Tay Ninh is called the Holy See *(Toa Thanh)*. The first disciple to make contact with Caodai, Ngo Minh Chieu, was invited to be the pope but declined the position, which was then offered to Le Van Trung, the highest-ranking Vietnamese member of the French Colonial Council and a

prominent businessman. Trung died in 1934, and on that very day a rival denomination was formed in Ben Tre, but its head, Nguyen Ngoc Tuong, was not allowed to return to the Holy See. Pham Cong Tac never renounced his own position as Ho Phap, and was thus unable to become pope, but he did take over executive powers and direct the Tay Ninh branch from 1936 to 1957, finally dying in exile in Cambodia in 1959. Three other Caodai denominations (Tien Thien, Ban Chinh Dao and Chon Ly) have Holy Sees that were once directed by a pope (all of them in the Mekong Delta: the first two in Ben Tre and the third in My Tho), but since 1960 no new popes have been elected, and at present the highest-ranking living dignitaries are archbishops, many of them female. (Women may rise to the rank of cardinal in Caodaism, and the first female cardinal is represented on the front of the Tay Ninh cathedral beside the first pope.)

2. An exception to this policy of respect is narrated in the (fictionalized) bestseller *The Green Berets*, which describes American Special forces blowing up what is called "a Cao-Dai pagoda," and describing Caodaists as "religious zealots" and "spook sheeted dick-heads" (Moore 1965, 129). One camp commander notes, more sympathetically: "Though he might well suspect that the local Cao-Dais, one hundred and fifty miles from the sect's main strength in Tay Ninh province, were being terrorized into helping the Viet Cong, still the religious bond they shared was stronger than most Westerners could realize" (Moore 1965, 129). The extensive damage we saw on Caodai temples, especially those in the Mekong Delta, makes it clear that it was perhaps not unusual.

3. The official statistics from Camp Pendleton, however unreliable, are the following: 55 percent were listed as Catholics, 27 percent as Buddhists, 11 percent as Confucians, and 5 percent as having no religion (Freeman 1997, 54). Catholics number about 8 percent of the total population of reunited Vietnam, with Buddhists counted as 15 percent, Caodaists as 8 percent, and Hoa Hao as 2 percent. Government statistics in Vietnam do not count "Confucians," but this might indeed have been a category that was used to "store" unidentified Caodaists in the United States. Since many Vietnamese boat people were ethnically Chinese, it is also likely that they made up a substantial number of the "Confucians."

4. Andrew Pham's *Catfish and Mandala* is a beautifully written memoir of the Vietnamese migration experience and the author's return to Vietnam that contains a vivid description of one paper conversion in Louisiana.

5. Statistics about Caodai membership are controversial. Here I have relied on the numbers collected by the ecumenical teaching organization the Co Quan Pho Thong Giao Ly in Saigon/Ho Chi Minh City (henceforth CQPTGL), and the widespread estimate of 5 million. Government statistics usually place the total number of Caodaists at four million, and in 2004 estimated that the number of Ban Chinh Dao followers was somewhat more than the followers of Tay Ninh. Tay Ninh still has the largest number of temples (500 temples to Ban Chinh Dao's 300), and Tay Ninh leaders maintain that it, as the "First Church of Caodaism," is and will remain the largest denomination (personal communication, fieldwork in Vietnam in 2004). There are twenty-three branches (*phái*) of Caodaism, but only nine are recognized according to the government rules and conditions for recognition, which require more than 50,000 members, and presence in more than three provinces.

6. The Mekong Delta denominations of Ban Chinh Dao (The Reformed Religion) and Tien Thien (Primordial Unity) are now seen as more politically correct than Tay Ninh, but they were also closed down by the government of reunified Vietnam from 1975 to 1997. They have recently been allowed to reopen their temples and expand their

membership in part because the pope of Ban Chinh Dao renounced spiritism back in 1934, and this denomination now practices only meditation and spiritual cultivation of the self. In 2003, several books, plays, and television shows appeared celebrating the heroism of Mekong Delta Caodaists Nguyen Ngoc Nhu, Nguyen Ngoc Bich, and Cao Trieu Phat in fighting with the Viet Minh, publicizing a more patriotic past for these groups. Tay Ninh is now run by a government-appointed management committee, but its disciples have been more resistant to government control than many of the smaller branches, emphasizing large-scale ritual congregations and ritual—including lavish music and processions—which are less important in the smaller denominations.

7. In 1997, the Silicon Valley had the second largest concentration of Vietnamese in the United States, and 1,645 Vietnamese engineers, 478 computer scientists, 289 managers, 2,272 secretaries and administrative support people, 2,472 engineering and science technicians, 1,299 other technicians, and 1,422 assemblers (Freeman 1997).

8. Ngasha Beck was called to Caodaism by a vision of the Divine Eye, which she now believes came from Victor Hugo: "It was in 1993, I believe. I was reclined in meditation when a shining image of the Divine Eye came shooting from infinity toward me, and at the time that it collided or encompassed me there was a very loud sound like a gun going off beside each ear, which jolted me upright. It was instantaneous; there was no thought, no sentiment other than wonder possible in the time frame of the vision. But unlike a dream, it did not fade as moments passed; instead, there was like an urgency to understand. And unlike most meditations, I did not emerge contented but rather searching my mind, seeking for answers. . . . I remembered that I had read or heard somewhere about a Vietnamese religion who worshipped an Eye and had Victor Hugo as a Saint. I hadn't been to school (proper) and didn't know who Victor Hugo was, other than he was famous for something. Even so, I felt right about asking Victor Hugo if he would guide me, to do so. Suddenly, everywhere I looked, the newspaper, TV, there was mention of Victor Hugo. There were just too many coincidences. I now believe that Victor Hugo is the one who named me" (e-mail to author, April 10, 2004).

9. The spirit message from Joseph Smith indicates that both Mormonism and Caodaism came from the same source—God—and that they share many goals, "so you do not need to abandon your religion and change to ours. . . . God's will is to have all religions united. . . . You need to make a wise decision. . . . To escape the huge earthquake which is coming soon. . . . You need to practice religions more and leave fame and wealth aside" (http://www.thienlybuutoa.org, accessed September 15, 2004).

10. Vietnamese text accessed September 15, 2004, at http://www.thienlybuutoa.org, translated with assistance from Judy Vy-Uyen Cao.

REFERENCES

Abdullah, Aslam. *The Minaret.* Los Angeles: Islamic Center of Southern California.

Abou El Fadl, Khaled. 2001. *And God Knows the Soldiers: The Authoritative and Authoritarian in Islamic Discourses.* New York: University Press of America.

———. 2003. "9/11 and the Muslim Transformation." In *September 11 in History,* edited by Mary L. Dudziak, 70–111. Durham: Duke University Press.

Ahlstrom, Sydney E. 1972. *A Religious History of the American People.* New Haven: Yale University Press.

Alemán, Eduardo, and Guadalupe Ortega. 2001. *Statistical Abstract for Latin America.* Los Angeles: UCLA Latin American Center.

Alinsky, Saul D. 1989. *Rules for Radicals: A Pragmatic Primer for Realistic Radicals.* New York: Vintage Books.

Allen, Jr., Ernest. 1998. "Identity and Destiny: The Formative Views of the Moorish Science Temple and the Nation of Islam." In *Islam on the Americanization Path?* edited by John L. Esposito and Yvonne Yazbeck Haddad, 201–266. Atlanta: Scholars Press.

Alumkal, Antony. 2003. *Asian American Evangelical Churches.* New York: LFB Scholarly.

Amesfoot, Hans von. 2004. "The Politics of Diaspora: Moluccan Migrants in the Netherlands." *Journal of Ethic and Migration Studies* 30 (1): 151–174.

Ammerman, Nancy Tatom. 1997. *Congregation and Community.* New Brunswick, NJ: Rutgers University Press.

———. 2005. *Pillars of Faith: American Congregations and Their Partners.* Berkeley: University of California Press.

Ammerman, Nancy Tatom, Arthur E. Farnsley, Tammy Adams, Penny Edgell Becker, and Brenda Brasher. 1997. *Congregation and Community.* New Brunswick, NJ: Rutgers University Press.

Anderson, Benedict. 1983. *Imagined Communities: Reflections on the Origin and Spread of Nationalism.* London: Verso.

Andreas, Peter. 2000. *Border Games: Policing the U.S.-Mexico Divide.* Ithaca: Cornell University Press.

Anzaldúa, Gloria. 1987. *Borderlands/The Frontera: The New Mestiza.* San Francisco: Aunt Lute Books.

Aquino, María Pilar. 1999. "Theological Method in U.S. Latino/a Theology: Toward an Intercultural Theology for the Third Millennium." In *From the Heart of Our People: Latino/a Explorations in Catholic Systematic Theology,* edited by Orlando O. Espín and Miguel H. Díaz, 6–48. Maryknoll, NY: Orbis Books.

Asani, Ali. 2002. "On Pluralism, Intolerance, and the Quran." *American Scholar* 71 (1): 52–60.

Associated Press. 2002. "Tombstone Militia Will Operate on Public Land, Leader Says." December 3, State and Regional Section. http://web.lexis-nexis.com/universe/document.

———. 2003a. "Civilian Border Watch Group Launches Spy Plane." *Associated Press*, May 1, BC cycle, State and Regional Section.

———.2003b. "Law Enforcement: Immigrant Extortion Growing Problem." *Associated Press*, July 29, BC cycle, State and Regional Section.

Bagby, Ihsan. 2004. *A Portrait of Detroit Mosques: Muslim Views on Policy, Politics and Religion.* Clinton Township, MI: Institute for Social Policy and Understanding.

Bagby, Ihsan, Paul M. Perl, and Bryan T. Froehle. 2001. *The Mosque in America: A National Portrait: A Report from the Mosque Study Project.* Washington, DC: Council on American-Islamic Relations.

Barry, Brian. 2002. *Culture and Equality: An Egalitarian Critique of Multiculturalism.* Cambridge, MA: Harvard University Press.

Bartra, Roger. 1980. *Estructura Agraria y Clases Sociales en México.* México: Ediciones Era.

Beaman, Lori G. 2003. "The Myth of Pluralism, Diversity, and Vigor: The Constitutional Privilege of Protestantism in the United States and Canada." *Journal for the Scientific Study of Religion* 42: 311–325.

Bellah, Robert N., Richard Madsen, William M. Sullivan, Ann Swidler, and Steven M. Tipton. 1985. *Habits of the Heart: Individualism and Commitment in American Life.* Berkeley: University of California Press.

Berger, Peter, and Richard John Neuhaus. 2000. "To Empower People: From State to Civil Society." In *The Essential Civil Society Reader: The Classic Essays*, edited by Don E. Eberly, 143–182. Lanham, MD: Rowman and Littlefield.

Bernardini, Pierre. 1974. *Le Caodaisme au Cambodge* (Thèse du troisième cycle), Université de Paris VII, Directeur Jean Chesnaux.

Bevans, Stephen. 2005. "Variations on a Theme by Anselm: Contemporary Reflections on a Classic Definition." *Toronto Journal of Theology* 21 (1): 33–48.

Beyer, Peter. 2003. "Constitutional Privilege and Constituting Pluralism: Religious Freedom in National, Global, and Legal Context." *Journal for the Scientific Study of Religion* 42: 333–339.

Billeaud, Jacques. 2003. "Kidnappings Rise as Migrants Smuggling Gets Lucrative." *Arizona Republic*, January 11.

Blagov, Sergei. 1999. *The Cao Dai: A New Religious Movement.* Moscow: Institute of Oriental Studies.

———. 2001. *Caodaism: Vietnamese Traditionalism and Its Leap into Modernity.* New York: Nova Science Publishers.

Bolivar, Wilfredo, Aaron Dorfman, Cristina Fundroa, and Gerard Pean. 2002. "Unleash the Power of Immigrants . . . Organize!" *Social Policy* 2: 30–36.

Bosh, Juan. 2001. "The Meaning of 'Catholic' Today." *Religious Life Asia* 3 (2): 70–74.

Bosniak, Linda. 1996. "Opposing Prop. 187: Undocumented Immigrants and National Imagination." *Connecticut Law Review* 28 (3): 555–619.

Bourgois, Philippe. 2001. "The Power of Violence in War and Peace: Post–Cold War Lessons from El Salvador." *Ethnography* 2 (1): 5–34.

Braude, Ann. 1997. "Women's History Is American Religious History." In *Retelling U.S. Religious History,* edited by Thomas A. Tweed, 87–107. Berkeley: University of California Press.

Bui, Hum Dac. 1996. *God Has Come: Messages from Vietnam.* Bilingual compilation in English and Vietnamese. Santa Ana, CA: Caodai Overseas Mission.

Bui, Hum Dac, and Ngasha Beck. 2000. *Cao Dai: Faith of Unity.* Fayetteville, AR: Emerald Wave Press.

Burke, Kevin F. 2005. "Thinking about the Church: The Gift of Cultural Diversity to Theology." In *Many Faces, One Church: Cultural Diversity and the American Catholic Experience,* edited by Peter C. Phan and Diana Hayes, 27–47. Lanham: Sheed & Ward.

Burns, Gene. 1996. "Studying the Political Culture of American Catholicism." *Sociology of Religion* 57: 37–54.

Busto, Rudy. 1996. "The Gospel According to the Model Minority? Hazarding an Interpretation of Asian American Evangelical College Students." *Amerasia Journal* 22: 133–147.

Buttinger, Joseph. 1967. *Vietnam: A Dragon Embattled.* 2 vols. New York: Praeger.

Camp, Roderic Ai. 2001. *Citizen Views of Democracy in Latin America.* Pittsburgh: University of Pittsburgh Press.

Campbell, David. 2002. "Beyond Charitable Choice: The Diverse Service Delivery Approaches of Local Faith-Related Organizations." *Nonprofit and Voluntary Sector Quarterly* 32: 207–230.

Campese, Gioacchino. 2004. "Behold the Beauty of the Lord: The Journey toward Dignity and Freedom of Undocumented Immigrants in the USA." In *Migration and Interculturality: Theological and Philosophical Challenges,* edited by Raúl Fornet-Betancourt, 133–150. Aachen, Germany: Missionswissenchaftliches Institut Missio e.V.

Campese, Gioacchino, and Pietro Ciallella, eds. 2003. *Migration, Religious Experience, and Globalization.* New York: Center for Migration Studies.

Campese, Gioacchino, and Flor María Rigoni. 2003. "Hacer Teología Desde el Migrante: Diario de un Camino." In *Migration, Religious Experience, and Globalization,* edited by Gioacchino Campese and Pietro Ciallella, 181–203. New York: Center for Migration Studies.

Carnes, Tony, and Fenggang Yang. 2004. "Introduction." In *Asian American Religions,* edited by Tony Carnes and Fenggang Yang, 1–37. New York: New York University Press.

Carroll, Susan. 2003a. "Series of Killings Tied to People-smuggling." *Arizona Republic,* January 6.

———. 2003b. "Civilians to 'assist' in patrol of border." *Arizona Republic,* January 25.

Casanova, Jose. 1994. *Public Religions in the Modern World.* Chicago: University of Chicago Press.

———. 1997. "Globalizing Catholicism and the Return to a 'Universal' Church." In *Transnational Religion and Fading States,* edited by S. H. Rudolph and J. Piscatori. Boulder, CO: Westview Press.

Castillo, Jorge Guerra. 2004. "Hacia una Teología de la Migración: Perspectivas Y Propuestas." *Chakana* 2 (3): 27–51.

Castles, Stephen. 2002. "Migration and Community Formation under Conditions of Globalization." *International Migration Review* 36 (4): 1141–1168.

———. 2004. "Why Migration Policies Fail." *Ethnic and Racial Studies* 27 (2): 205–227.

Castles, Stephen, and Mark J. Miller. 2003. *The Age of Migration: International Population Movements in the Modern World.* 3rd ed. New York: Guilford Press.

Chang, Robert. 1997. "A Meditation on Borders." In *Immigrants Out! The New Nativism and the Anti-Immigrant Impulse in the United States,* edited by Juan F. Perea, 244–253. New York: New York University Press.

Chavez, Leo R. 1992. *Shadowed Lives: Undocumented Immigrants in American Society.* Orlando: Harcourt Brace Jovanovich.

———. 2001. *Covering Immigration: Popular Images and the Politics of the Nation.* Berkeley: University of California Press.

Chen, Carolyn. 2002. "The Religious Varieties of Ethnic Presence: A Comparison between a Taiwanese Immigrant Buddhist Temple and an Evangelical Christian Church." *Sociology of Religion* 63 (2): 215–238.

Chong, Denise. 2000. *The Girl in the Picture: The Story of Kim Phuc, the Photograph, and the Vietnamese War.* London: Penguin.

Cohen, Jean L. 1999. "Does Voluntary Association Make Democracy Work?" In *Diversity and Its Discontents: Cultural Conflict and Common Ground in Contemporary American Society,* edited by Neil J. Smelser and Jeffrey Alexander, 263–292. Princeton, NJ: Princeton University Press.

Coleman, John. 1997. "Coleman Revisited: Religious Structures as a Source of Social Capital." *American Behavioral Scientist* 5: 587–595.

Collins, Patricia Hill. 1986. "Learning from the Outsider Within: The Sociological Significance of Black Feminist Thought." *Social Problems* 33: 6–34.

"Colocarán otra barrera." 2005. *(Phoenix, AZ) La Voz*, January 12.

Coolidge, David Orgon. 2001. "Evangelicals and the Same-Sex 'Marriage' Debate." In *A Public Faith: Evangelicals and Civic Engagement*, edited by Michael Cromartie, 93–100. Lanham, MD: Rowman and Littlefield.

Copeland, M. Shawn. 2002. "Racism and the Vocation of the Christian Theologian." *Spiritus* 2 (1): 15–29.

Counts, Laura. 1999a. "A Clean Fight: Shabby Building Spurs Formation of Unlikely Tenants Coalition." *Oakland Tribune*, April 19, Local.

———. 1999b. "Oak Park Complex Stuck in Legal Battle: Owner Declares Bankruptcy." *Oakland Tribune*, June 25, Local.

Coutin, Susan Bibler. 1993. *The Culture of Protest: Religious Activism and the U.S. Sanctuary Movement*. Boulder, CO: Westview Press.

———. 1998. "From Refugees to Immigrants: The Legalization Strategies of Salvadoran Immigrants and Activists." *International Migration Review* 32: 901–925.

———. 2000. *Legalizing Moves: Salvadoran Immigrants' Struggle for U.S. Residency*. Ann Arbor: University of Michigan Press.

Curtis, Edward E., IV. 2002. *Islam in Black America: Identity, Liberation, and Difference in African-American Islamic Thought*. Albany: State University of New York Press.

Dacyl, Janina. 1996. "Sovereignty versus Human Rights: From Past Discourses to Contemporary Dilemmas." *Journal of Refugee Studies* 9: 136–165.

Dagger, Richard. 1997. *Civic Virtues: Rights, Citizenship, and Republican Liberalism*. New York: Oxford University Press.

Dahl, Robert A. 1967. *Pluralist Democracy in the United States: Conflict and Consent*. Chicago: Rand McNally.

Davy, Lucy, trans. 1992. *Phap Chanh Truyen Dai Dao Tam Ky Pho Do: The Religious Constitution of Caodaism*. Sydney: Caodaist Association of Australia NSW Chapter.

Deck, Allan Figueroa. 1989. *The Second Wave: Hispanic Ministry and the Evangelization of Cultures*. New York: Paulist Press.

Deck, Allan Figueroa, Yolanda Tarango, and Timothy M. Matovina. 1995. *Perspectivas: Hispanic Ministry*. Kansas City, MO: Sheed & Ward.

DeFao, Janine. 1999. "New Attack on Oakland Slumlords: City Levies Fins, Disgruntled Renters Sue." *San Francisco Chronicle*, October 29.

———. 2000. "Oakland Tenants Get Big Settlement: Decrepit Apartments to Be Fixed Up." *San Francisco Chronicle*, October 17.

Demerath, N. J., III. 2003. *Crossing the Gods: World Religions and Worldly Politics*. New Brunswick, NJ: Rutgers University Press.

Dillon, Michele. 1999. *Catholic Identity: Balancing Reason, Faith and Power*. New York: Cambridge University Press.

Do, Merdeka Thien-Ly Huong. 1994. *Cao Daism: An Introduction*. California: Centre for Dai Dao Studies.

Dolan, Jay P. 1987. *The American Catholic Parish: A History from 1850 to the Present*. New York: Paulist Press.

———. 1992. *The American Catholic Experience: A History from Colonial Times to the Present*. Notre Dame: University of Notre Dame Press.

———. 2002. *In Search of an American Catholicism: A History of Religion and Culture in Tension.* Oxford: Oxford University Press.

Dolan, Timothy M. 2005. "The Bishops in Council." In *First Things* 152 (April): 20–25.

Dong Tan. 2000. *Tim Hieu Dao Cao Dai.* Victoria, Australia: Nha Xuat Ban Cao Hien.

Dunn, Timothy. 1996. *The Militarization of the U.S.-Mexico Border, 1978–1992: Low Intensity Conflict Doctrine Comes Home.* Austin: University of Texas Press and Center for Mexican American Studies.

Dutton, Thomas E. 1970. "Caodai History, Philosophy and Religion." Master's thesis, University of California, Berkeley.

Ebaugh, Helen Rose, and Janet Saltzman Chaftez, eds. 2000. *Religion and the New Immigrants: Continuities and Adaptations in Immigrant Congregations.* Walnut Creek, CA: AltaMira Press.

———. 2002. *Religion across Borders: Transnational Immigrant Networks.* Walnut Creek, CA: AltaMira Press.

Eck, Diana. 2001. *A New Religious America.* San Francisco: HarperSanFrancisco.

Elizondo, Virgilio P. 1981. *La Morenita, Evangelizadora de las Americas.* Liguori, MO: Liguori Publications.

———. 1997. *Guadalupe, Mother of the New Creation.* Maryknoll, NY: Orbis Books.

Elkholy, Abdo A. 1966. *The Arab Moslems in the United States: Religion and Assimilation.* New Haven, CT: College and University Press.

Ellacuría, Ignacio. 2000. *Escritos Teológicos.* Vol. 1. San Salvador: UCA Editores.

Emerson, Michael, and Christian Smith. 2000. *Divided by Faith: Evangelical Religion and the Problem of Race in America.* New York: Oxford University Press.

Eschbach, Karl, Jacqueline Hagan, and Nestor Rodríguez. 1999. "Death at the Border." *International Migration Review* 33 (2): 430–454.

———. 2003. "Deaths during Undocumented Migration: Trends and Policy Implications in the New Era of Homeland Security." In *In Defense of the Alien,* vol. 26, edited by Joseph Fugolo. New York: Center for Migration Studies.

Espín, Orlando O. 2000. "Immigration, Territory, and Globalization: Theological Reflections." *Journal of Hispanic/Latino Theology* 7 (3): 46–59.

Espiritu, Yen Le. 2003. *Home Bound: Filipino American Lives across Cultures, Communities, and Countries.* Berkeley: University of California Press.

Etzioni, Amitai, ed. 1995. *The New Communitarian Thinking: Persons, Virtues, Institutions, and Communities.* Charlottesville: University Press of Virginia.

Fall, Bernard. 1955. "The Political-Religious Sects of Vietnam." *Pacific Affairs* 27: 235–53.

———. 1963. *The Two Viet-Nams: A Political and Military Analysis.* New York: Praeger.

———. 1967. *Vietnam Witness, 1953-66.* New York: Praeger.

Finke, Roger. 1997. "The Illusion of Shifting Demand: Supply Side Interpretations of American Religious History." In *Retelling U.S. Religious History,* edited by Thomas A. Tweed, 108–124. Berkeley: University of California Press.

Finke, Roger, and Rodney Stark. 1992. *The Churching of America, 1776–1990: Winners and Losers in Our Religious Economy.* New Brunswick, NJ: Rutgers University Press.

Fiscus, Chris. 2003. "Arizona a Hub for Human Trafficking." *Arizona Republic,* October 11.

Fisher, David Hackett. 1991. *Albion's Seed: Four British Folkways in America.* New York: Oxford University Press.

Fitzgerald, David. 2005. "A Nation of Immigrants? Statecraft, Church-Building, and Nationalism in Mexican Migrant Source Communities." Ph.D. diss., University of California, Los Angeles.

Flannery, Austin, ed. 1975. *Vatican Council II: The Conciliar and Post Conciliar Documents.* Collegeville: Liturgical Press.

Flores, William V., and Rina Benmayor, eds. 1997. *Latino Cultural Citizenship*. Boston: Beacon Press.

Flynn, Michael. 2002. "U.S. Anti-Migration Efforts Move South." Americas Program. Silver City, MD: Interhemispheric Resource Center, July 8.

Freeman, James M. 1997. *Hearts of Sorrow: Vietnamese-American Lives*. Palo Alto: Stanford University Press.

———. 1999. *Changing Identities: Vietnamese-Americans, 1975–1995*. Boston: Allyn and Bacon.

Fujiwara, Lynn H. 2005. "Immigrant Rights are Human Rights: The Reframing of Immigrant Entitlement and Welfare." *Social Problems* 52: 79–101.

Gill, Jerry H. 2003. *Borderland Theology*. Washington, DC: EPICA.

———. 2004. *BorderLinks II: Still on the Road*. Tucson, AZ: BorderLinks.

Gilliam, Harold. 1993. "Bursting at the Seams: California's Immigration Crisis." *San Francisco Chronicle*, February 21.

Gittins, Anthony J. 2002. *A Presence That Disturbs: A Call to Radical Discipleship*. Liguori, MO: Liguori/Triumph.

Glendon, Mary Ann. 1991. *Rights Talk: The Impoverishment of Political Discourse*. New York: Free Press.

———. 1998. "'Absolute' Rights: Property and Privacy." In *The Essential Communitarian Reader*, edited by Amitai Etzioni, 107–114. Lanham, MD: Rowman and Littlefield.

Gobron, Gabriel. 1949. *Histoire et Philosophie du Caodaisme: Bouddhisme rénové, spiritisme vietnamien, religion nouvelle en Eurasie*. Paris: Dervy.

Goborn, Marguerite. 1949. *Images du Caodaisme*. Paris: Dervy.

Golden, Renny, and Michael McConnell. 1986. *Sanctuary: The New Underground Railroad*. Maryknoll, NY: Orbis Books.

Golden, Timothy. 1996. "If Immigrants Lose U.S. Aid, Local Budgets May Feel Pain." *New York Times*, July 19.

Goldstein, Warren. 2005. "A Liberal Dose of Religious Fervor." *Chronicle of Higher Education*, July 8.

Gonzalez, Daniel. 2003. "Gangs Are Menacing 'Coyotes,' Immigrants." *Arizona Republic*, August 17.

González, Justo L. 1992. *Out of Every Tribe and Nation: Christian Theology at the Ethnic Roundtable*. Nashville: Abingdon Press.

González, Justo L., and Zaida Maldonado Pérez. 2002. *An Introduction to Christian Theology*. Nashville: Abingdon Press.

Goodstein, Laurie. 2004. "Muslim Women Seeking a Place in the Mosque." *New York Times*, July 22.

Gordon, Milton Myron. 1964. *Assimilation in American Life: The Role of Race, Religion, and National Origins*. New York: Oxford University Press.

Grayson, George W. 2003. "Mexico's Southern Flank: A Crime-Ridden 'Third U.S. Border.'" *Hemisphere Focus* 11 (32): 1–3.

Greenberg, Brad A. 2005. "Christians Chide Governor." *San Bernadino County Sun*, May 10.

Greene, Graham. 1955. *The Quiet American*. London: William Heineman. Reprinted in the Viking Critical Library with additional texts and criticism selected by John Clark Pratt (New York: Penguin Books, 1996).

Grenier, Guillermo J., and Alex Stepick. 1992. Introduction to *Miami Now! Immigration, Ethnicity and Social Change*, edited by Guillermo J. Grenier and Alex Stepick, 1–17. Gainesville: University Press of Florida.

Guerrero, Andres G. 1987. *A Chicano Theology*. Maryknoll, NY: Orbis Books.

Guest, Kenneth J. 2003. *God in Chinatown: Religion and Survival in New York's Evolving Immigrant Community*. New York: New York University Press.

Guth, James L., John C. Green, Corwin E. Smidt, Lyman A. Kellstedt, and Margaret M. Poloma. 1997. *The Bully Pulpit: The Politics of Protestant Clergy.* Lawrence: University Press of Kansas.

Gutierrez, Lorraine, Anne Alvarez, Howard Nemon, and Edith Lewis. 1996. "Multicultural Community Organizing: A Strategy for Change." *Social Work* 5: 501–508.

Habermas, Jurgen. 1970. *Toward a Rational Society: Student Protest, Science, and Politics.* Boston: Beacon Press.

———. 1973. *Legitimation Crisis.* Boston: Beacon Press.

Hagan, Jacqueline. Forthcoming a. "Border Crosses: Religion as Resource in Preparing for the Migration Journey." In *Migration and Theology,* edited by Daniel Groody and Gioacchino Campese. Notre Dame, IN: University of Notre Dame Press.

———. Forthcoming b. "Making Theological Sense of the Migration Journey from Latin America: Catholic, Protestant and Interfaith Perspectives." *American Behavioral Scientist.* Special issue, Cecilia Menjívar, ed., Public Religion and Immigration across National Contexts.

———. 2002. "Religion and the Process of Migration: A Case Study of a Maya Transnational Community." In *Religion across Borders: Transnational Religious Networks,* edited by Helen Rose Ebaugh and Janet Chafetz. Walnut Creek, CA: Alta Mira Press.

Hagan, Jacqueline, and Helen Rose Ebaugh. 2003. "Calling upon the Sacred: Migrants' Use of Religion in the Migration Process." *International Migration Review* 37 (4): 1145–1162.

Hagan, Jacqueline, and Nestor Rodriguez. 2004. "Church vs. the State: Borders, Migrants and Human Rights." Paper presented at the Annual Meeting of the American Sociological Association, San Francisco, August.

Hall, John A. 1987. *Liberalism: Politics, Ideology and the Market.* Chapel Hill: University of North Carolina Press.

Hamilton, Nora, and Norma Stoltz Chinchilla. 2001. *Seeking Community in a Global City: Guatamalans and Salvadorans in Los Angeles.* Philadelphia: Temple University Press.

Hammerback, John C., and Richard J. Jensen. 1998. *The Rhetorical Career of Cesar Chavez.* College Station: Texas A&M University Press.

Hammer-Tomizuka, Zoe, and Jennifer Allen. 2002. "Hate or Heroism: Vigilantes on the Arizona-Mexico Border." Tucson: Border Action Network.

Han, Ju Hui Judy. 2005. "Missionary Destinations and Diasporic Destiny: Spatiality of Korean/American Evangelism and the Cell Church." ISSC Fellows Working Papers, Institute for the Study of Social Change, University of California, Berkeley.

Harris, Frederick. 1994. "Something Within: Religion as a Mobilizer of African American Political Activism." *Journal of Politics* 56: 42–68.

Hartney, Christopher. 2004. "A Separate Peace: Cao Dai's Manifestation in Australia." Ph.D. diss., University of Sydney, Australia.

Hartz, Louis. 1955. *The Liberal Tradition in America.* New York: Harcourt, Brace.

Hatch, Nathan O. 1989. *The Democratization of American Christianity.* New Haven, CT: Yale University Press.

Hehir, J. Bryan. 2003. "With No Vision, People Perish." In *All Come Bearing Gifts.* Proceedings of the National Migration Conference 2003. Washington, DC: U.S. Conference of Catholic Bishops.

Herberg, Will. 1983. *Protestant, Catholic, Jew: An Essay in American Religious Sociology.* Chicago: University of Chicago Press.

Hickey, Gerald C. 1964. *Village in Vietnam.* New Haven, CT: Yale University Press.

Hicks, Jonathan P. 2004. "In Primary Upset for Queens Assembly Seat, Signs of a Changing District." *New York Times,* September 18.

Higher Education Research Institute. 1998. "Academic and Political Engagement among Nation's College Freshman Is at All-Time Low, UCLA Study Finds." American

Freshman National Norms Survey, Higher Education Research Institute, University of California Los Angeles. Accessed April 14, 2005, at http://www.gseis.ucla.edu/heri/norms_pr_97.html.

Hirschman, Charles. 2004. "The Role of Religion in the Origins and Adaptation of Immigrant Groups in the United States." *International Migration Review* 38:1206–1233.

Holthouse, David, and Amanda Scioscia. 2000. "Phoenix or Busted: The Valley Is Now the Prime Way Station for Ruthless Smugglers Engaged in Lucrative Trafficking of Human Cargo—Illegal Immigrants." *New Times*, April 6.

Hondagneu-Sotelo, Pierrette, Genelle Gaudinez, Hector Lara, Billie C. Ortiz. 2004. "There's a Spirit that Transcends the Border: Faith, Ritual, and Postnational Protest at the U.S.-Mexico Border." *Sociological Perspectives* 47 (2): 133–159.

Hoover, Robert (Robin). 1998. "Social Theology and Religiously Affiliated Nonprofits in Migration Policy." Ph.D. diss., Texas Tech University.

———. 2004. "The Story of Humane Borders, Inc." Humane Borders pamphlet.

Hoyt, Joshua. 2002. "Reflections on Immigrant Organizing and the 'Universals.'" *Social Policy* 2: 37–42.

Huntington, Samuel P. 1981. *American Politics: The Promise of Disharmony.* Cambridge, MA: Harvard/Belknap Press.

———. 2004. *Who Are We? The Challenges to America's National Identity.* New York: Simon & Schuster.

Huspek, Michael. 2001. "Production of State, Capital, and Citizenry: The Case of Operation Gatekeeper." *Social Justice* 28 (2): 51–68.

Innes, S. 2005. "Entrant-Helping Case Is Targeted." http://www.aztarnet.com/dailystar/metro/98701. Accessed November 10, 2005.

———. 2006. "Former Arizona Chief Justice Will Represent One of Two Defendents in Entrant-Aid Case." February 7. http://www.azstarnet.com/metro/114777. Accessed March 9, 2006.

Isasi-Díaz, Ada María. 2004. *La Lucha Continues: Mujerista Theology.* Maryknoll, NY: Orbis Books.

Islamic Horizons. Plainfield, IN: Islamic Society of North America.

Jackson, Sherman A. 2003. "Islam(s) East and West: Pluralism between No-Frills and Designer Fundamentalism." In *September 11 in History,* edited by Mary L. Dudziak, 112–135. Durham: Duke University Press.

———. 2005. *Islam and the Blackamerican: Looking toward the Third Resurrection.* Oxford: Oxford University Press.

Jasper, James M. 1997. *The Art of Moral Protest: Culture, Biography and Creativity in Social Movements.* Chicago: University of Chicago Press.

Jensen, Carsten. 2000. *I Have Seen the World Begin: Travels through China, Cambodia and Vietnam.* Translated by Barbara Haveland. New York: Harcourt Books.

Jeung, Russell. 2004. *Faithful Generations: Race and the New Asian American Churches.* New Brunswick: Rutgers University Press.

———. 2005. "Related by Faith: Asian American Ministers' Religious Discourse on Multiethnicity." Paper presented at the 2005 Association for Asian American Studies Conference, Los Angeles, April.

Jones, Dale E. 2002. *Religious Congregations and Membership in the United States 2000: An Enumeration by Region, State and County Based on Data Reported for 149 Religious Bodies.* Nashville: Glenmary Research Center.

Jones-Correa, Michael, and David Leal. 2001. "Political Participation: Does Religion Matter?" *Political Research Quarterly* 54: 751–770.

Joseph, Suad. 1999. "Against the Grain of the Nation—The Arab." In *Arabs in America: Building a New Future,* edited by Michael Suleiman, 257–271. Philadelphia: Temple University Press.

Kaufman, Jason. 1999. "Three Views of Associationalism in Nineteenth-Century America: An Empirical Examination." *American Journal of Sociology* 104: 1296–1345.

Kelly, Gail Paradise. 1977. *From Vietnam to America: A Chronicle of the Vietnamese Immigration to the United States.* Boulder, CO: Westview Press.

Kelly, Paul, ed. 2002. *Multiculturalism Reconsidered.* Cambridge, UK: Polity Press.

Khan, Mohommed A. Muqtedar. 1998. "Muslims and American Politics: Refuting the Isolationist Arguments." *American Muslim Quarterly* 2 (1–2): 60–69.

———. 2002. *American Muslims: Bridging Faith and Freedom.* Beltsville, MD: Amana Publications.

Kil, Sang Hea, and Cecilia Menjívar. Forthcoming. "The Criminalization of Immigrants and Militarization of the Border: Recent Lessons from Arizona." In *Immigration and Crime: Race, Ethnicity, and Violence,* edited by Ramiro Martínez Jr. and Abél Valenzuela Jr. New York: New York University Press.

Kilgannon, Corey. 2004. "Asian Immigrants Become Political Force in Flushing." *New York Times,* September 30.

Kim, Kwang Chung, and Shin Kim. 2001. "Ethnic Roles of Korean Immigrant Churches in the United States." In *Korean Americans and Their Religions: Pilgrims and Missionaries from a Different Shore,* edited by Ho-Youn Kwon, Kwang Chung Kim, and R. Stephen Warner, 71–94. University Park: Pennsylvania State University Press.

Kim, Rebecca. 2004. "Negotiation of Ethnic and Religious Boundaries by Asian American Campus Evangelicals." In *Asian American Religions,* edited by Tony Carnes and Fenggang Yang, 141–159. New York: New York University Press.

Kim, Sharon. 2003. "Replanting Sacred Spaces: The Emergence of Second Generation Korean American Churches." *Dissertation Abstracts International,* 65 (05), 1977 (UMI No. AAT3133295). Abstract obtained from Dissertation Abstracts Online.

Kjærum, Morten. 2002. "Refugee Protection between State Interests and Human Rights: Where Is Europe Heading?" *Human Rights Quarterly* 24: 513–536.

Kraut, Benny. 1998. "Jewish Survival in Protestant America." In *Minority Faiths and the American Protestant Mainstream,* edited by J. Sarna, 15–60. Urbana: University of Illinois Press.

Kurashige, Scott. 2000. "Pan-Ethnicity and Community Organizing: Asian Americans United Campaign against Anti-Asian Violence." *Journal of Asian American Studies* 2: 163–190.

Kurien, Prema. 1998. "Becoming American by Becoming Hindu: Indian Americans Take Their Place at the Multicultural Table." In *Gatherings in Diaspora: Religious Communities and the New Immigration,* edited by R. Stephen Warner and Judith Wittner, 37–70. Philadelphia: Temple University Press.

Kurtz, Lester, and Kelly Goran Fulton. 2002. "Love Your Enemies? Protestants and United States Foreign Policy." In *The Quiet Hand of God: Faith-Based Activism and the Public Role of Mainline Protestantism,* edited by R. Wuthnow and J. H. Evans, 364–380. Berkeley: University of California Press.

Kurzman, Charles, ed. 1998. *Liberal Islam: A Source Book.* New York: Oxford University Press.

Kushner, Tony, and Katharine Knox. 1999. *Refugees in an Age of Genocide: Global, National and Local Perspectives during the Twentieth Century.* London: Frank Cass.

Kymlicka, Will. 1989. *Liberalism, Community and Culture.* New York: Oxford/Clarendon Press.

———. 1995. *Multicultural Citizenship: A Liberal Theory of Minority Rights.* New York: Oxford University Press.

Laguerre, Michel S. 1984. *American Odyssey: Haitians in New York City.* Ithaca, NY: Cornell University Press.

———. 1999. "State, Diaspora, and Transnational Politics: Haiti Reconceptualised." *Millennium* 28: 633–651.

Lattin, Don. 2004a. "The Battle Over Same Sex Marriage: Newsom Faces Wrath of God, Fundamentalist Leaders Say." *San Francisco Chronicle,* April 15.

———. 2004b. "Presbyterian Culture Clash: Many Asian American Members Oppose Liberal Leaning. *San Francisco Chronicle*, June 23.

Lauren, Paul Gordon. 1998. *The Evolution of International Human Rights: Visions Seen.* Philadelphia: University of Pennsylvania Press.

Lawrence, Bruce B. 2004. *New Faiths, Old Fears: Muslims and Other Asian Immigrants in American Religious Life.* New York: Columbia University Press.

Leege, David C., and Joseph Germillion. 1984. "The U.S. Parish Twenty Years after Vatican II." *Notre Dame Study of Catholic Parish Life* I: n.p.

Leonard, Karen. 2002a. "American Muslims, before and after September II, 2001." *Economic and Political Weekly* 37 (24): 2292–2302.

———. 2002b. "South Asian Leadership of American Muslims." In *Sojourners to Citizens: Muslims in Western Diasporas*, edited by Yvonne Yazbeck Haddad, 233–249. New York: Oxford University Press.

———. 2003. *Muslims in the United States: The State of the Research.* New York: Russell Sage Foundation.

———. 2004. "American Muslims: Race, Religion and the Nation." *ISIM Newsletter*, June, 16–17.

Levitt, Peggy. 2001. *The Transnational Villagers.* Berkeley: University of California Press.

———. 2002. "Two Nations under God? Latino Religious Life in the United States." In *Latinos: Remaking America*, edited by Marcelo M. Suarez-Orozco and Mariela M. Paez, 150–164. Berkeley: University of California Press and Rockefeller Center for Latin American Studies at Harvard University.

Lewis, Norman. 2003. *A Dragon Apparent: Travels in Cambodia, Laos and Vietnam.* London: Eland.

Lichterman, Paul. 2005. *Elusive Togetherness: Church Groups Trying to Bridge America's Divisions.* Princeton, NJ: Princeton University Press.

Lien, Pei-te. 2001. *The Making of Asian America through Political Participation.* Philadelphia: Temple University Press.

———. 2004a. *Pilot National Asian American Political Survey (PNAAPS), 2000–2001.* ICPSR version. Produced by Interviewing Service of America, Inc., Van Nuys, CA. Distributed by Inter-university Consortium for Political and Social Research, Ann Arbor, MI.

———. 2004b. "Religion and Political Adaptation among Asian Americans: An Empirical Assessment from the Multi-Site Asian American Political Survey." In *Asian American Religions: Borders and Boundaries*, edited by Tony Carnes and Fenggang Yang, 450–483. New York: New York University Press.

Lien, Pei-te, and Tony Carnes. 2004. "The Religious Demography of Asian American Boundary Crossing." In *Asian American Religions: Borders and Boundaries*, edited by Tony Carnes and Fenggang Yang, 67–87. New York: New York University Press.

Lien, Pei-te, M. Margaret Conway, and Janelle Wong. 2004. *The Politics of Asian America: Diversity and Community.* New York: Routledge.

Lipset, Seymour Martin. 1979. *The First New Nation: The United States in Historical and Comparative Perspective.* New York: Norton.

———. 1996. *American Exceptionalism: A Double-Edged Sword.* New York: W. W. Norton.

Lloyd, David, and Paul Thomas. 1998. *Culture and the State.* New York: Routledge.

Louie, Miriam Ching. 1992. "Immigrant Asian Women in Bay Area Garment Sweatshops: 'After Sewing, Laundry, Cleaning and Cooking, I Have No Breath Left to Sing.'" *Amerasia Journal* I: I–26.

Ma, Jason. 2000. "Straight from the Church: How Korean American Churches in California Rallied against Gay Rights" *AsianWeek* 21 (21): I–13.

Machado, Daisy L. 2002. "The Unnamed Woman: Justice, Feminists, and the Undocumented Woman." In *Reader in Latina Feminist Theology: Religion and Justice*, edited by

María Pilar Aquino, Daisy L. Machado, and Jeanette Rodríguez, 161–176. Austin: University of Texas Press.

Marrus, Michael Robert. 2002. *The Unwanted: European Refugees from the First World War through the Cold War.* Philadelphia: Temple University Press.

Martinez, Michael. 2005. "Man Provides Water for Illegal Immigrants at Mexican Border." *Kansas City Star,* May 3.

Marzheuser, Richard. 1995. "A Revitalized Theology of Catholicity: Toward Better Communication with Those Who Talk Differently than We Do about the Church." *New Theology Review* 8 (4): 48–55.

Massey, Douglas S. 2002. "The New Immigration and Ethnicity in the United States." In *American Diversity: A Demographic Challenge for the Twenty-First Century,* edited by Nancy A. Denton and Stewart E. Tolnay, 75–98. New York: State University of New York Press.

———. 2003. "Beyond Smoke and Mirrors: Paradoxes of U.S. Immigration Policy." In *Points of Migration Quarterly Issue.* Princeton, NJ: Center for Migration and Development, Princeton University. http://cmd.princeton.edu/files/pom-aug.pdf.

Massey, Douglas S., Joaquín Arango, Graeme Hugo, Ali Kouaouci, Adela Pellegrino, and J. Edward Taylor. 1993. "Theories of International Migration: A Review and Appraisal." *Population and Development Review* 19 (3): 431–466.

Matovina, Timothy M., and Gary Riebe-Estrella. 2002. *Horizons of the Sacred: Mexican Traditions in U.S. Catholicism.* Ithaca, NY: Cornell University Press.

McAdam, Doug. 1982. *Political Process and the development of Black Insurgency, 1930–1970.* Chicago: University of Chicago Press.

———. 1985. *Political Process and the Development of Black Insurgency, 1930–1970.* Chicago: University of Chicago Press.

McGreevy, John T. 2003. *Catholicism and American Freedom: A History.* New York: W. W. Norton.

McRoberts, Omar M. 2003. *Streets of Glory: Church and Community in a Black Urban Neighborhood.* Chicago: University of Chicago Press.

Meillon, Gustave. 1962. "Le Caodaisme." In *Les Messages Spirites de la trosième Amnistie de Dieu en Orient,* edited by Tran Quang Vinh. Tay Ninh: Sainte Siège du Caodaisme. This article first appeared in 1955 in *La revue des membres de la Legion d'Honneur "le Ruban Rouge."*

Menjivar, Cecilia. 1999. "Religious Institutions and Transnationalism: A Case Study of Catholic and Evangelical Salvadoran Immigrants." *International Journal of Politics, Culture and Society* 12 (4): 589–612.

———. 2000. *Fragmented Ties: Salvadoran Immigrant Networks in America.* Berkeley: University of California Press.

———. 2001. "Latino Immigrants and Their Perceptions of Religious Institutions: Cubans, Salvadorans, and Guatemalans in Phoenix, AZ." *Migraciones Internacionales* 1 (1): 65–88.

———. 2003. "Religion and Immigration in Comparative Perspective: Catholic and Evangelical Salvadorans in San Francisco, Washington, D.C. and Phoenix." *Sociology of Religion* 64: 21–45.

Messner, Michael A. 1990. "Men Studying Masculinity: Some Epistemological Questions in Sport Sociology." *Sociology of Sport Journal* 7 (2): 136–153.

Miller, Donald E. 1997. *Reinventing American Protestantism: Christianity in the New Millennium.* Berkeley: University of California Press.

Miller, Donald E., Jon Miller, and Grace R. Dyrness. 2001. *Immigrant Religion in the City of Angels.* Los Angeles: Center for Religion and Civic Culture, University of Southern California.

Miller, Jake C. 1984. *The Plight of Haitian Refugees.* New York: Praeger.

Mills, C. Wright. 1959. *The Power Elite.* New York: Oxford University Press.

———. 1959. *The Sociological Imagination.* New York: Oxford University Press.

Min, Anselm. 1999. "From Autobiography to Fellowship of Others: Reflections on Doing Ethnic Theology Today." In *Journeys at the Margin: Toward an Autobiographical Theology in American-Asian Perspective,* edited by Peter C. Phan and Jung Young Lee, 135–159. Collegeville, MN: Liturgical Press.

———. 2004. *The Solidarity of Others in a Divided World: A Postmodern Theology after Postmodernism.* New York: T & T Clark International.

Min, Pyong Gap. 1992. "The Structure and Social Functions of Korean Immigrant Churches in the United States." *International Migration Review* 26: 1370–94.

———. 2002. "Introduction." In *Religions in Asian America,* edited by Pyong Gap Min and Jung Ha Kim, 1–14. Walnut Creek, CA: Alta Mira Press.

Mitra, Kana. 1982. "Human Rights in Hinduism." In *Human Rights in Religious Traditions,* edited by Ann Swidler, 79–84. New York: Pilgrim Press.

Moltmann, Jürgen. 1993. *The Church in the Power of the Spirit: A Contribution to a Messianic Ecclesiology.* Minneapolis: Fortress Press.

Montero, Daniel. 1979. *Vietnamese-Americans: Patterns of Resettlement and Socioeconomic Adaptation in the United States.* Boulder, CO: Westview Press.

Moody, Michael. 2002. "Caring for Creation: Environmental Advocacy by Mainline Protestant Organizations." In *The Quiet Hand of God: Faith-Based Activism and the Public Role of Mainline Protestantism,* edited by Robert Wuthnow and John H. Evans, 237–264. Berkeley: University of California Press.

Mooney, Margarita. 2005. "Upward Climb or Downward Slide? Religion and Mediating Social Capital in the Haitian Immigrant Communities of Miami, Montreal and Paris." Ph.D. diss., Princeton University.

Moore, Robin. 1965. *The Green Berets.* New York: St. Martin's Paperbacks.

Moore, Solomon, and Mai Tran. 2004. "Vietnam Flight to Make History." *Los Angeles Times,* December 9.

Morris, Aldon D. 1984. *The Origins of the Civil Rights Movement: Black Communities Organizing for Social Change.* New York: Free Press.

Morris, Charles R. 1997. *American Catholic: The Saints and Sinners Who Built America's Most Powerful Church.* New York: Times Publishers.

Moyers, Bill. 2005. *Bill Moyers on America: A Journalist and His Times.* New York: Anchor Books.

National Conference of Catholic Bishops of the United States. 1988. *People on the Move: A Compendium of Church Documents on the Pastoral Concern for Migrants and Refugees.* Washington, DC: U.S. Conference of Catholic Bishops.

Nawyn, Stephanie J. 2006. "Faith, Ethnicity and Culture in Refugee Resettlement." *American Behavioral Scientist* 49(33): 1509–1527.

Nealon, Sean. 2002. "Budding Influence: One Man's Effort to Awaken Flushing's Asian Voters." *Race and Ethnicity in the New Urban America.* http://www.jrn.columbia.edu/studentwork/race/2002/voters-nealon.shtml.

Nelson, Robert H. 2001. *Economics as Religion: From Samuelson to Chicago and Beyond.* University Park: Pennsylvania State University Press.

Nepstad, Sharon Erickson. 2004. *Convictions of the Soul: Religion, Culture, and Agency in the Central America Solidarity Movement.* New York: Oxford University Press.

Nérestant, Micial M. 1994. *Religions et politique en Haïti.* Paris: Éditions Karthala.

Nichols, J. Bruce. 1988. *The Uneasy Alliance: Religion, Refugee Work, and U.S. Foreign Policy.* New York: Oxford University Press.

Noden, Kirk. 2002. "Building Power in Forty Languages: A Story about Organizing Immigrants in Chicago's Albany Park." *Social Policy* 2: 47–52.

Noll, Mark A. 2001. *American Evangelical Christianity*. Boston: Blackwell Publishing.

Novak, Michael. 1989. *Catholic Social Thought and Liberal Institutions: Freedom with Justice.* New Brunswick, NJ: Transaction.

Nuruddin, Yusuf. 1998. "African-American Muslims and the Question of Identity: Between Traditional Islam, African Heritage, and the American Way." In *Muslims on the Americanization Path?* edited by Yvonne Yazbeck Haddad and John L. Esposito, 215–262. Atlanta: Scholars Press.

Oates, Mary. 1995. *The Catholic Philanthropic Tradition in America*. Bloomington: Indiana University Press.

Ochs, Mary, and Mayron Payes. 2003. "Immigrant Organizing: Patterns, Challenges and Opportunities." *Social Policy* 4: 19–24.

Oliver, Victor, L. 1976. *Caodai Spiritism: A Study of Religion in Vietnamese Society*. Leiden: E. J. Brill.

Olson, Laura R. 2002. "Mainline Protestant Washington Offices and the Political Lives of Clergy." In *The Quiet Hand of God: Faith-Based Activism and the Public Role of Mainline Protestantism*, edited by R. Wuthnow and J. H. Evans, 54–79. Berkeley: University of California Press.

Ong, Aihwa. 2003. *Buddha Is Hiding: Refugees, Citizenship, and the New America*. Berkeley: University of California Press.

"Out of the Political Closet." 2000. *AsianWeek*, January 24, p. 4.

Pacific Institute for Community Organizations. 1997. "Reweaving the Fabric of America's Communities." Oakland, CA: Pacific Institute for Community Organizations.

Palacios, Joseph M. 2004. "Oakland Community Organizations' 'Faith inAction': Locating the Grassroots Social Justice Mission." In *Living the Catholic Social Tradition: Cases and Commentary*, edited by Kathleen Maas Weigert and Alexia K. Kelley, 125–138. Lanham, MD: Rowman and Littlefield.

Passel, Jeffrey. 2004. "Mexican Immigration to the U.S.: The Latest Estimates," in *Migration Information Source*. March 1. http://www.migrationinformation.org/feature/cfm?ID-208. Accessed March 15, 2006.

———. 2005. "Estimates of the Size and Characteristics of the Undocumented Population." March 21. Washington, DC: Pew Hispanic Center Report.

Pateman, Carole. 1970. *Participation and Democratic Theory*. Cambridge: Cambridge University Press.

Pew Forum on Religion and Public Life. 2005. *A Faith-Based Partisan Divide*. Accessed February 27, 2004, at http://pewforum.org/publications/reports/religion-and-politics-report.pdf.

Phái, Chieu-Minh. 1950. *Le Grand Cycle de l'Esoterisme* [Spirit Messages in French from the Founding Branch of Caodai Esoterism]. Saigon: Cénacle de Chieu-Minh.

Pham, Andrew. 1999. *Catfish and Mandala*. New York: Farrar Strauss Giroux.

Phan, Peter C. 1999. "Betwixt and Between: Doing Theology with Memory and Imagination." In *Journeys at the Margin: Toward an Autobiographical Theology in American-Asian Perspective*, edited by Peter C. Phan and Jung Young Lee, 113–133. Collegeville, MN: Liturgical Press.

———. 2003. "The Experience of Migration in the United States as Source of Intercultural Theology." In *Migration, Religious Experience, and Globalization*, edited by Gioacchino Campese and Pietro Ciallella, 143–169. New York: Center for Migration Studies.

———. 2004. "Cultures, Religions, and Power: Proclaiming Christ in the United States Today." *Theological Studies* 65 (4): 714–740.

Phan Truong, Manh. 1950. *La voie du salut Caodaique*. Saigon: Imprimerie Ly Cong Quan.

———. 1951. *Qu'est-ce que le Caodaisme? J'éclaire et J'unis*. Saigon: Imprimerie Ly Cong Quan.

Platt, Gerald M., and Rhys H. Williams. 1997. "Religion, Ideology, and Electoral Politics." In *Cultural Wars in American Politics: Critical Reviews of a Popular Myth*, edited by R. H. Williams, 221–236. Hawthorne, NY: Aldine de Gruyter.

———. 2002. "Ideological Language and Social Movement Mobilization: A Sociolinguistic Analysis of Segregationists' Ideologies." *Sociological Theory* 20 (3): 328–359.

Portes, Alejandro, and Alex Stepick. 1993. *City on the Edge: The Transformation of Miami*. Berkeley: University of California Press.

Putnam, Robert. 2000. *Bowling Alone: The Collapse and Revival of American Community*. New York: Simon and Schuster.

Putnam, Robert D., Robert Leonardi, and Raffaella Y. Nanetti. 1993. *Making Democracy Work: Civic Traditions in Modern Italy*. Princeton, NJ: Princeton University Press.

Redman, Nina, and Lucille Whalen. 1998. *Human Rights: A Reference Handbook*. Santa Barbara, CA: ABC-CLIO.

Revue Caodaiste, Cao Dài Giao Ly No 1–20, Saigon 1930–1932. Revived under a new editor 1949–50. Photocopies of bilingual journal received from the files of the Co Quan Pho Thong Giao Ly Dai Dao, Ho Chi Minh City, 2004.

Riley, Michael. 2003. "A Grim Gamble: Mexican Immigrants Bet Their Lives They Can Make It across the U.S. Border through the Blazing Arizona Desert." *Denver Post*, October 19.

Rodgers, Daniel T. 1987. *Contested Truths: Keywords in American Politics since Independence*. New York: Basic Books.

Rodriguez, Jeanette. 1994. *Our Lady of Guadalupe: Faith and Empowerment among Mexican-American Women*. Austin: University of Texas Press.

Rodriguez, Nestor. 2002. "Crossing the Mexican Gauntlet: Trials and Challenges of Central American Migration to the United States." Paper presented at the Latin American Conference on "The Other Latinos," Harvard University, April.

Roof, Wade Clark. 2001. *Spiritual Marketplace: Baby Boomers and the Remaking of American Religion*. Princeton, NJ: Princeton University Press.

Rosaldo, Renato. 2003. *Cultural Citizenship in Island Southeast Asia: Nation and Belonging in the Hinterlands*. Berkeley: University of California Press.

Rosenblum, Nancy L., ed. 1989. *Liberalism and the Moral Life*. Cambridge, Mass.: Harvard University Press.

Rotstein, Arthur H. 2004. "Migrant Deaths in Arizona down from Heat, up Overall through June." Associated Press, State and Regional Section, July 4.

Rouse, Carolyn Moxley. 2003. *Engaged Surrender: African American Women and Islam*. Berkeley: University of California Press.

Ruiz, Olivia Marrujo. 2003. "Immigrants at Risk, Immigrants as Risk: Two Paradigmsof Globalization." In *Migration, Religious Experience, and Globalization*, edited by Gioacchino Campese and Pietro Ciallella, 17–28. New York: Center for Migration Studies.

Rumbaut, Ruben G. 1989. "The Structure of Refuge: Southeast Asian Refugees in the United States, 1975–1985." *International Review of Comparative Public Policy* 1:97–129.

Russell, James C. 2004. *Breach of Faith: American Churches and the Immigration Crisis*. Raleigh, NC: Representative Government Press.

Safi, Omid, ed. 2003. *Progressive Muslims: On Justice, Gender, and Pluralism*. Oxford: Oneworld Publications.

Sailer, Steve. 2003. "Feature: Serving Christ in the Borderlands." *UPI National Correspondent*, June 23.

Saramago, José. 2001. "El Factor Dios." *La Insignia*, September 18.

Sarna, Jonathan D., editor. 1998. *Minority Faiths and the American Protestant Mainstream*. Urbana: University of Illinois Press.

Satinover, Jeffrey. "The Evangelical Response to Homosexuality: A Survey, Critique, and Advisory." In *A Public Faith: Evangelicals and Civic Engagement*, edited by Michael Cromartie, 69–91. Lanham, MD: Rowman and Littlefield.

Savani, A. M. 1952. *Le Caodaisme: Notions Sommaires*. Saigon: Imprimerie de la Sainte Siège, Tay Ninh.

Schmitz, Dan. 2001. "Landlord Lawsuit Puts Gospel into Real-Life Context." Covenant News, April 26. Accessed at http://www.covchurch.org/cov/news/item1505.html.

Schneiders, Sandra M. 1986. *Women and the Word*. New York: Paulist Press.

Schreiter, Robert J. 1997. *The New Catholicity: Theology between the Global and the Local*. Maryknoll, NY: Orbis Books.

———. 2003. "Theology's Contribution to (Im)Migration." In *Migration, Religious Experience, and Globalization*, edited by Gioacchino Campese and Pietro Ciallella, 170–180. New York: Center for Migration Studies.

Seligman, Adam B. 1992. *The Idea of Civil Society*. New York: Free Press.

Shapiro, Ian. 1986. *The Evolution of Rights in Liberal Theory*. Cambridge: Cambridge University Press.

Sherry, Norman. 1994. *The Life of Graham Greene, Volume 2: 1939–1955*. New York: Viking.

Shupe, Anson, and Bronislaw Misztal, eds. 1998. *Religion, Mobilization, and Social Action*. Westport, CT: Praeger Press.

Simmons, Gwendolyn Zoharah. 2000. "Striving for Muslim Women's Human Rights—Before and Beyond Beijing." In *Windows of Faith: Muslim Women Scholar-Activists in North America*, edited by Gisela Webb, 197–225. Syracuse: Syracuse University Press.

Skerry, Peter. 1993. *Mexican Americans: The Ambivalent Minority*. Cambridge, MA: Harvard University Press.

Skocpol, Theda. 2003. *Diminished Democrqacy: From Membership to Management in American Civic Life*. Norman: University of Oklahoma Press.

Skocpol, Theda, and Morris P. Fiorina. 1999. "Making Sense of the Civic Engagement Debate." In *Civic Engagement in American Democracy*, edited by Theda Skocpol and Morris P. Fiorina, 1–23. New York: Russell Sage Foundation.

Slingerland, Edward. 2004. "Conceptual Metaphor Theory as Methodology for Comparative Religion." *Journal of the American Academy of Religion 72*: 1–31.

Smith, Christian. 1991. *The Emergence of Liberation Theology: Radical Religion and Social Movement Theory*. Chicago: University of Chicago Press.

Smith, Ralph B. 1970. "An Introduction to Caodaism." *Bulletin of the School of Oriental and African Studies* (University of London) 33 (2–3): 335–349.

Sobrino, Jon. 1988. *Spirituality of Liberation: Toward Political Holiness*. Maryknoll, NY: Orbis Books.

———. 1995. "La teología y el 'Principio Liberación.'" *Revista Latinoamericana de teología* 12: 115–140.

———. 2003. *Witnesses to the Kingdom. The Martyrs of El Salvador and the Crucified Peoples*. Maryknoll, NY: Orbis Books.

Stark, Rodney, and Roger Finke. 2000. *Acts of Faith: Explaining the Human Side of Religion*. Berkeley: University of California Press.

Steensland, Brian. 2002. "The Hydra and the Swords: Social Welfare and Mainline Advocacy, 1964–2000." In *The Quiet Hand of God: Faith-Based Activism and the Public Role of Mainline Protestantism*, edited by Robert Wuthnow and John H. Evans, 213–236. Berkeley: University of California Press.

Stepick, Alex. 1992. "The Refugees Nobody Wants: Haitians in Miami." In *Miami Now! Immigration, Ethnicity and Social Change*, edited by Guillermo Grenier and Alex Stepick, 57–82. Gainesville: University Press of Florida.

Stevens-Arroyo, Anthony M. 2004. "From Barrios to Barricades: Religion and Religiosity in Latino Life." In *The Columbia History of Latinos in the United States since 1960*, edited by David G. Gutierrez, 303–354. New York: Columbia University Press.

Stotzky, Irwin P. 2004. "Haitian Refugees and the Rule of Law." Unpublished manuscript in possession of the author, University of Miami School of Law.

Swarns, Rachel L. 2005. "Bill on Illegal-Immigrant Aid Draws Fire." *New York Times*, December 30.

Swidey, Neil. 2003. "God in the Squad." *Boston Globe*, November 30.

Swidler, Ann. 1986. "Culture in Action: Symbols and Strategies." *American Sociological Review* 51: 273–286.

Tac, Pham Cong. 1953. *Ho Phap la constitution religieuse du Caodaisme*. Paris: Dervy.

Tai, Hue-Tam Ho. 1983. *Millenarianism and Peasant Politics in Vietnam*. Cambridge, MA: Harvard University Press.

Tassello, Graziano G. 2001. "Los migrantes: Profetas de la Catolicidad." *Spiritus* 42 (2): 113–124.

Taylor, Charles, and Amy Gutmann. 1994. *Multiculturalism: Examining the Politics of Recognition*. Princeton, NJ: Princeton University Press.

Taylor, Verta, and Leila J. Rupp. 1993. "Women's Culture and Lesbian Feminist Activism: A Reconsideration of Cultural Feminism." *SIGNS: A Journal of Women in Culture and Society* 19: 32–61.

Thien, Ly Buu Toa. 1986. *Dai Giac Thanh Kinh and Kinh Thanh Giao Phap*. San Jose, CA: Papyrus Press.

———. 1998. *Phap Bao Tam Kinh*. San Jose, CA: Papyrus Press.

———. 2000. *Dai Thua Chon Giao*. San Jose, CA: Papyrus Press.

Thomas, William Isaac, and Florian Znaniecki. 1927. *The Polish Peasant in Europe and America*. New York: Alfred A. Knopf.

Thompson, Virginia. 1937. *French Indochina*. New York: Octagon Books, 1968.

Tocqueville, Alexis de. 1995. *Democracy in America*. New York: Everyman's Library.

Tomasi, Silvano M., ed. 2000. *For the Love of Immigrants: Migration Writings and Letters of Bishop John Baptist Scalabrini, 1839–1905*. New York: Center for Migration Studies.

Tran Quang Vinh, ed. 1961. *Les messages spirites de la trosième Amnistie de Dieu en Orient*. Tay Ninh: Sainte Siège du Caodaisme.

Tran Thu Dung. 1996. "Le Caodaisme et Victor Hugo." Ph.D. diss., University of Paris.

Tweed, Thomas A. 1997. *Our Lady of the Exile: Diasporic Religion at a Cuban Catholic Shrine in Miami*. New York: Oxford University Press.

Ufford-Chase, Rick. 2004. "Crisis on the Mexican Border: Dying in the Desert." *The Christian Century: Thinking Critically, Living Faithfully*. BorderLinks pamphlet, Tucson, AZ.

Urrutia-Rojas, Ximena, and Nestor Rodriguez. 1997. "Potentially Traumatic Events among Unaccompanied Migrant Children from Central America." In *Health and Social Services among International Labor Migrants: A Comparative Perspective*, edited by Antonio Ugalde and Gilberto Cardenas, 151–166. Austin: Center for Mexican American Studies, University of Texas.

U.S. Commission on Civil Rights. 1997. "Federal Immigration Law Enforcement in the Southwest: Civil Rights' Impacts on Border Communities." Arizona, California, New Mexico, and Texas Advisory Committees. Washington, DC: U.S. Commission on Civil Rights.

U.S. Conference of Catholic Bishops. 1986. *Together a New People*. Washington, DC: U.S. Conference of Catholic Bishops.

———. 1988. *People on the Move: A Compendium of Church Documents on the Pastoral Concern for Migrants and Refugees*. Washington, DC: U.S. Conference of Catholic Bishops.

———. 1997. "Migration and Refugee Services Mission Statement." Washington, DC: U.S. Conference of Catholic Bishops.

———. 1998. *One Family under God.* Rev. ed. Washington, DC: U.S. Conference of Catholic Bishops.

———. 2000. *Welcoming the Stranger among Us: Unity in Diversity.* Washington, DC: U.S. Conference of Catholic Bishops.

———. 2001. *Asian and Pacific Presence: Harmony in Faith.* Washington, DC: U.S. Conference of Catholic Bishops.

U.S. Conference of Catholic Bishops and Conferencia del Episcopado Mexicano. 2003. *Strangers No Longer: Together on the Journey of Hope.* Washington, DC: U.S. Conference of Catholic Bishops.

U.S. Immigration and Naturalization Service. 1999. *Statistical Yearbook of the Immigration and Naturalization Service, 1997.* Washington, DC: U.S. Government Printing Office.

Valentín, Benjamín. 2004. "Going Public: Latino(a) Theology as Public Discourse." *Perspectivas Occasional Papers* 8: 9–26.

Verba, Sidney, Kay Lehman Schlozman, and Henry E. Brady. 1995. *Voice and Equality: Civic Voluntarism in American Politics.* Cambridge, MA: Harvard University Press.

Villa, Juan. 2005. "Ya van 20 fallecimientos de inmigrantes en 2005." *(Phoenix, AZ) La Voz,* January 12.

Vo, Kim Quyen. 1950. *Prières aux Quatre Heures Canoniques.* Ben Tre, Vietnam: Ecole Nam Phuong.

Wadud, Amina. 1999. *Qur'an and Woman: Rereading the Sacred Text from a Woman's Perspective.* New York: Oxford University Press.

Wallis, Jim. 2003. "Dangerous Religion: George Bush's Theology of Empire." In *Sojourners to Citizens: Muslims in Western Diasporas,* edited by Yvonne Yazbeck Haddad, 20–26. New York: Oxford University Press.

Warren, Mark R. 2001. *Dry Bones Rattling: Community Building to Revitalize American Democracy.* New York: Oxford University Press.

Warner, R. Stephen. 1993. "Work in Progress Toward a New Paradigm for the Social Scientific Study of Religion in the United States." *American Journal of Sociology* 98:1044–1093.

———. 1999. "Changes in the Civic Role of Religion." In *Diversity and Its Discontents,* edited by N. Smelser and J. C. Alexander, 229–243. Princeton, NJ: Princeton University Press.

———. 2004. "Coming to America." *Christian Century,* February 10, 20–23.

Warner, R. Stephen, and Judith Wittner. 1998. *Gatherings in Diaspora: Religious Communities and the New Immigration.* Philadelphia: Temple University Press.

Watanabe, Teresa. 2006. "Immigrants Gain the Pulpit." *Los Angeles Times,* March 1.

Watt, Alan J. 1999. "The Religious Dimensions of the Farm Worker Movement." Ph.D. diss., Vanderbilt University.

Webb, Gisela, ed. 2000. *Windows of Faith: Muslim Women Scholar-Activists in North America.* New York: Syracuse University Press.

Weigel, George, and Robert Royal, eds. 1991. *A Century of Catholic Social Thought: Essays on "Rerum Novarum" and Nine Other Key Documents.* Washington, DC: Ethics and Public Policy Center.

Weigert, Kathleen Maas, and Alexia K. Kelley, eds. 2005. *Living the Catholic Social Tradition: Cases and Commentary.* Lanham, MD: Rowman & Littlefield Publishers.

Werner, Jayne. 1976. *The Cao Dai: The Politics of a Vietnamese Syncretic Religious Movement.* Ph.D. diss., Cornell University.

———. 1981. *Peasant Politics and Religious Sectarianism: Peasant and Priest in the Cao Dai in Vietnam.* New Haven, CT: Yale University Southeast Asia Studies.

Wilbanks, Dana W. 1996. *Re-Creating America: The Ethics of U.S. Immigration and Refugee Policy in a Christian Perspective*. Nashville: Abingdon Press.

Williams, Gwyneth I., and Rhys H. Williams. 1995. "'All We Want Is Equality': Rhetorical Framing and the Father's Rights Movement." In *Images of Issues*, 2nd ed., edited by Joel Best, 191–212. New York: Aldine de Gruyter.

Williams, Rhys H. 1995a. "Constructing the Public Good: Cultural Resources and Social Movements." *Social Problems* 42 (1): 124–144.

———. 1995b. "Breaching the 'Wall of Separation': The Balance between Religious Freedom and Social Order." In *Armageddon in Waco: Critical Perspectives on the Branch Davidian Conflict*, edited by Stuart A. Wright, 299–322. Chicago: University of Chicago Press.

———. 2002. "From the 'Beloved Community' to 'Family Values': Religious Language, Symbolic Repertoires, and Democratic Culture." In *Social Movements: Identity, Culture and the State*, edited by David S. Meyer, Nancy Whittier, and Belinda Robnett, 247–265. New York: Oxford University Press.

Williams, Rhys H., and Timothy J. Kubal. 1999. "Movement Frames and the Cultural Environment: Resonance, Failure, and the Boundaries of the Legitimate." *Research in Social Movements, Conflict, and Change* 21: 225–248.

Williams, Rhys H., and John P. N. Massad. Forthcoming. "Religious Diversity, Civil Law, Institutional Isomorphism." In *Religious Organizations in the United States: A Study of Identity, Liberty, and the Law*, edited by J. A. Serritella, T. C. Berg, W. C. Durham Jr., E. M. Gaffney Jr., and C. B. Mousin. Durham, NC: Carolina Academic Press.

Wolfe, Alan. 2003. *The Transformation of American Religion*. Washington, DC: Free Press.

Wong, Janelle. 2006. *Democracy's Promise: American Civic Institutions and Political Mobilization among Asian American and Latino Immigrants*. Ann Arbor: University of Michigan Press.

Wood, Richard. 1997. "Social Capital and Political Culture: God Meets Politics in the Inner City." *American Behavioral Scientist* 5: 595–606.

———. 2002. *Faith in Action: Religion, Race and Democratic Organizing in America*. Chicago: University of Chicago Press.

Woodside, Alexander. 1971. *Vietnam and the Chinese Model: A Comparative Study of Nguyen and Ch'ing Civil Government in the First Half of the Nineteenth Century*. Cambridge, MA: Harvard University Press.

———. 1976. *Community and Revolution in Modern Vietnam*. Boston: Houghton Mifflin.

Wuthnow, Robert. 1988. *The Restructuring of American Religion: Society and Faith since World War II*. Princeton, NJ: Princeton University Press.

———. 1998. *After Heaven: Spirituality in America since the 1950s*. Berkeley: University of California Press.

———. 2004. *Saving America? Faith-Based Services and the Future of Civil Society*. Princeton, NJ: Princeton University Press.

Wuthnow, Robert, and John H. Evans, eds. 2002. *The Quiet Hand of God: Faith-Based Activism and the Public Role of Mainline Protestantism*. Berkeley: University of California Press.

Yang, Fenggang. 1999. *Chinese Christians in America: Conversion, Assimilation, and Adhesive Identities*. University Park: Pennsylvania State University Press.

———. 2004. "Gender and Generation in a Chinese Christian Church." In *Asian American Religions: Borders and Boundaries*, edited by Tony Carnes and Fenggang Yang, 205–222. New York: New York University Press.

Yang, Fenggang, and Helen Rose Ebaugh. 2001. "Transformations in New Immigrant Religions and Their Global Implications." *American Sociological Review* 66 (2): 269–288.

Yoo, David. 1999. *New Spiritual Homes: Religion and Asian Americans*. Honolulu: University of Hawaii Press.

Zhou, Min, and Carl L. Bankston. 1998. *Growing up American: How Vietnamese Children Adapt to Life in the United States*. New York: Russell Sage Foundation.

Zinoman, Peter. 2001. *The Colonial Bastille: A History of Imprisonment in Vietnam, 1862–1940*. Berkeley: University of California Press.

———. 2002. "Introduction." In *Dumb Luck: A Novel by Vu Trong Phung*. Translated by Nguyen Nguyen Cam. Ann Arbor: University of Michigan Press.

NOTES ON CONTRIBUTORS

GIOACCHINO CAMPESE is professor of theology at the Scalabrinian International Migration Institute in Rome. As a Scalabrinian Brother, he at worked the Casa del Migrante in Tijuana for seven years, and he has co-organized two national conferences on migration and theology.

GENELLE GAUDINEZ is a Ph.D. student in the Department of Sociology at the University of Southern California. Her research focuses on race relations and the legacies of U.S. colonialism experienced by Puerto Ricans and Filipino Americans in the United States.

JACQUELINE HAGAN is associate professor in the Department of Sociology at the University of North Carolina, Chapel Hill. Her research has examined Central American migration to the United States, as well as gender, social networks, religion, and social justice.

PIERRETTE HONDAGNEU-SOTELO is professor in the Department of Sociology at the University of Southern California. Her research has focused on gender and Latino immigration, global paid domestic work, and religion and immigrant rights mobilizations.

JANET HOSKINS is professor in the Department of Anthropology at the University of Southern California. Her research has focused on culture, religion, and gender in Indonesia, and most recently on the Caodai religion among the Vietnamese diaspora.

JANE NAOMI IWAMURA is assistant professor of Religion and American Studies and Ethnicities at the University of Southern California. Her research focuses on Asian American religions, race, and popular culture in the United States.

RUSSELL JEUNG is assistant professor in the Department of Asian American Studies at San Francisco State University. His research interest focuses on the

Asian Pacific Islander second generation, race and religion, community organizing and social movements.

HECTOR LARA is a graduate student in social work at the University of Southern California. His research interests include public policy and Latino social issues.

KAREN LEONARD is professor of anthropology and Asian American Studies at the University of California, Irvine. Her research interests include the social history of India, caste, ethnicity, and gender, and South Asians and Muslims in the United States.

CECILIA MENJÍVAR is associate professor in the Department of Sociology at Arizona State University. Her research focuses on Salvadoran and Guatemalan immigrants, social networks, gender, family, and religion.

MARGARITA MOONEY is research associate in the Office of Population Research at Princeton University. Her research focuses on international migration and development, Haitians, and religion.

STEPHANIE NAWYN is assistant professor of sociology at Michigan State University. She received her Ph.D. in the Department of Sociology at the University of Southern California, and her research has examined gender, refugee resettlement, and ethnicity.

JOSEPH PALACIOS is assistant professor in the Department of Sociology and Anthropology at Georgetown University. His research interests include Latin America, Latino Sociology, and the study of religion, political culture, and civil society.

RHYS H. WILLIAMS is professor of sociology at the University of Cincinnati and the editor of the *Journal for the Scientific Study of Religion*. His research interests are mainly in the sociology of religion and the sociology of American culture.

JANELLE S. WONG is assistant professor of Political Science and American Studies and Ethnicities at the University of Southern California. Her research interests include race, ethnicity, and politics, with a particular focus on Asian Americans and Latinos.

INDEX